Policy Styles in Western Europe

Policy Styles in Western Europe

Edited by
Jeremy Richardson
University of Strathclyde

London
GEORGE ALLEN & UNWIN
Boston   Sydney

George Allen & Unwin (Publishers) Ltd,
40 Museum Street, London WC1A 1LU, UK

George Allen & Unwin (Publishers) Ltd,
Park Lane, Hemel Hempstead, Herts HP2 4TE, UK

Allen & Unwin, Inc.,
9 Winchester Terrace, Winchester, Mass. 01890, USA

George Allen & Unwin Australia Pty Ltd,
8 Napier Street, North Sydney, NSW 2060, Australia

First published in 1982

British Library Cataloguing in Publication Data

Policy styles in Western Europe.
    1. Europe–Politics and government, 1945-
I. Richardson, Jeremy
320.94   JN94.A2
ISBN 0-04-350062-5

Library of Congress Cataloging in Publication Data

Main entry under title:

    Policy styles in Western Europe.

Includes index.
1. Europe – Politics and government – 1945-
– Addresses, essays, lectures. 2. Comparative government
– Addresses, essays, lectures. 3. Policy sciences –
Addresses, essays, lectures. I. Richardson, J. J.
(Jeremy John)
JN94.A91P64 1982   320.3'094   82-11415
ISBN 0-04-350062-5

Set in 10 on 11 point Ehrhardt by Fotographics (Bedford) Ltd
and printed in Great Britain by
Billing and Sons Ltd, London and Worcester

Contents

Preface

It is now almost commonplace to argue that modern Western European governments are 'overloaded', that policy failure rather than success is the norm and that citizens and groups are more inclined towards acts of 'non-compliance'. In short, it is believed that the 'business of government' is somehow more difficult in the 1980s than it was in the 1970s. In turn, the 1970s was seen as a more 'difficult' decade for many Western European countries than the 1960s, notwithstanding the widespread student disorders in the latter.

In analysing the degree to which government might be becoming more difficult, it is important to focus on one of the central activities of modern governments – the making and implementing of public policies. The growth of the modern state has in practice meant a rapid expansion of public policies. The state has widened its areas of concern such that virtually all aspects of societal activity are now subject to some form of regulation (in the broadest sense of the term) through public policies. The last decade has seen political science in Europe develop a recognition of the central role of policies in the political system. Increasingly, we recognise that many policy problems are common to all industrialised democracies. For example, unemployment, inflation, crime, threatened energy shortages, pollution and the intransigence of organised groups are common features of every Western European nation today. Policy responses to these problems may also be quite similar (for instance, in dealing with unemployment). Moreover, analysis of single-country studies of policy process suggests that the similarities in the *processes* by which responses are formulated and implemented are much greater than the differences. What each analyst may see as features unique to his own country often turn out to be equally evident elsewhere. For example, interest groups are often seen as 'uniquely powerful' in single-country studies, whereas it is a feature of most Western European democracies that interest groups are accorded a very central role in all stages of the policy process.

Could it be, then, that problems and policy responses, and the political *processes* adopted in formulating those responses, are converging in Western Europe? Do Western European democracies have a particular 'way of doing things' in the policy field from which we can identify certain key characteristics? Is it possible to identify the primary characteristics of the policy processes in individual countries with a view to classifying them according to a simple typology of *policy styles*? Are there truly national characteristics in the policy field as well as in, say, social life?

The present collection of essays is an exploration of these questions. We use the word exploration advisedly, for one of the chief problems in such an exercise is that because the amount of policy-making and implementing activity of the modern state *is* so massive, our knowledge of it can at best be patchy. Do we at present have enough detailed knowledge of the policy process, across a range of policy sectors and over a period of time, in order to identify its key characteristics, if indeed there *are* key characteristics? In practice the data for each European country are neither fully systematic, nor fully comparable. Yet because of the importance of policy studies in political science, we do know a good deal about policy processes in Europe. As is clear from the list of authors, the contributors to this volume are all highly experienced observers of the policy processes in their selected countries. They have tried to reflect, within the limits of available data, on attitudes and behaviour in the policy process. Our hope is that we have gone some way towards highlighting the most salient features of policy processes in Western Europe, through the concept of policy style, as well as pointing out the need for more systematic policy research, both in terms of single-country studies and in terms of comparative public policy.

The contributors wish to acknowledge the generous support of the Nuffield Foundation for a workshop, held at the University of Keele, England, in January 1981. We benefited greatly from being able to meet and argue and, hopefully, to agree on an approach which is sufficiently coherent to bind the individual studies together, yet allows each author the flexibility demanded by his data base and by the special features of his selected country. As editor of the volume I am especially grateful to the individual contributors for accepting the difficult challenge of adequately covering a country's policy process in a single chapter. If nothing else, they are all radical/heroic rather than incremental/humdrum in their approach to policy studies! I also wish to thank Kim Pickerill, of the Politics Department at Keele, for her work in the preparation of the manuscript and Paul Smart for his assistance with the preparation of the index.

September 1981   JEREMY J. RICHARDSON

1 The Concept of Policy Style

JEREMY RICHARDSON, University of Strathclyde;
GUNNEL GUSTAFSSON, University of Umeå;
GRANT JORDAN, University of Aberdeen

Introduction

A number of writers have attempted to identify the central characteristics of the policy process in particular countries and some attempts have been made to develop comparative analyses (Rokkan, 1966; Anton, 1969; Heisler, and Kvavik, 1974; Hayward, 1974, 1976; Kvavik, 1976; Richardson and Jordan, 1979). For example, Hayward has linked the study of economic planning with the notions of 'humdrum' and 'heroic' approaches to policy-making (Hayward, 1974, pp. 388–400).

In Britain there is a well-developed body of literature describing the predilection for consultation and the strong desire to avoid action that might challenge well-entrenched interests. Such description differs from conventional analysis of France, which presents a policy system characterised by secrecy, limited consultation, immobilism and stagnation most of the time, and an assertive government and abrupt and radical change some of the time. Descriptions of Sweden have, in the past, emphasised consultation, but in contrast to Britain more 'rational' processes of search for solutions were found and more radical outcomes were said to emerge. In contrast to France, however, the Swedish state was less likely to resort to coercive behaviour.

These examples, which could be easily expanded and augmented, treat policy styles as *divergent*. In contrast, there is a case that the policy routines of various West European countries are essentially similar: policy styles are *convergent*. In an earlier work (Richardson and Jordan, 1979) we noted how a series of what were intended as descriptions of unique national policy procedures, ended up with a close family resemblance: there may well be a European policy style (Heisler and Kvavik, 1974). The chapters in the rest of this book attempt to assemble available evidence to allow us to speculate on whether policy styles are essentially divergent or convergent. Are there trends making societies more dissimilar or similar? If there are changes, what forces are at work?

Anton has argued that political scientists need to shift their focus of concern from the single decision to the structure of the relationship between participants and the norms which serve to maintain or change the relationship through time: the focus shifts, in other words, from *decision to systems of decision-making* (Anton, 1969). We see policy styles as different systems of decision-making, different procedures for making societal decisions.

By policy style we perhaps, more cumbersomely, really mean policy-*making* and *implementation* style. Our interest is thus not limited to policy-making, but also encompasses policy execution. We are interested in whether societies develop 'standard operating procedures' for making and implementing policies. It is also possible to argue that most societies develop legitimising norms for policy activity. These reflect often deep-rooted values in society (sometimes even in the form of constitutional and legal rules). For example, in the Swedish case, 'belief in science and secular rationality' is seen as a core modern value related to the 'belief in the use of knowledge to shape the environment, which no country does more than Sweden' (Tomasson, 1970; Wittrock, 1980). This is, of course, not to say that the 'match' between *normative* values relating to the policy process and *actual behaviour* will always be close. The two can diverge for a number of reasons. A society might place a high value on consultation and it may, therefore, be necessary to surround policy-making with a plethora of consultative committees or to go through long and wide-ranging consultation processes. Yet in practice these consultations can be a sham to hide the real locus of decision. (In Britain, for example, it is common for environmental groups to claim that public inquiries into new road-building schemes or nuclear-power proposals give no real opportunity for them to influence actual policy outcomes.) Consultations involving literally hundreds of pressure groups and thousands of individuals may be used to disguise what may be termed 'inner-circle negotiation', involving a very limited range of groups who 'matter'. There may also be a conflict not only between the normative values and actual practice, but also between the normative values themselves. Thus, it might be felt that 'governments should govern' *and* that 'governments should consult and seek consensus'. These two values can, in certain circumstances, be in conflict. Thus, electorates may vote for 'strong government' yet reject a government whose policies lead to 'confrontation'.

Difficulties in Identifying Policy Style

In practice, we believe that policy-makers (be they politicans or civil servants) will often try to develop standard operating procedures for handling issues which arrive on the political agenda (that is, there is a behavioural policy style). The flow of issues on to the agenda is never-ending and procedures have to be devised for 'processing' them. Though difficult, we believe that it should eventually be possible for political scientists to identify the *main* characteristics of the ways in which a given society formulates and implements its public policies. We, of course, recognise that the processes are complex and the task difficult. Morever, we would not wish to argue that in any one society public policies are *always* formulated and implemented in a particular way. Even if a predominant style can be identified, exceptions will always occur. For example, the reorganisation of the water industry in Britain (Jordan *et al.*, 1977) can be seen as a rather unusual departure from what observers have seen as the main characteristic of the British approach to policy-making – namely, a predilection for consultation, avoidance of radical policy change and a strong desire to avoid actions which might challenge well-entrenched interests (Hayward, 1974; Brown, 1974). The 'water' case was certainly contrary to the norm of passing only acceptable policies (acceptable, that is, to the interested groups).

One of the biggest difficulties in trying to identify a predominant style is, of course, presented by the now familiar phenomenon of the sectorisation of policy-making. Thus, if policies are formulated independently in each policy sector (in fact , this itself could be identified as one of the primary characteristics of a political system) – in what can be termed 'policy com-munities', 'policy networks' and 'policy circuits' (Jordan, 1981) – then this itself may invalidate a search for one policy style. If each policy area develops into a semi-watertight compartment, ruled by its own 'policy elite', then quite different policy styles may develop within the same political system (Richardson, 1979). A model which accurately describes one policy area may be inappropriate as a description of another and quite misleading descriptions of national systems can result. Indeed, any one policy sector may itself exhibit more than one policy style.

It may also be the case that the policy issue itself may be a determinant of the way in which a problem is 'processed'. Thus Lowi, in what is the best-known categorisation of issues, has argued that different types of policy promote different types of political activity (Lowi, 1964). In other words, he notes that a variety of different political behaviours (what we would term policy styles) exist in society and feels that he can explain these behaviours by reference to the *types* of issue at stake. Lowi can be crudely summarised in the following proposition, that public policies can be divided into three main types (distributive, regulatory and redistributive) and that the kind of politics associated with these policies differs along lines determined by the basic policy type. He presents his argument in one key diagram (see Table 1.1).

Table 1.1 can be interpreted as being a description of three styles of decision-making. Lowi's argument is that type of policy is one of the 'conditions that cause variations in the procedural characteristics of political systems'. Lowi would presumably dissent from the notion of *national* policy style and could instead demand that the policy content would have to be first stipulated. The Lowi approach has appeal based on logic. In other words, the idea that relations will vary when the state is attempting to distribute benefits and when it is enforcing regulations is attractive.

Table 1.1   *Arenas and Political Relationships: A Diagrammatic Summary*

Arena	Primary political unit	Relation among units	Power structure	Stability of structure	Primary decisional locus	Implementation
Distribution	Individual, firm, corporation	Log-rolling, mutual non-interference, uncommon interests	Non-conflictual elite with support groups	Stable	Congressional committee and/or agency	Agency centralised to primary functional unit ('bureau')
Regulation	Group	'The coalition', shared subject-matter interest, bargaining	Pluralistic multi-centred, 'theory of balance'	Unstable	Congress, in classic role	Agency decentralised from centre by 'delegation', mixed control
Distribution	Association	The 'peak association', class, ideology	Conflictual elite, i.e. elite and counter-elite	Stable	Executive and peak associations	Agency centralised towards top (above 'bureau'), elaborate standards

Source: Lowi, 1964, p. 713.

The Lowi scheme, however, has had more admirers than followers, and it seems difficult to use his categories in practice. Moreover, his types of policies do not appear to be exhaustive and the relationship to types of process is not exact. For example, James Wilson makes several objections to Lowi's typology, though in the sense that he also sees a causal relationship between issues and processes, he is not in conflict with the basic principles of the Lowi scheme (Wilson, 1973). Wilson's preference is to distinguish between policy innovation and policy adaptation. He postulates that there is a substantially different kind of politics over innovation than over revision. The difficulty, as with Lowi, is that because most examples are ambiguous, it is difficult to fit them into very refined schemes.

Our own position is that authors such as Lowi and Wilson are absolutely correct in pointing out that all policies are not handled in the same way. We would argue, however, that it is equally true to say that policies are not so distinctive as to prevent them being accommodated in a basic simple typology of policy styles. Moreover, if there are common trends in liberal democracies, then it might well be the case that not only is there a convergence of national styles, but that cross-sectoral differences, and differences between types of policies, will be gradually eroded. Are there forces at work which, like the impact of high fuel prices on motor-car designs, lead to some conformity? Are there forces which encourage all policy sectors to behave similarly in any one country – to adopt common operating procedures? In particular, do the increased mobilisation of interest groups and the development of what may be called 'unconventional participation' bring with them certain practical imperatives in the policy-making and implementing process, irrespective of policy sectors?

Overcrowding and Unconventional Participation

Writing in 1975 Heclo referred to the 'crowded policy environment' in the sense that 'partitions which were previously assumed to separate policy areas are more often being called into question ... The interplay of what were once thought to be exogenous factors for a given program is increasingly seen as integral to its very substance' (Heclo, 1975, p. 404). Elsewhere we have argued that Western democracies are subject to a different form of 'overcrowding' of policy sectors, in addition to the increasing interdependence of policy problems described by Heclo (Gustafsson and Richardson, 1979; 1980). We have suggested that many policy sectors are now subject to participation by increased numbers of interest groups (and sometimes ordinary citizens, too) and that this participation is causing an 'overcrowding', leading to increased difficulty in reaching agreed decisions in each policy sector. We see this as an important phenomenon in what have been called 'post-industrial' societies.

Even before the 'post-industrial period', interest groups in most Western democracies exercised influence through informal and formal contacts with decision-makers. Thus, writers on Britain have long seen the role of interest groups as quite central to the policy process (Beer, 1956; Finer, 1958; Eckstein, 1960; Hayward, 1974, 1976; Richardson and Jordan, 1979). Observers of the USA have seen consultation, bargaining and negotiation with interest groups as a central feature of the US political system (Dahl,

1967; Lowi, 1969). In Scandinavia very similar labels have been used. Rokkan's description of numerical democracy and corporate pluralism is well known (Rokkan, 1966, p. 107). His view was echoed in Kvavik (1976) and by Christensen and Rønning (1977). In Sweden Elvander has concluded that there is possibly the strongest interest group system in the world (Elvander, 1974). Lijphart's study of Holland (though see van Putten's study in this volume for an important qualification), where he coined the term 'the politics of accommodation', clearly fits this pattern (Lijphart, 1968), and even in France there is a suggestion that we may all have underestimated the degree of group involvement in the policy process (Suleiman, 1974). There is a possibility that we have been bemused by the more spectacular defeats of groups in France, because these have been the object of so many studies, and have missed the quieter activity of the organised interests in some sectors.

What we have seen with the onset of post-industrialisation is an intensification of these developments – hence the flourishing debate on corporatism (Ruin, 1974; Schmitter, 1974, 1977; Pahl and Winkler, 1976; Panitch, 1977, 1980; Cawson, 1978, 1979; Heisler, 1979; Cox, 1981). Alongside this development, there may well have been a change in the nature of some of the demands which decision-makers have to process. In particular, the development of non-materialistic values may have rather important consequences for the policy process. Increasingly, conflict within 'policy communities' is not just about the distribution of material benefits to different sections of society, but is also concerned with what Inglehart has identified as non-materialistic values (Inglehart, 1977). The role of environmentalists, in articulating non-material values, has been particularly significant. As Cotgrove and Duff argue, disagreement with the central values and beliefs of the dominant social paradigm can often run deep: 'Not only do they [the environmentalists] challenge the importance attached to material and economic goals, they by contrast give much higher priority to the realisation of non-material values – to social relationships and community, to the exercise of human skills and capacities, and to increased participation in decisions that affect our daily lives' (Cotgrove and Duff, 1980, p. 34). A further development is the apparent increase in what can be termed 'unconventional participation'. Put simply, many new groups, and following their example some long-established groups as well, have exhibited behaviour quite outside the 'rules' of the normally well-regulated policy systems.

Overcrowding

It is not difficult to show that the number of interest groups seeking an active role in policy-making, at both national and local levels, has increased very considerably. The 'environmentalist' groups again provide a good example. In the United Kingdom, for example, it was estimated that the vast majority (85 per cent) of local amenity societies were formed after 1957 (Barker, 1976). The number of groups nationally active in the environmental field also increased in the 1960s and 1970s. Many of these groups brought a new holistic and ecological perspective to bear on environmental and pollution problems (Brookes and Richardson, 1975). Even long-established 'preservationist' groups became more active and determined to influence policy. By 1975 it was estimated that membership of the environmental movement in Britain had possibly reached 2 million (Lowe, 1975). In West Germany it has been estimated that the new 'grass-roots' organisations (groups) have more participants than the political parties (Mayer-Tasch, 1976). An official Danish survey demonstrated that the number of local administrations which had contact with grass-roots organisations increased from 36 to 51 per cent over 1973–6 (Gundelach, 1978). Even in France, hardly thought to be the cradle of 'interest group liberalism', it has been estimated that during the period 1967–76 an average of 25,000 voluntary associations (mostly local) were established annually, compared with only 1,000 in the interwar period (Hayward, 1979, p. 29). It is almost a truism to say that the arrival of these large numbers of groups on the political scene has made the task of the decision–maker much more difficult. For example, the lead time for large development projects such as road building, power stations and airports has been adversely affected by the need to accommodate the demands of such groups and some projects have had to be abandoned. What might have been a routine and rather technical decision about, say, road construction in 1950, is now often a hotly debated issue, involving rather wide participation and quite new values in society. In the United Kingdom policy-makers became so worried (by the growth in groups in the field of road planning) that they commissioned outside consultants to advise them on procedures for identifying groups which might have an interest in a given road scheme. Deliberately excluding some groups was not really a viable alternative, as they would force their way into the policy process one way or another.

Sweden is a particularly interesting example of the demand for participation. Despite having a very well-developed system for integrating groups through the use of the Royal Commission and 'remiss' systems, it has nevertheless been a significant example of what we see as potential over-crowding. The strong demands for participation, which have characterised all Western democracies during the post-industrial period, have resulted in Sweden in extending the accommodation of both new and old groups to almost every decision-making situation. The Swedish case is an important example of not only overcrowding, but also of the potential impact of new groups bringing new, non-materialistic values with them. There has been a vigorous debate in Swedish society over the nuclear energy issue, and this debate has had rather clear post-materialistic overtones. Gradually the debate came to include discussion not just of the safety or economics of nuclear power generation, but also of the issue of what kind of society the Swedes really want. If society decides to emphasise the provision of non-materialistic things, for example, more time with one's family, as much as or more than purely materialistic objects such as more Volvos, then the whole nuclear question may be quite irrelevant – or so the argument goes. The West German case, particularly in the field of nuclear energy, has seen the coming together of all these groups articulating non-material values through highly unconventional participation. The severe riots in West Germany in early 1981 were all too obvious a sign that the political system was having as much difficulty 'processing' the nuclear issue as it was in processing the actual nuclear waste.

Unconventional Participation

We recognise, of course, that the term 'unconventional' participation contains a degree of ambiguity. For example, at what point does a form of participation become so common and well established that it is no longer unconventional? Also what may be quite common (and hence conventional) in one country may be regarded as very unconventional in another. French farmers have traditionally resorted to direct action, for example, blocking roads or pouring milk down the street, in order to force the government to grant higher prices or better subsidies. British farmers have generally adopted very well-ordered behaviour to achieve their aims through the annual farm price review-type procedure, but even they have occasionally copied the French model and have resorted to direct action. But for the purposes of this chapter we see unconventional participation as behaviour which does not conform to the regularised processes of consultation, considered argument and debate, presentation of evidence, acceptance of rules and procedures for handling conflict or, indeed, respect for the law. Thus, the sit-in – though clearly a form of participation – is unconventional in this sense. In the 1960s students concluded that consultation with university vice-chancellors and rectors was unlikely to bring about the desired change. University administrators throughout the world found themselves having to deal with occupied offices, rifled filing cabinets and even arson.

As it turned out, the mass media gave such 'participation' a great deal of publicity – the non-traditional always being more newsworthy. This publicity had the effect of causing the spread of this form of participation throughout society and, indeed, across national boundaries. New forms of participation of this unconventional nature thus become quickly 'internationalised', as do the issues with which they are concerned. Because of the media attention, 'sit-ins' and other forms of direct action had arrived on the political agenda as an issue in themselves, whether decision-makers liked it or not. Workers also came to see the effectiveness of the sit-in and the work-in as additions to more conventional trade union behaviour and bargaining.

Public authorities have, of course, faced similar situations and have had to cope with such examples of unconventional participation as mothers blocking roads in support of their demands for children's crossings and day care facilities. In the United Kingdom the public inquiry system was placed under great stress in the period 1970–9 by the quite unprecedented behaviour of anti-road groups in disrupting the hearings. While quite 'disapproved of', these actions nevertheless secured concessions in the form of changed procedures and rules, allowing the presentation of much broader arguments against new road schemes. Thus, unconventional participation can be quite effective in producing procedural and structural change in the policy process. It is no accident that we have seen a large number of experiments in participation in countries such as Sweden (Gidlund, 1978), Denmark (Tonboe *et al.*, 1977) and the United Kingdom (Richardson, 1978). It has been in the area of physical planning that we have seen the most examples of unconventional participation. Public authorities have therefore had to respond with new procedures and new structures for consultation, and have had to recognise more groups as having a legitimate interest, in order to return to a more stable and ordered policy-making environment.

It is, of course, not always the case that procedural or structural change is sufficient to stabilise the policy-making environment. Some situations are not so easily managed and it is not so easy to negotiate order from the chaos caused by unconventional participation. Unconventional participation may, in fact, create a situation where the decision-maker has to accept defeat. Stockholm's famous 'battle of the elms' is a good example of this. At the end of the day the subway station could not be built on the planners' desired location. Today the trees continue to grow in the threatened park and the new subway station is located at a site where it is little used by travellers! In other cases, of course, the decision-maker neither introduces procedural change, nor accepts defeat. He decides to enforce his decision.

Sectorisation and Bureaucratisation as Trends

Other writers have also suggested that there is a certain 'logic' arising from the nature of advanced industrial democracies. Thus, Dahl has described how, because of its inherent requirements, an advanced economy and its supporting social structures automatically distribute political resources and political skills to a vast variety of individuals, groups and organisations. This disaggregated power (and skills) means that there is a tendency to negotiation and bargaining rather than direction. This helps 'to foster a political sub-culture with norms that legitimate negotiating, bargaining, log-rolling, give and take, the gaining of consent as against unilateral power of coercion' (Dahl, 1971, pp. 66–77). The tendency to develop a disaggregated approach to policy-making has also been linked to the 'logic' of bureaucracy. Thus, Lindberg has suggested that sectorisation is a congenital feature of bureaucracy. He suggests that individuals in bureaucratic settings typically deal with challenges presented by rapidly changing complex and interactive problems in ways that reinforce a disaggregated and sectoral approach to policy' (Lindberg, 1977, p. 372). The disaggregation of the policy system into sectors brings with it the phenomenon of clientelism (La Palombara, 1964). Wildavsky has put the general position as follows:

> Every agency wants more money; the urge to survive and expand is built in. Clientele groups, on whom an agency depends for support, judge the agency by how much it does for them. The more the clients receive, the larger they grow, the more they can help the agency. (Wildavsky, 1975, p. 7.)

Habermas, too, has emphasised the degree to which public policy-making can become 'privatised'. He sees a 'rationality deficit' because 'authorities, with little information and planning capacity . . . are dependent on the flow of information from their clients. They are thus unable to preserve the distance from them necessary for independent decisions' (Habermas, 1976, p. 62). The bureaucratisation of problems means that bargains can be struck between professionals who respect the limitation on resources. A rapidly developing jargon has emerged in an attempt to describe this 'new politics'. Beer has coined the term 'professional-bureaucratic complex' (Beer, 1956), and Heclo uses the term 'technopols' and policy-making by the 'journeymen of issues' (Heclo, 1978, pp. 105–6). These 'policy watchers' do not share opinions, but share an understanding and language that 'comes from sustained attention to a given policy debate' (Heclo, 1978, p. 99).

The symbiosis between bureaucrats, groups and policy professionals, which many writers detect, is often matched by the desire of politicians to reach consensus and avoid conflict. Indeed politicians may, more than other actors in the policy process, see consensus as the objective of policy-making, rather than solving problems in a more technical sense (Gustafsson and Richardson, 1979). As Neustadt suggests, command decisions are politically expensive (Neustadt, 1980). By resolving conflict in 'private government', issues are kept off an already crowded political agenda.

A Simple Basic Typology of Policy Styles

Our discussion of Lowi's typology of policy issues and processes has indicated the complexity which such an exercise can involve. The reader

Table 1.2 *Attempted Comprehensive Matrix*

Issue style	*Policy initiator*	*Arena of decision*	*Decision technique employed by participants*	*Type of decision**	*Type of resolution*	*Implementation*
Compensatory	Group	Bureaucratic	All Rationalist	(1) Political-high	Command	Self-executing
Distributive	Media	Political	All Incrementalist	(2) Technical	Consensus,	Bargained implementa-
Regulatory	Department	Community	All Bounded rationality	(3) Political-specific	etc.	tion
Redistributive	Parties	Parliamentary	Rationality/	(4) Departmental,		
Self-regulatory	Environmental	Party, etc.	Incrementalist	etc.		
Constitutional, etc.	change, etc.		permutations, etc.			

* Adapted from Boyle (1980).

will no doubt be able to devise new categories of both policies and processes, each more complex than the last. We ourselves tried combining various categorisations, such as Lowi's, with others (for example, Boyle, 1980) and produced the matrix in Table 1.2. (For another attempt, see Chapter 3.) This matrix tries to combine typologies of issues, arenas of decision, decision techniques, type of decision, type of enforcement and type of implementation. The exercise was based on the premiss that there are differences in the way policies are determined and executed both within and between societies. We would argue that such an exhaustive model as that in the table (even this preliminary form has several thousand permutations!) is unmanageable. In a search for a typology of policy style which was at least manageable, and which was sufficiently flexible to facilitate cross-national comparisons, we concluded that we must retain a very simple and basic matrix.

Our necessarily brief review of what observers have identified as a characteristic policy 'style' (though not necessarily using that term) suggests that it is useful to concentrate on what we see as the two *primary features* of policy-making systems in devising a typology of policy styles. In identifying what we saw as the primary features we were, of course, conscious of the fact that there is unlikely to be agreement on what the primary features of a policy system are. Even if agreement could be reached, then the primary features would still only convey a very basic description of the system. It does appear, however, that many descriptions of individual policy systems are more or less related to two factors. (1) A government's approach to problem-solving – often characterised in terms of the incrementalist/rationalist debate. An examination of national case studies suggests that some policy processes are seen as incrementalist in their basic features, while others were (comparatively at least) thought to be more 'rational'. The two principal characterisations of government approaches to problem-solving were then (with key words):

Incrementalist – with conflict over values, analysis at the margins, mutual adjustment, a premium placed on consultation and agreement, successive limited comparisons, low coercion, 'managerial' change, and so on.
Rationalist – central authority, high coercion ability, limited conflict over values, wide search for options, clear objectives, a possibility of radical change, and so on.

The difficulty with this rather popular approach is that it runs the risk of being embroiled in the rationalist/incremental debate and in questions of what *is* rational. We have elsewhere discussed some of these issues (Gustafsson and Richardson, 1979). In terms of formulating a typology of policy styles we think it is more useful to characterise approaches to problem-solving in terms of governments taking either an *anticipatory/*

active attitude towards societal problems, or taking an essentially *reactive* approach to problem-solving.

(2) The second 'primary' factor appears to be a government's relationship to other actors in the policy-making and implementing process. For example, how do governments 'deal' with the interest groups in society? Is a government very accommodating and concerned to reach a *consensus* with organised groups, or is it more inclined towards *imposing* decisions notwithstanding opposition from groups?

Our hope is that these two primary factors will at least be generally accepted as central aspects of the policy system in any one country, even if readers would see other factors of equal importance. Certainly, it would be easy to justify extending the list. For example, Premfors (1981) has argued that degree of *centralisation*, degree of *openness* and degree of *deliberation* should be added as central features of a policy process. Our own preference remains for simplicity in order to increase the heuristic value of our typology in comparative terms (that is, one should avoid a country-specific typology, if it is to be used for comparative analysis). We would, therefore, define policy style as *the interaction between* (a) *the government's approach to problem-solving and* (b) *the relationship between government and other actors in the policy process.*

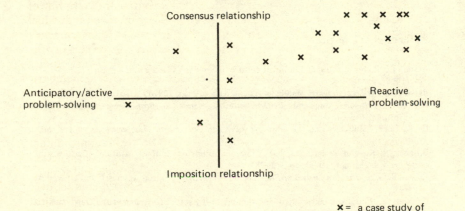

Figure 1.1   *A national policy style*

Such a definition enables us to categorise societies into four basic 'policy styles'. Thus, some societies seem to be located in a category which we might see as emphasising consensus and a reactive attitude to problem-solving. Others appear to be located in a category also stressing consensus but with a set of normative values which emphasise an anticipatory or active approach to problem-solving. Others are seemingly less concerned with consensus, but see the role of the state as being rather active and being willing (even having a duty) to impose policy change in the face of opposition from organised interests. A fourth category into which we suspect most post-industrial societies may be moving, is where governments are increasingly reactive rather than anticipatory in their approach to problem-solving yet, if any policy change is to be achieved, it has to be enforced against the resistance of at least some organised groups.

By concentrating on our two primary factors in the policy process we produced a simple basic typology of policy styles as shown in Figure 1.1.

Our working premiss is that (*a*) this basic typology has value in comparative terms and can be 'stretched' or amended to fit a range of countries, and (*b*) an analysis of a range of case studies would enable the researcher to 'map' a policy system. Thus, we would expect case studies to be 'clustered' in one sector of our diagram, enabling the researcher to identify the predominant policy style for any given country. Our hope, therefore, is that this basic typology will be both useful in analysing the policy systems of individual countries, and in helping to identify any cross-national trends.

References: Chapter 1

Anton, T., 'Policy-making and political culture in Sweden', *Scandinavian Political Studies*, vol. 4, (1969), pp. 88–102.

Barker, A., *The Local Amenity Movement* (London Civic Trust, 1976).

Beer, S. H., 'Pressure groups and parties in Britain', *American Political Science Review*, vol. L, no. 1 (1956), pp. 613–50.

Boyle, Lord, 'Ministers and the administrative process', *Public Administration*, vol. 8, no. 1 (1980).

Brookes, S. K., and Richardson, J. J., 'The environmental lobby in Britain', *Parliamentary Affairs*, vol. 28, no. 4 (1975), pp. 312–28.

Brown, R. G. S., *The Administrative Process as Incrementalism* (Milton Keynes: Open University, 1974).

Cawson, A., 'Pluralism, corporatism and the role of the state', *Government and Opposition*, vol. 13, no. 2 (1978), pp. 178–98.

Cawson, A., 'Representational crises and corporatism in capitalist societies', paper presented at the ECPR Workshops, Brussels, Belgium, 1979.

Christensen, G., and Rønning, R., *Organizational Participation in Governmental Politics* (Colchester: European Consortium for Political Research, 1977).

Cotgrove, S., and Duff, A., 'Environmentalism, middle class radicalism and politics', *Sociological Review*, vol. 28, no. 2 (1980), pp. 333–51.

Cox, A., 'Corporatism as reductionism: the analytical limits of the corporatist thesis', *Government and Opposition*, vol. 16, no. 1 (1981), pp. 78–95.

Dahl, R. A., *Pluralist Democracy in the United States* (Chicago: Rand McNally, 1967).

Dahl, R. A., *Polyarchy* (New Haven, Conn./London: Yale University Press, 1971).

Eckstein, H., *Pressure Group Politics: The Case of the British Medical Association* (London: Allen & Unwin, 1960).

Elvander, N., 'Interest groups in Sweden', *Annals*, vol. 413 (May, 1974), pp. 27–43.

Finer, S. E., *Anonymous Empire* (London: Pall Mall, 1958).

Gidlund, J., 'The responsiveness of decision-makers on the local level in Sweden', paper presented at the ECPR Workshops, Grenoble, France, 1978.

Gundelach, P., 'Grass-roots organisations: can they be subversived?', paper presented at the ECPR Workshops, Grenoble, France, 1978.

Gustafsson, G., and Richardson, J. J., 'Concepts of rationality and the policy process', *European Journal of Political Research*, vol. 7, no. 4 (1979), pp. 415–36.

Gustafsson, G., and Richardson, J. J., 'Post-industrial changes in policy style', *Scandinavian Political Studies*, vol. 3 (new series), no. 1 (1980), pp. 21–37.

Habermas, J., *Legitimation Crisis* (London: Heinemann, 1976).

Hayward, J. E. S., 'National aptitudes for planning in Britain, France and Italy', *Government and Opposition*, vol. 9, no. 4 (1974), pp. 397–410.

Hayward, J. E. S., 'Institutional inertia and political impetus in France and Britain', *European Journal of Political Research*, vol. 4, no. 4 (1976), pp. 341–59.

Hayward, J. E. S., 'Interest groups and the demand for state action', in J. E. S. Hayward and R. N. Berki (eds), *State and Society in Contemporary Europe* (Oxford: Robertson, 1979).

Heclo, H., 'Frontiers of social policy in Europe and America', *Policy Sciences*, vol. 6, no. 4 (1975), pp. 403–21.

Heclo, H., 'Issue networks and the executive establishment', in A. King (ed.), *The New American Political System* (Washington, DC: American Enterprise Institute, 1978).

Heisler, M. O., 'Corporate pluralism revisited: where is the theory?', *Scandinavian Political Studies*, vol. 2 (new series), no. 3 (1979), pp. 277–97.

Heisler, M. O., and Kvavik, R. B., 'Patterns of European politics: the "European polity" model', in M. O. Heisler (ed.), *Politics in Europe* (New York: McKay, 1974).

Inglehart, R., 'Political dissatisfaction and mass support for social change in advanced industrial society', *Comparative Political Studies*, vol. 10, no. 3 (1977), pp. 455–72.

Jordan, A. Grant, 'Iron triangles, woolly corporatism and elastic nets: images of the policy process', *Journal of Public Policy*, vol. 1, pt 1 (February 1981), pp. 95–123.

Jordan, A. Grant, Richardson, J. J. and Kimber, R. H., 'The origins of the Water Act 1973', *Public Administration*, vol. 55 (Autumn, 1977), pp. 317–34.

Kvavik, R. S., *Interest Groups in Norwegian Politics* (Oslo: Universitetsforlaget, 1976).

La Palombara, J., *Interest Groups in Italian Politics* (Princeton, NJ: Princeton University Press, 1964).

Lijphart, A., *The Politics of Accommodation: Pluralism in the Netherlands* (Berkeley, Calif.: University of California Press, 1968).

Lindberg, L. N., 'Energy policy and the politics of economic development', *Comparative Political Studies*, vol. 10, no. 3 (1977).

Lowe, P. D., 'The environmental lobby: political resources', *Built Environment Quarterly*, June 1975, pp. 73–6.

Lowi, T., 'American business, public policy, case studies, and political theory', *World Politics*, vol. XVI, no. 4 (1964), pp. 677–715.

Lowi, T., *The End of Liberalism* (New York: Norton, 1969).

Mayer-Tasch, P. C., *Die Bürgerinitiativebewegung: Der aktive Bürger als rechts und politikwissenschaftliches Problem* (Hamburg: Rowohlt, 1976).

Neustadt, R. E., *Presidential Power: The Politics of Leadership* (New York: Wiley, 1980).

Pahl, R. E. and Winkler, J. T., 'Corporatism in Britain', in *The Corporate State – Reality or Myth?* (London: Centre for Studies in Social Policy, 1976).

Panitch, L., 'The development of corporatism in liberal democracies', *Comparative Political Studies*, vol. 10, no. 1 (1977), pp. 61–90.

Panitch, L., 'Recent theorizations of corporatism: reflections on a growth industry', *British Journal of Sociology*, vol. 31, no. 2 (1980), pp. 159–87.

Premfors, R., *The Politics of Higher Education in a Comparative Perspective: France, Sweden, United Kingdom*, Studies in Politics No. 15, Stockholm (1981).

Richardson, J. J., 'Public participation and policy styles: rational policy-making vs public participation', paper presented at the ECPR Workshops, Grenoble, France, 1978.

Richardson, J. J., 'Policy-making and rationality in Sweden: the case of transport', *British Journal of Political Science*, vol. 9, no. 3 (1979), pp. 314–53.

Richardson, J. J. and Jordan, A. G., *Governing Under Pressure: The Policy Process in a Post-Parliamentary Democracy* (Oxford: Robertson, 1979).

Rokkan, S., 'Norway: numerical democracy and corporate pluralism', in R. A. Dahl (ed.), *Political Oppositions in Western Democracies* (New Haven, Conn.: Yale University Press, 1966), pp. 70–115.

Ruin, O., 'Participatory democracy and corporativism: the case of Sweden', Scandinavian Political Studies, vol. 9 (1974), pp. 171–84.

Schmitter, P. C., 'Still the century of corporativism?', *Review of Politics*, vol. 36 (January 1974), pp. 85–131.

Schmitter, P. C., 'Modes of interest intermediation and models of societal change in Western Europe', *Comparative Political Studies*, vol. 10, no. 1 (1977) pp. 7–38.

Suleiman, E., *Politics, Power and Bureaucracy in France* (Princeton, NJ: Princeton University Press, 1974).

Tomasson, R. F., *Sweden: Prototype of Modern Society* (New York: Random House, 1970).

Tonboe, J. C., Bovin, B. and Meulengracht, K., *Regionalplandebat: En sociologisk undersøgelse på Bornholm 1975–6* (Copenhagen: Statens Byggeforskningsinstitut, SBI-Byplan lægning 33, 1977).

Wildavsky, A., *Budgeting: A Comparative Theory of Budgetary Processes* (Boston, Mass.: Little, Brown, 1975).

Wilson, James Q., *Political Organisations* (New York: Basic Books, 1973).

Wittrock, B., *Mögligheter och gränser* (Stockholm: Liber, 1980), ISBN 91-38-05511-2.

2 West Germany: The Search for a Rationalist Consensus

KENNETH DYSON, University of Bradford

Introduction

The West German policy process is extremely diversified and complex. Policy is made in different ways not only between sectors, but also in the same sector. Nevertheless, it is possible to identify an element of order in the policy process. West German policy style is distinctive; it reflects a particular historical experience and the cultural attitudes that have emerged from that experience. It can be broken down into a set of models, and the dynamics of change of policy style over time can be explored. Collapse of the Weimar Republic, the experience of the Third Reich and of the devastation of war, and the labour of reconstruction have led West German political leaders to spell out the normative framework of policy to a greater degree than is typical of West European societies. West German policy style rests on an explicit normative code that has been modified by the experience of past political crisis and war. There are, nevertheless, interesting and important elements of continuity.

One aspect of policy style is the intellectual style of policy, the approach to problem-solving. West Germany is characterised by a high-minded and didactic style of thought about policy that focuses on *Sachlichkeit* (objectivity) and on public-regarding attitudes and that has its cultural roots in a tradition of distaste for the materialism of politicking. The aspect of style can take the form of a reactive style that emphasises the essentially passive and responsive character of government. Reactive policy style rests on a neo-liberal view of the importance of the state–society distinction and of the impartial role of government as a referee. The reactive style is deductivist and pursues a language of principles. An anticipatory policy style is the opposite intellectual style of problem-solving. This pre-emptive style focuses on the importance of acquiring information and knowledge as the basis of an engaged, innovative role of government. It rests on a 'social-state' ideology and pursues a language of goals, options, appraisal and effectiveness. The shift from a reactive to a more anticipatory policy style during the 1960s was reflected intellectually by changing views of the function of the state as the conception of the state as a framework of order was displaced by the conception of the state as a public-service organisation with a function of development. The shift was prompted politically by the entry of the Social Democratic Party into federal government in 1966 and administratively by the recruitment of *Beamte* (higher officials), who were more politically engaged, had more varied career backgrounds and were more open and tolerant in their political outlook (Dyson, 1977). The shift was also prompted circumstantially in 1965–7 by the first major post-war experience of economic recession and of problems of control of public expenditure.

The other main aspect of policy style involves culturally conditioned attitudes towards the relationship between government and other actors in the policy process. The character of the relationship reflects different conceptions of state and society. A style of negotiation and consensus building is based on a conception of the interdependence of state and society and of the importance of consensus in policy. This style is rooted in the power-sharing that is implicit in the co-operative norms of the 'social-state' ideology, of German federal arrangements and of coalition politics. The authoritative style of imposition is based on a conception of state vs society: the overriding common good must be guaranteed by imposing the technically correct solution. In the first case group power is legitimated; groups acquire officially recognised status and privileged access as useful and respectable bodies. In the second case groups are regarded as potentially irresponsible and disruptive. Imposition has been particularly important in the policy sector of currency management. It has also been an important feature of policy style across sectors in the form of the law. In the Roman law tradition law is conceived to be a coherent, self-sufficient body of norms that will yield a technically correct solution to a dispute. Where negotiation fails to secure consensus, and an interest or party fears a politically imposed solution, it is likely to attempt to close down the issue by seeking an authoritative legal resolution. Hence the nuclear issue has found its way to the administrative courts, lock-outs to the labour courts and issues like abortion, co-determination and Eastern policy to the Federal Constitutional Court. The role of judges and bankers as authoritative decision-makers underlines an important feature of West German policy style – the distrust and fear of party political imposition. If in the end 'governments must govern', the agencies of imposition are removed, or at least distanced, from the realm of partisan politicking. Nevertheless, outside the sectors of currency management and police, imposition of the technically correct solution is a last resort. Negotiation appears the major feature of the relationship between government and groups. Of course, imposition by judges or central bankers may be central in another sense; the possibility of imposition as a last resort encourages participants in the policy process to make negotiation work.

West Germany possesses a relatively stable, higher-order normative code that underpins its policy style. This normative policy style involves an enduring conception of the nature of public authority, with reference to which standards of judgement of policy are made (Dyson, 1980). It does not necessarily describe the behavioural style of policy-makers, which may be characterised by deception and even self-deception. It does, however, permeate their institutional context and the process of their socialisation. The normative policy style is part and parcel of the politicking that is also characteristic of the policy process. Consequently, in certain policy sectors it may be adopted as an expedient tool or camouflage for self-seeking behaviour. Such a tactical use of normative policy style does, nevertheless, suggest its cultural significance. It forms part of the thought processes of policy-makers as a shared way of looking at, and responding to, problems. The language of German policy is thematic and intellectual, remote from colloquial speech. It utilises a carefully delimited vocabulary of theoretical concepts that centre primarily on *Staat* (state) and attempts rational persuasion by fostering an image of competence and *Sachlichkeit*. The language of policy focuses on 'impressive' nouns like *Staat*, *Sicherheit* (security), *Stabilität* (stability), *Verantwortung* (responsibility), *Kooperation* and *Partner*: and on 'creative' verbs like to achieve, to realise and to serve. Both the intellectual and the accommodative styles of West German policy style are historically and culturally conditioned and rest on a normative code that is more explicit than, and different from, that of Britain.

These two dimensions of policy style yield four types of models of policy style in West Germany (see Figure 2.1). In the cases of the models of concertation and status preservation a common emphasis is placed on co-operative, trustworthy 'professional' organisations which acquire privileged, institutionalised status. Status preservation involves a politics of routine, day-to-day relationships, of quiet collaboration between 'insider groups' and governments. Examples are provided by the policy sectors of agriculture, health and the public service. By contrast, concentration is characterised by the pursuit of enlightenment and innovation via a politics of summit diplomacy. Examples are provided by *Konzertierte Aktion* (see p. 35); by the three federal state joint tasks (*Gemeinschaftsaufgaben*) of regional structural policy, agricultural structural policy and investment in higher education; by financial planning; and by the case of the Saar steel rescue. The background and limits of both types of policy style are defined by the prospect of disruptive 'wildcat' action, of a rank-and-file disobedience that jeopardises consensus and the prospects for collaboration. The viability of the styles of status preservation and concertation depends on strong, highly organised groups which are capable of aggregating opinion.

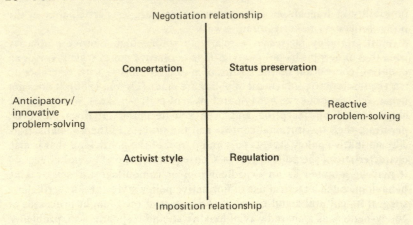

Figure 2.1   *A model of policy style in West Germany*

Regulation and 'activism' are authoritative styles of imposition and differ with respect to the form of problem-solving that they involve. Both styles are aloof and detached compared to the styles of status preservation and concertation. Regulation is the traditional style of bureaucratic legalism, which embodies the highly formalised character of the *Rechtsstaat* (state ruled by law) conception and a neo-liberal political outlook (Dyson, 1980). Perhaps the best examples are provided by the exercise of the police power and by the ordinary courts; both see themselves as applying the law authoritatively in the Roman-law tradition. Other instances might include economic policy and nuclear policy in the 1950s and the notorious attempt to exclude extremists from the public service by application of the Radicals Decree of 1972 (Dyson, 1975). The context and limits of regulation are defined by the prospect of a politics of ideological protest: witness, for example, the citizen action groups (*Bürgerinitiativen*) which were provoked by the Radicals Decree. 'Activism' is an innovative style of imposition of the will of public authorities which perceive themselves to be better informed. As a general rule 'activism' on the part of government is a short-term, exceptional feature of German public policy. The cultural hostility to political 'activism' means that this style is only resorted to in one of two circumstances: when agreement is assumed with respect to a particular and pressing problem (for example, nuclear policy in 1973–6); or when a con-sensus politics of negotiation fails to, or is perceived as unlikely to, create agreement and a solution is seen as pressing (for example, the approach of the Ministry of Labour and Social Affairs to health insurance reform in

1958–60). Nuclear policy and health insurance policy (including the period of the birth of statutory health insurance from the 1880s to the First World War) illustrate how activist government intervention creates new forms of organised political opposition that soon neutralise the will to innovate of government.

This model of policy style seeks to make comprehensible the extraordinary complexity of the West German policy process without losing sight of its variety and the contradictions and tensions that it contains. A given policy sector or a particular case may display various policy styles as well as shifts in the dominant policy style over time. For instance, the Radicals Decree exhibited an activist style in the stage of policy initiation when the attempt was made to anticipate the threat of 'the slow march through the institutions' from the left; and a regulative style in its stages of policy formulation and implementation. The currency management of the Bundesbank embodies in part a regulative style that sees the measures of the Bundesbank as the application of the terms of the law, and in part an activist style that has been suggested by its use of monetary targets in the 1970s. Policy sectors reveal interesting shifts of policy style through time. For instance, the regulative and status preservation ethos of the transport policy sector has been disturbed from the mid-1960s by a threat of political 'activism' that has at least changed the terms of negotiation. Nuclear policy has been characterised by styles of regulation and status preservation in the 1950s and 1960s; by the activism of the early 1970s; and by the search for concertation in the late 1970s. The policy sectors of health and industrial policy have revealed a similar tendency from the mid-1960s: dominant styles of regulation and status preservation have been overlaid by an emphasis on concertation, for instance, in industrial crisis management and in the form of a 'concerted action' that involves a new type of collaboration between the health insurance funds and the doctors' professional organisations.

At a general level it is possible to identify a shift of dominant policy style during the 1960s. There has been a shift from regulation and status preservation to concertation and status preservation as the dominant styles of the policy process. In particular, while regulation remains an important feature of the policy process, it is no longer as characteristic of German public policy as in the 1950s. This gradual change of policy style reflects the politicisation that West Germany experienced in the 1960s and a growing recognition of the disruptive power of both well-organised groups and ad hoc citizen action groups. Consensus was an increasingly important object of German public policy at the expense of concern with realisation of the 'will' of the state. At the same time during the 1970s a new and different development took place. The 'activism' of the Bundesbank created a 'resource squeeze' that made the authoritative style of currency management more significant across all policy sectors and especially in the economic policy sector. Nevertheless, the notable characteristic of West German policy style that distinguishes it from French style is the highly partisan nature of the conception of a politically activist policy style. The demands of the SPD and of the trade unions for an 'active' employment policy and an 'active' structural policy for the economy are controversial. Only the autonomous realms of central banking and law approximate to a French boldness of will. It is the boldness of intellect of West German public policy that constitutes the chief contrast with British policy style and the closest approximation to French policy style.

West German public policy has been shaped by two types of policy-related norms. One norm is that the threat of crisis requires determined leadership. Memories of past economic and political crisis have produced widespread acceptance of the need for imposed change in policy areas like currency management, radicalism (witness the conception of a 'militant' democracy) and human rights and the limitation of power. Another different and more characteristic norm is a reaction to the leadership principle of the Third Reich: power sharing is essential to the restraint of government. The relationship between these norms and the behaviour of policy-makers is established and mediated by the institutional structure of the Federal Republic. Central bankers and judges are powerful institutional actors who act as guarantors of determined leadership. The Bundesbank acts autonomously to fulfil the statutory requirement that it must safeguard the currency; and the significance of the judicial 'activism' of the Federal Constitutional Court has been increased by the provision that it can be drawn quickly into the resolution of an issue of policy through the device of a request that it undertake an abstract review of legislation. Coalition politics and federal politics are institutional guarantors of power sharing and respond to deep cultural fears of a concentration of political power. There is a complex interlocking between the federal and state levels in both policy making, and implementation. With the exception of the policy sectors of education, local government and police, state governments find that most legislation of any importance emanates from Bonn. On the other hand, federal government depends on the states for the implementation of most federal laws 'as a matter of their own concern' and on the experience and expertise that state governments acquire in the administrative process. In addition the federal government faces the powerful Bundesrat, in which sit the state governments. The Bundesrat is a federal legislative organ, has an absolute veto on matters that affect the administrative, financial and territorial interests of the states (in other words, most legislation) and offers the possibility of a dual majority at the federal level. For instance, the 1970s saw the emergence of a different majority in the Bundesrat (CDU/CSU) from that in the Budestag (SPD/FDP). A style of negotiation is well adapted to a political system that is characterised by a wide dispersal of responsibility. Although the gradual establishment of stable and responsible party government has been a novel feature of the Federal Republic, its impact on policy style has been limited. Responsible party government has encouraged resort to an activist political language. However, this political style has been vague and abstract and presented in ideological or personalised terms. It has been notably lacking in the behaviour of the political parties within the policy process. They have preferred a quieter style of collaborative negotiation; electoral changes in relative majorities of parties have served mainly to alter the terms of negotiation.

The characteristics of West Germany's policy style are to be understood against the background of the elements of continuity and change in postwar Germany. The element of continuity is provided by the importance of public officials, especially *Beamte*, in political life. Their influence on policy formation and implementation derives from their presence both in the public bureaucracy, and in the political arena of parties and parliaments (Dyson, 1977). The proportion of *Beamte* and other public officials in the Bundestag has grown continuously from 16·8 per cent in 1949–53 to 41·9 per cent in 1976-80. In some states this group accounts for over 50 per cent of parliamentarians. *Beamte* alone made up 12·3 per cent of CDU (Christian Democratic Union) members in 1978, 13·2 per cent of CSU (the Bavarian Christian Social Union, the sister-party of the CDU) members in 1978, 10 per cent of SPD members in 1977 and 14 per cent of FDP (Free Democratic Party) members in 1977. The reasons for this political presence are complex and relate to the political privileges that are enjoyed by *Beamte*. These privileges include a pension as well as a parliamentary allowance and the prospect of returning to an official carrier. Because they have always been judged by the parties as possessing a special political competence, *Beamte* have been over-represented throughout German parliamentary history, especially as party officeholders. The continuation of their political privileges is ensured by their parliamentary significance and their dominant role in the parliamentary committees that deal with public service affairs. This political presence of the *Beamte* in ministerial organisation, in parliamentary committees and in party committees reinforces the strength of technical values of *Sachlichkeit*, particularly legal values, and an expert attention to detail in the policy process. The faculties of law and economics, in which most public servants are trained, continue to disseminate a language of service to the abstract, impersonal state and a Roman-law tradition of the coherence, consistency, certainty and sense of mission of administrative action. German officials are trained in an intellectual model that emphasises the technical rationality of the *Rechtsstaat*, a conception of a state ruled by law that has been reaffirmed and strengthened after the experience of the Third Reich.

As we have seen, West German policy style is deeply marked by the Third Reich. As far as objectivity and 'public-regarding' attitudes are concerned, an attempt was made to restate tradition. The element of discontinuity in policy style is also the product of reactions to the Third Reich. Quite simply, a policy style of enforcement of change or *dirigisme* has been made difficult by this experience of the 'total state'. Methods and style of economic management and of industrial policy have been notably constrained by the prevailing ideology of the social market economy which in general denied the value of detailed interventions in the economic process. However, within the severe limits of this economic ideology, enforcement was seen to be essential in the policy field of currency management. The closed and authoritative character of this policy field was emphasised because of its cross-sectoral implications and because it was seen as of central importance to the effective functioning of the market economy as well as to the stability of the regime itself. Otherwise enforcement has been an exceptional style of policy in West Germany. The prevailing style of dialogue finds its legitimation in the concept of the *Sozialstaat* and the collaborative ethic of social partnership with which that concept is associated. Traditionally important associations of economic interests have achieved a new official status in the rules of procedure of the federal government. The key 'summit' organisations or *Spitzenverbände* enjoy intimate access to government – the Federation of German Employers' Associations (BDA) contains several hundred individual employers' associations; the Federation of German Industry (BDI) unites some forty national industrial associations, each structured on a federal basis; and another 'peak' organisation integrates the local and district chambers of industry and commerce. These associations employ some 120,000 permanent officials. The leadership style of Chancellors like Konrad Adenauer (CDU), Willy Brandt and Helmut Schmidt was characterised by close and direct contacts to relevant interests, especially to economic interests such as the big banks and the BDI and, under the two SPD Chancellors, to the trade union leaders. A similar 'official' status is enjoyed by powerful 'status' groups which enjoy a monopoly position in the fields of agricultural, banking, health and public service policy. Economic and status groups were represented by so-called *Vertrauensleute im Staatsapparat* (confidants in the state apparatus), by former group officials who had been appointed civil servants in the relevant federal ministry. Thus, during the late 1970s the head of the currency policy division of the Federal Finance Ministry had previously been an official of the Federal Association of German Banks. Groups liked also to appoint senior officials who had long experience of, and intimate contacts within, the Bonn bureaucracy. For instance, for many years the director-general of the BDI was Fritz Neef, former State Secretary in the Economics Ministry; he was replaced by a former State Secretary in the Defence Ministry. Economic and status groups are also strongly represented in the Bundestag committees that deal with their sector of policy. Group representation was especially high in the committees for agriculture (77·8 per cent), labour and social policy (70·4 per cent), economics (63 per cent) and youth, family and health (63 per cent) during the 8th Bundestag. Group officials accounted for some 25 per cent of parliamentarians, the largest group after *Beamte*. Such intimate contacts to a ministry and representation within its relevant parliamentary committee form the basis for the conclusion that the farmers through the *Bauernverband* has achieved a co-determination of agricultural policy (Ackerman, 1970). The claims of groups to have their representatives in positions of authority have been processed through the political parties which, for example, even during the years of CDU–CSU rule, ensured trade union representation in the Ministry of Labour and Social Affairs. Collaborative relationships between the state apparatus and social groups are legitimated by reference not only to the conception of the *Sozialstaat*, but also by reference to the conception of the *Parteienstaat* (party state). The parties were seen as the central institutions guaranteeing a mediation between state apparatus and society (Dyson, 1977).

West German policy style is not easy to label as radical or non-radical, heroic or humdrum. It has radical and non-radical implications. On the one hand, the stress on objectivity and 'public-regarding' attitudes gives a radical dimension to policy style. The correct answer is supposed to be derived from a 'root-and-branch' analysis that starts from first principles. On the other hand, the emphasis on collaborative dialogue can suggest stagnation. In the context of a stable, well-defined and closed policy community like health policy, the policy process is threatened by a sterile and conservative veto politics. Alternatively, if new forms of unconventional participation emerge, as in nuclear policy, the policy process is liable to overcrowding and blockage. Ad hoc organisations or citizen action groups (*Bürgerinitiativen*) have posed new problems for the policy process during the 1970s, notably the problem of how to adopt policy style to larger, more fluid policy communities. Intellectual style remains rationalist and radical. Accommodative style faces greater problems of consensus building.

Having established the general character of West German policy style and the context of that style, an attempt will now be made to highlight some of the variety that is to be found within the German policy process. Particular attention will be given to nuclear policy because of its impact on the consciousness of policy-makers, to health policy as an example of the 'reform deficit' that has worried many Germans and to economic policy because of its central significance in German politics.

Nuclear Energy Policy: The Limits of Political Activism

Nuclear energy policy has had a great impact on the consciousness of policy-makers in the 1970s. This impact derived in part from the development of nuclear energy as a major political issue during the decade, and in part from its illustration, in a dramatic form, of changes that were occurring in other policy areas like housing, transport and the environment. Citizen action groups (*Bürgerinitiativen*) were not a new phenomenon in the West German policy process. There was, indeed, evidence of administrative support for citizen action groups; they served as useful 'early-warning' devices for the policy process. Moreover, in sociological terms these groups had much in common with the administrative system – low working-class representation and over-representation of well-educated and professional people. The search for greater sector rationality in the form of policy planning was an important factor in the development of citizen action groups. The 1970s saw the appearance of long-term housing programmes, education plans, transport plans, environmental programmes (*Unwelt-programme*) and land-use programmes (*Raumordnungsprogramme*). Correspondingly, citizen action groups proliferated and were most active in housing followed by education, conservation, transport and regional planning. They arrived somewhat later on the scene in energy policy. Opponents of the peaceful use of nuclear energy were provided with an organisational model of self-organisation in order to promote values of community and self-realisation on the political agenda. These new political associations were to challenge on a much larger scale the traditional role, power and values of economic interest groups in a central policy sector. A small, exclusive and relatively closed policy community of professionals was confronted by an anti-nuclear movement that was very heterogeneous in both sociological and programmatic senses.

Citizen action groups were not able to establish themselves as a decisive presence in nuclear energy policy as long as the ecological issue was primarily abstract. A change in the character of nuclear energy policy after 1973 was the precondition of the new problems of 'managing' this policy sector as groups sought to force other problems and issues on to the policy agenda. Nuclear energy policy can be divided into two periods (1955–67 and 1968 onwards) and four stages (Kitschelt, 1980). In the first period nuclear energy was defined as research policy. Till 1963 a neo-liberal economic philosophy suggested a policy of regulation and distribution according to a general formula. Emphasis was on a framework of rules with reference, for instance, to safety and international co-operation. The policy community was clearly defined and divided roughly into two opposed groupings: on the one hand, the reactor construction industry, the German Atom Commission and the Federal Ministry of Atomic Affairs; and on the other, the Federal Economics Ministry, the Federal Finance Ministry and the electricity supply companies. The scientific world was firmly behind the pro-nuclear lobby. In the second stage (1963–7) nuclear energy began to be defined as structural policy for technology. An active research policy that concentrated resources towards a few giant industrial undertakings stemmed from a concern about the longer-term competitiveness of these firms at home and abroad in the context of the USA's technological lead. In particular, SPD policy-makers began to see nuclear energy as a key industry for modernisation of the economy. An SPD commitment to the industry was reflected in the priority that it received from successive ministers of the new Federal Ministry of Research and Technology after 1972 (Horst Ehmke, Hans Matthöfer and Volker Hauff) as well as from Chancellor Schmidt. Its importance derived not just from its capacity to meet energy needs after the oil crisis and from the export potential, but also from the employment that it generated in the electrical, engineering and chemical industries. During this stage the policy community remained small but was characterised by greater internal consensus.

The decisive change came in 1967–8 with the commissioning of the first commercial reactor. Nuclear energy was now defined as a pre-emptive infrastructural and redistributive policy that was concerned to secure the long-term conditions for growth of the economy. Although new regional and ecological issues were raised, procedures of approval and choice of sites remained the preserve of a rather closed policy community. The policy community did, nevertheless, change. In particular, planning authorities at the local and state (*Land*) levels became involved. On the one hand, the policy sector faced new problems of implementation. Growing political pressures from affected interests produced conflicts and competition within the policy community, for instance, between local and state planning authorities. On the other hand, the policy sector remained wedded to an essentially administrative process of problem resolution. Policy was a professional process of satisfying and guaranteeing the energy needs of society. Political parties, trade unions and citizen action groups did not play, and were not expected to play, an active role within the policy community. Administrative changes within the policy sector sought to emphasise the neutrality (*Überparteilichkeit*) of the state. According to the Science Minister, Klaus von Dohnanyi, in 1972: 'The federal government is not a party to the dispute between supporters and opponents of nuclear energy, but the independent advocate of the common good.' Hence, research administration was reorganised in 1971 by reducing the number of permanent advisory committees in favour of ad hoc committees; and the promotion of nuclear research and control of project development were separated within the administration.

The importance of nuclear energy as both economic and environmental policy was underlined by the energy crisis of the 1970s. As a growing number of sites were named, the problem of nuclear energy achieved a new political visibility. Political mobilisation was a reaction to these plans and to a fear that a technical perspective of policy was neglecting considerations of safety and the ecological and human aspects of energy policy. The federal government, the nuclear industry and the trade unions were presenting nuclear energy as a *Sachzwang*, a requirement of a competitive and expansive economy. There were new conflicts about priorities (economy vs ecology), about the time scale of implementation as well as about the structure of participation itself. Greatest controversy was unleashed by the proposals to develop sites like Brokdorf, Wyhl and Gorleben in rural, agricultural areas (Kitschelt, 1980). The motor of the movement was the mass demonstration and occupation of the Wyhl site in February 1975, while the repressive police measures at Brokdorf in November 1976 marked a new intensity of politics. A previously clearly defined policy community broke down and during 1976–7 was submerged in the larger political process. Nuclear energy had not been an issue in the federal election of 1976 despite growing alarm in the political parties at the local and regional levels about the strength of citizen protests and about how best to realise the nuclear programme. However, the big demonstrations and occupations in the winter of 1976–7, followed by the electoral successes of the Green Lists in some local and state elections, confronted the parties, notably the SPD/FDP coalition, with a serious political problem. Internal party controversy and electoral threat opened up fresh divisions within the policy community. A complex combination of ideological sympathy for the ecological concerns of the so-called Greens, of disillusion with the appeal of the economism of political leadership and of electoral anxiety created new problems of unifying the governing parties, especially the SPD, which threatened to become divided between trade union and environmental camps. SPD and FDP Party congresses, which were shocked by the repressive measures of the CDU state government of Schleswig-Holstein to secure the Brokdorf site, were concerned to toughen the criteria that had to be fulfilled before construction could begin. However, after their silence on the nuclear issue before and during the 1976 election the role of the political parties in nuclear policy was essentially reactive to unconventional forms of participation that had erupted. By general and ambivalent statements they sought to neutralise a politically explosive issue and smooth over internal party divisions that threatened their image as 'catch-all' parties (*Volksparteien*). At the federal administrative level there was conflict between, on the one hand, the Economics (FDP) and Research (SPD) ministries, both of which shared a pessimistic scenario of mounting energy shortages and were pledged to the imperative of the development of nuclear energy and, on the other hand, the Interior Ministry (FDP) which was concerned with the problem of consent. The nuclear issue caused also federal/state conflicts, especially between the SPD–FDP coalitions in Bonn and Düsseldorf over the relative priorities of coal and nuclear energy. In 1977 the government of North-Rhine Westphalia announced a five-year moratorium on nuclear sites. In late 1978 a spectacular showdown occurred in the FDP over the fast-breeder reactor. The dispute between the FDP economics ministers in Bonn and Düsseldorf about this proposal was followed by the threat of all four FDP ministers to resign from the Bonn cabinet; if they were not supported by their parliamentary colleagues. State governments were also divided over the question of how to implement the nuclear programme. The tough approach of the CDU state government of Schleswig-Holstein was exceptional. By contrast the CDU state government of Baden-Würtemberg emphasised enlightenment and dialogue with respect to the Wyhl site. Between November 1975 and February 1976 there were six conferences between citizen action groups, on the one hand, and the state government and the electricity supply company Baden Werke, on the other.

The key development within the policy community was, of course, the emergence of the citizen action groups. Their threat to the manageability of the policy arena was further heightened by the division between these new groups. They were divided about the use of violence (which was advocated by some communist groups) and about the formation of political parties to fight local and state elections. For instance, two Green Lists fought the state election at Hamburg. Another important new institution in the politics of nuclear energy was the administrative courts. As is typical of public policy issues in West Germany, judges were elevated to an important role in its resolution. The administrative courts blocked the final approval of atomic power stations until adequate facilities had been provided for the disposal of atomic waste. This criterion proved to be the stumbling-block of the whole nuclear programme. The federal government had planned to construct a concentrated 'atomic park' in Lower Saxony. At Gorleben the largest atomic project in the world was to offer facilities for waste reprocessing and underground disposal. However, in 1978 Ernst Albrecht, the CDU Minister-President of Lower Saxony, rejected this proposal in the face of mounting public resistance and of doubts about its safety as a disposal site. There was now the prospect of an ever-growing tonnage of atomic waste without adequate facilities for its disposal.

In the face of growing conflict policy-makers sought to design procedural policies of agenda management and consensus. Their attention shifted from a policy to meet the problem of future energy needs to the search for a policy that would deal with the problem of conflict. In other words, the problem was redefined. Policy-makers pursued a symbolic politics of legitimacy. In particular, corporatist devices were established in order to achieve dialogue between opponents within the newly expanded policy community. Various such devices were attempted. The 'citizen dialogue nuclear energy' of the Federal Research and Technology Ministry was greeted with scepticism by both the nuclear industry (which saw it as an expensive anti-nuclear platform) and the citizen action groups (which saw it as an ineffective forum); the 'study group for environmental questions' was composed of four groups with different views (federal government, states, industry, unions and environmental associations) and sought to anticipate future problems like Wyhl by early information and co-ordination; the Research and Technology Ministry built on the model of concerted 'action by establishing a discussion group on nuclear energy with representatives from the parties, citizen action groups, industry, organised groups and the churches; and the centre of government a nuclear council of party politicians, industrialists and scientists was formed in order to achieve a better co-ordination between the traditional actors within the policy community.

The destabilisation of the policy community after 1973 prompted consideration of a policy for policy (metapolicymaking) in nuclear energy. The new equilibrium which was established at the end of the 1970s involved political and administrative stalemate in the construction of nuclear power stations. At the end of 1977 the blockage of the nuclear programme meant the loss of over 1·6 billion marks per annum in construction orders and, to the irritation of the trade unions, of more than 20,000 jobs. Whereas a French nuclear plant could be completed on the basis of an original authorisation, German plants needed a step-by-step approval that lengthened lead times to eight to ten years. This process of destabilisation and the new equilibrium of stalemate suggest two features of the West German policy process. First, policy-makers displayed on the whole an unwillingness to impose change. Procedural change and acceptance of defeat were preferred responses of policy-makers. Emphasis on complex procedures of approval and corporatist devices were indicative of the 'social-state' (*sozialstaatlich*) outlook as opposed to the old *Obrigkeitsstaat* view of the authoritarian sovereign state. An abrasive use of public power was anathema. Despite criticism of the so-called 'atomic state', on the one hand, and of the nuclear industry, on the other, politicians proved able and willing to respond to the number of new citizen action groups seeking influence, to the non-materialistic values that they represented and to the unconventional forms of participation through direct action that were seen at Brokdorf, Wyhl and Gorleben. Secondly, the complex character of the West German 'party state' was revealed. Overcrowding of the nuclear policy sector, unconventional forms of behaviour and the formation of Green Lists to fight state elections and a Green Party to contest the 1980 federal election suggested that the traditional parties were not adequately representing new interests and values in post-industrial society and might be in electoral danger. Despite the popularity of the values that were advocated by the Greens, their electoral performance in the federal election was disappointing, in part because the major parties began to take on board the ecological issue. While the traditional parties displayed their responsiveness in this way, party leaderships that were enmeshed in the complex machinery of state at federal and state levels and saw party as an essential pillar of the state exhibited discomfort in the face of these new conflicts. Their preference was for policy discussion in functional and technical terms rather than in the adversary terms of rival party positions that are rooted in contrasting ideologies. Co-operative elite problem-solving was attempted through institutions like the high-level nuclear council. The nuclear energy issue (and other issues like the Saar steel crisis) revealed the possibility of a dangerous development within the West German policy process. A gap could appear between grass-roots opinion which was shifting towards non-materialistic values and the corporatist ethos of organised leaderships which emphasised material values and technological achievement.

The Politics of Status Preservation: The Case of Health Policy

The term 'reform deficit' has been frequently applied to health policy. This policy sector combines in a paradoxical fashion institutional dispersion with a high concentration of power. On the one hand, the policy community is characterised by a complexity of relatively autonomous institutions or subsystems: for instance, there are three types of hospital. They frustrate co-ordination in the senses of a coherent health policy and of a capacity and willingness to co-operate effectively in the provision of medical services. On the other hand, the politics of health policy is determined by a narrow circle of policy-makers; and within this circle the administrators of the doctors' associations exert the greatest influence. The organisational complexity of the health policy community is offset and managed by the close working relationships between the administrators of its various institutions (Rauskolb, 1971). Health policy has proved a relatively closed and specialised policy sector except when under pressure the doctors' associations have taken their case to the public (for instance, in 1958–60).

German health policy bears the marks of its origin in 1882 when Bismarck took the initiative and established statutory health insurance. This system has been extended in terms both of the numbers covered (over 90 per cent in 1975), and of the types of benefits and services provided (in 1975 it accounted for 6 per cent of GNP). Hence statutory health insurance has become the key arena of contest in health policy. From the beginning the system of statutory health insurance was collaborative in character. Statutory health insurance was not administered directly by the government. This new state function was devolved to certain types of institution, notably the new local sickness funds (*Ortskrankenkassen*), which were required to build up reserves and invest in order to avoid tax financing. The *Ortskrankenkassen* were independent of the local authorities and were self-governing with representation of employers and workers. They have emerged both as administrative institutions, and as new interest groups in health policy, encompassing the interests of employers and workers. The influence of the local sickness funds arises in part from their role in carrying out devolved state functions, and in part from their large staffs of expert officials. The local sickness funds (of which there were 341 in 1974) are not the only health insurance institutions. In 1975 there were in total 1,469 such funds which included an array of separate institutions for artisans, coal-miners, farmers, large firms, seamen and voluntary insurance. The most important of the federal associations of these funds remains, however, the *Bundesverband der Ortskrankenkassen*. These federal associations are intimately concerned with health policy and have a reputation as conser-vative bodies whose federal directors seek to present a common defensive front against their mutual enemies – doctors, hospitals and drug firms. There is in fact little political threat to the existing institutions of statutory health insurance. All the major parties (CDU/CSU, FDP and SPD) are committed both to the principle of self-government and the collaborative style of the insurance institutions and to the principle of competition between institutions in order to offer greater freedom of choice to clients and to restrict the number of those covered by statutory insurance. Such a decentralised policy system suits politicians also in the sense that it clears relations (*Arbeitsrecht*), a conception that is also embodied in the adminis-trative responsibility of the Federal Ministry of Labour and Social Affairs for health insurance. This style involves a negotiation between the 'social partners' in which the trade unions represent client demands and the employers' associations attempt to reduce the burdens that fall on industry and to restrict the number of those covered by statutory insurance. Such as decentralised policy system suits politicians also in the sense that it clears some difficult problems from their agenda. In other words, problems of health policy are exported to decentralised institutions.

The power of the health insurance institutions is offset by a range of other actors, which makes health the most complex of all the sectors of social policy. Among the different subsystems with which the health insurance institutions must deal are the doctors' associations, the different types of organisations (notably the Catholic Church) that run hospitals, the dispensing chemists, the pharmaceutical industry and, on an increasing scale, the paramedical professions (especially the public service union ÖTV). This interaction is regulated in two ways by public policy. A statu-tory framework exists for the interaction of the doctors and the health insurance institutions; and the social courts adjudicate on matters of social insurance. In comparison to Britain the interesting feature of German health policy is the public status of most members of the policy community. Besides the public institutions of statutory health insurance, German doctors' associations grew up within the context of a state-instituted system of representation (Rauskolb, 1971).

The reform deficit in health policy was underlined by two failures of reform. First, there were the abortive attempts to reform statutory health insurance in 1958–61 and again in 1963 (Naschold, 1967; Safran, 1967); secondly, the cost-explosion crisis after 1960 saw a new recognition of the need for structural reform but only palliative measures to tackle the crisis.

Despite the inability of the health insurance institutions to resist the doctors' demands and despite the SPD's belief in an integrated health service, no serious attempt was made either in 1958–61, or after the social-liberal coalition came to power in 1969, to reform the institutions of statutory insurance. The policy initiatives of the social-liberal coalition recognised the role and power of the doctors' associations, which displayed considerable aggression towards the government. Important changes had taken place in the health policy community by the end of the 1970s. It was more complex than in the 1950s and rent by more divisions and particularly by the greater numerical significance of hospital doctors. By 1974 more doctors worked in hospitals than in general practice. Another change in the balance of power within the policy community was the enlargement of the paramedical professions and the greater role of the trade union ÖTV and of its demands for hospital reform. There were also protests from radical doctors: for example, in 1974 the Ärztetag (the actual conference of the *Bundesärztekammer*, the federal chamber of doctors) in Berlin was broken up by a group of 200 young doctors who demanded reform of the health system. Nevertheless, it remained a tightly knit policy community which was dominated by the professional administrators of public-law institutions and in which citizen action groups showed little sign of activity. The clients of statutory health insurance failed notably to increase their organisational effectiveness within the policy community.

German health policy is a peculiar synthesis of public-law regulation and private interest organisation. According to the dominant conception of health policy, which is articulated by the doctors' associations, the function of the state is the provision of a framework of order for a decentralised policy system. Governmental reforms that are concerned to improve the quality of medical services and to develop medical policy are seen as a threat to the autonomy of the medical profession as a *Stand* (estate). In this view, which is influenced by a traditional conception of the *Ständestaat* as well as by economic self-interest, the professional associations are concerned with the development of medical services. The health system is organised on the principle of social partnership or collaboration in health insurance administration and on commercial and individualistic principles of service provision, particularly of the individual's responsibility to protect himself. There is strong institutional resistance to the idea that health provision is primarily a matter of government's social policy. All participants in the policy community emphasise public-regarding attitudes and seek to relate their proposals and actions to general principles of the political order. However, it is difficult to disentangle the doctors' claims to assert the principles of freedom and responsibility under law from their advocacy of their own economic interests; and to counter the claim that they use the language of rhetoric to disguise their self-interested motives. Government has proved unwilling and unable to act on behalf of its own conception of the public interest and in the name of co-ordination. From the standpoint of general political reform, health policy has been characterised by a stalemate of opposed interests and consequent immobility of policy.

Economic and Industrial Policy Sectors: The Search for Concertation

It is helpful to consider the two sectors of economic and industrial policy together because the interconnections between them are so notably and distinctively close in West Germany. Economic policy has been directed at, even subordinated to, the requirements of an internationally competitive industry; while industrial policy, which has emerged since the early 1960s, has been seen primarily as an aspect of neo-liberal economic policy. The absence of an equivalent of an industry ministry on British or French lines (at federal or state levels) is indicative not only of the extent to which both sectors are inter-related, but also of the problem that industrial policy has had in establishing itself as a distinct sector. Since the establishment of the Federal Research and Technology Ministry in 1972, successive SPD ministers have entertained the ambition of converting it into a new 'structural' ministry, one that would pursue an active technological policy for the modernisation of industry. Structural policy has, however, remained firmly in the hands of the neo-liberal Economics Ministry; its two FDP ministers since 1972 have effectively resisted the ambitions of this new rival. The influence of the Economics Ministry has ensured that government's economic and industrial policies have been characterised by an unwillingness to impose change and by a preference for reliance on the self-regulation and the self-healing process of the market. As we shall see, these characteristics were notably evident in the management of the Saar steel rescue crisis.

The economic and industrial policy community is complex, differentiated and transcends public and private sectors. It comprises government's economic policy, which is managed by the federal economic and finance ministries; the currency management of the autonomous Bundesbank; the collective bargaining of the 'social partners'; and the industrial policies of government and of the big commercial banks. The Federal Chancellor presides over this policy community and provides one of the main pillars of co-ordination (Dyson, 1981). In particular, Helmut Schmidt has worked closely with the ministers of economics and finance and cultivated close personal contacts to senior industrialists, trade union leaders and bankers as well as to the Bundesbank (in other words, to the sources of economic and industrial power). Government's economic policy has been characterised by the co-operation and rivalry between the economics and finance ministries, whose styles have contrasted. The

Finance Ministry has had the arduous administrative function of good housekeeping in support of the stability policies of the Bundesbank. By contrast, under Professor Ludwig Erhard (1949–63) and Professor Karl Schiller (1966–72: during 1969–72 he was Minister of Economics and Finance) the Economics Ministry developed an intellectual and detached style of policy leadership. It became and remained a political spokesman for the doctrine of social market economy. The rationalistic character of this educative function was extended in 1967 by the Law on Stability and Growth, which was informed by Schiller's conception of the 'enlightened' social market economy. In fact, even before the Grand Coalition (SPD/ CDU/CSU) of 1966, officials within the Economics Ministry had begun to be converted to the value of forward looks at the development of economic aggregates (including financial planning of public expenditure); of an independent, critical and rational analysis of economic policy options; and of a 'positive' co-ordination of economic actors, notably of the social partners, with reference to the so-called 'magic square' of goals of economic policy (price stability, high level of employment and external balance with continuous economic growth). The overall concern was an objectification of policy, especially wages policy, in order to facilitate a new 'global steering' of macroeconomic aggregates. Under Schiller prognoses became a major instrument of economic policy as government sought to enlighten the various economic actors (notably through *Konzertierte Aktion*, or Concerted Action) about the assumptions behind its policy measures and about the consequences of their behaviour for growth, employment and price stability; the *Sachverständigenrat* (Council of Economic Advisers) was created as early as 1963 to analyse the effectiveness of economic policy measures with reference to the 'magic square' in an objective manner; and an attempt was made to co-ordinate public sector action through a variety of planning institutions like the *Konjunkturrat* (Counter-Cyclical Advisory Council), the *Finanzplanungsrat* (Financial Planning Council) and the joint federal/state committee for the planning of regional economic structure – all established during 1967–9. The economic uncertainties and disappointments of the 1970s were to reveal the limitations of macroplanning of economic aggregates. Nevertheless, a central characteristic of the West German economic policy process remained a faith in the possibility of collaborative dialogue on the basis of an intellectual rationality that was rooted in, and expedited by, common interest and a 'matter-of-fact' objectivity. Policy style emphasised not just dialogue in order to generate confidence and stable, realistic expectations and to foster a global perspective, but also expertise in order to ensure the relevance and objectivity (*Sachlichkeit*) of that dialogue. Continuous mutual information was to enable rational and objective decisions in terms of the public interest. In this way an effective 'global steering' of macroeconomic aggregates could be achieved with a minimum of detailed governmental intervention. This policy style could function because of widespread political agreement on the character of the economic order and on the need for 'positive' adjustment to market forces.

Although *Konzertierte Aktion* was in 1967–77 the most important institutional expression of the ideal of social partnership, this term has been a major part of the language of economic policy before and after its arrival. *Konzertierte Aktion* was an occasion for the government to present 'orientation data' to unions and employers, so that they would be better informed about the consequences of their prospective policies. It did not produce binding decisions. The objective was to co-ordinate the assumptions of public authorities, employers and unions with respect to the 'magic square' of goals that were laid down in the law of 1967. In fact, to the irritation of the unions, the scope of discussion narrowed down to wages, and it proved impossible to co-ordinate the authoritative decisions of the Bundesbank through this forum. Their withdrawal from *Konzertierte Aktion* in 1977 and a series of bitter industrial disputes after 1976 suggested a change in the climate of industrial relations. Despite these developments wage settlements remained remarkably moderate; and government sought informally to encourage industrial attitudes that were favourable to stability and growth. From the perspective of government, responsible collective bargaining was viewed as essential to effective economic management and as dependent on consensus through dialogue. From the perspective of both sides of industry, the principle of *Tarifautonomie* (autonomy of price and wage determination) was dependent on some measure of collaboration with reference to the public interest. Worker participation on the supervisory boards of industrial companies was further extended in 1976 and kept alive the habit of collaboration with reference to market principles as well as reduced the likelihood of an autonomous union strategy.

The most distinctive aspect of the economic policy community is the Bundesbank on which has fallen the burden of economic stabilisation since 1972. Its peculiarly important role is only to be understood by reference to the sanctity that the term 'stability' has enjoyed in postwar political and economic debate. Stability has been seen as the fundamental principle of the social market economy, one that was the precondition of the attainment of specific goals of economic policy. Specifically, a stable structure of relative prices was essential to investment in real growth and lasting employment. Germany had also a recent experience of two hyperinflations, one of which had played an important part in undermining loyalty to the Weimar Republic. Inflation has, therefore, been political and economic enemy number one of the Federal Republic. This historical and intellectual context gave birth to the idea of an independent, neutral force that could take a detached, analytical perspective and create the objective conditions for economic stability. Accordingly, in the law of 1957 that established the modern Bundesbank an attempt was made to remove currency management from the realm of partisan politics and consensus politics to that of autonomous technical determination. The Bundesbank has interpreted its statutory requirement to 'safeguard the currency' as a mandate to act as policy leader with respect to economic stability and even, in the last report, to impose the necessary monetary measures despite reluctant governments or aggrieved industrial interests. Not surprisingly it has been mainly criticised for doing its job too well, at the expense of excessive loss of output and jobs. As the Bundesbank is not subject to the directives of the government when exercising its power to safeguard the currency, opportunities for conflict between these two centres of economic decision-making exist. For instance, the Bundesbank was noticeably sceptical about Schmidt's political initiative to bring greater stability into the world's currency markets, the European Monetary System that came into operation in March 1979. The Bundesbank not only persuaded the Chancellor to reduce the number of participants in the system, but also reserved for itself the right to suspend interventions in currency markets unilaterally if support of the EMS threatened its duty to safeguard the currency. In practice the Bundesbank and the government have worked closely together. The Bundesbank has recognised that the success of its monetary policies depend ultimately on the consensus that government can help provide and on government's decisions on exchange rate policy and on the size and financing of its budgetary deficit. Conversely, governments have realised that the Bundesbank's legal and intellectual authority gives it considerable room for manoeuvre to safeguard what it sees as the longer-term requirements of stability against political expediency. In the process government has exported a difficult political problem. By keeping a united front with the Bundesbank government can succeed in neutralising a potentially highly partisan issue. Political perception of the priority of economic stability has combined with legal authority to create the conditions for a policy leadership role of the Bundesbank on terms that are not typical of the West German policy process.

The arrival of a co-ordinated, rationalistic government policy towards industry was signalled by the publication under Schiller of the 'Principles of Sectoral Policy' in 1966 and the 'Principles of the Federal Government's Sectoral and Regional Economic Policy' in 1968. Even before Schiller's appointment various factors had combined to convert many officials of the Economics Ministry to a limited conception of a structural policy: the impact of the EEC on different sectors, worries about the 'technological gap', labour scarcity in some sectors and investment problems in others. The aim was to solve similar problems of industrial adaptation in different sectors with a common set of instruments which were to be applied with reference to five general principles: structural intervention was only justifiable when the difficulties concerned the whole sector and were based on lasting economic changes; the entrepreneurs and managers were to be primarily responsible for the necessary structural adaptation; the government's role was to support measures of self-help, provided these measures promised to strengthen, on some lasting basis, the competitiveness of the enterprises concerned; special governmental aids or other interventions could only be considered if the individual sectors were undergoing major changes at a rapid rate, and if the changes would generate undesirable economic and social consequences: the aids should be temporary, should be gradually withdrawn and should not cripple the competitive process. Structural policy was clearly rationalistic and oriented to market principles in line with the theory of the social market economy. However, the fourth of these principles introduced political and social goals into industrial policy, even if in a restrictive manner, and was the cause of the large proportion of federal subsidies and allowances (66 per cent in 1970) that were spent on the declining industries. Support for industrial innovation and technology became the special responsibility of the new Research and Technology Ministry, which by 1977 was spending 13·3 billion marks (over three times the amount spent on the function in 1967). The response of the ministry to this rapid expansion and the complexity of the resultant state-industry complex was to attempt greater direction and control through an elaborate research planning system and an annual plan of its advisory system.

A major characteristic of industrial policy has been the promotion of concerted action by government. One form of concerted action was the voluntary self-limitation agreement as a type of market regulation: for instance, the agreement with the oil companies in the late 1960s to restrict imports in order to support the coal industry. Concerted action was also used to achieve rationalisation of certain industries by concentration: for instance, the formation of the Ruhrkohle AG from twenty-six coalmining companies in 1968 and its operation in a pattern of close co-operation among the Economics Ministry, the enterprises and the unions concerned. This policy style found perhaps its best expression in the form of crisis regulation that was adopted for the ailing Saar steel industry in 1977/8 (Esser *et al*, 1979). Small production units, inadequate investment and failure to concentrate on specialised steel products combined with locational disadvantages to ensure that the Saar steel industry was particularly hit by the recession. When mass redundancies were announced in 1977 the Saar government and the federal government decided that a massive steel rationalisation programme was urgently required. While the Saar's political parties conducted an ideological debate about state vs private reconstruction, the state government and the federal government negotiated in great privacy with the Luxembourg steel firm Arbed and the union IG Metall. This informal 'crisis cartel' brought together public and private actors in the search for a mutually satisfactory solution. From the point of view of the federal and state governments, the test of an agreement was that it should do something for the real problem of jobs and redundancies and take a difficult issue off the political agenda by pacifying the union. Arbed stepped in to take over the affected companies and to produce an economic rationalisation programme that was to have the approval of the public accountancy firm Treuarbeit AG and to meet certain conditions of the state government; the IG Metall received guarantees of social measures to protect employment and reduce hardship; and, in return for a restructuring of the Saar steel industry and for union agreement, the federal government provided massive financial aid of over 1 billion marks to cover Arbed's risks and to help finance the social plan. The device of 'selective corporatism' enabled government to take industrial initiative without assuming direct responsibility for rationalisation; the social partners were relied upon to work out acceptable economic solutions. Concerted action proved a convenient device for issue management and consensus formation in the face of politically sensitive industrial problems like coal and steel. It was also readily legitimated by reference to the *Sozialstaat* ideology of co-operation and partnership.

Industrial rescue operations by government have, in fact, been exceptional. Adaptability and resilience of industry have been strengthened by the attention to market research, financial discipline and long-term credit that has been encouraged by the close and complex bank–industry nexus. Government has been insulated to a greater degree than in Britain from the complex and detailed business of monitoring and responding to the adjustment problems of big industrial corporations. A first line of defence has been provided by the universal banking system, which was founded against the background of a shortage of private funds for industrial investment in the nineteenth century and has encouraged the emergence of an industrial banking oligarchy or a group of industrial statesmen in the world of banking. Through their combination of commercial with investment banking the big banks (Deutsche, Dresdener and Commerzbank) have developed an extraordinary network of involvement in industry, one which has tended to grow during periods of depression. The banks' power within industry derives from three major sources: large bank shareholdings in some companies, much of which (for instance, in construction) were procured after the world wars when outstanding credits were converted into bank-held shares and bonds to assist reconstruction; exercise of proxy rights for shares that they have on deposit from customers (in fact, most shares); and seats on the supervisory boards of companies. The result has been a network of reciprocal influence in which, on the one hand, industry has access to sources of long-term finance and financial expertise for its corporate planning and, on the other hand, the banks are able to exert financial discipline within industry. In 1975 the banks held 179 or 14·9 per cent of the seats on the supervisory boards of the top 100 companies; only twenty-five of these companies had no bank representative, and in thirty-one cases a bank provided the chairman. The voting rights of the banks (including proxies) amounted to 26 per cent of the total in the top 100 companies. Against this background industrial rescue tends to take on a different character from that in Britain. The *Hausbank* plays a decisive role in *Sanierung* (rationalisation): it presses for the appointment of external management consultants to design rationalisation programmes, provides (often by putting together a bank pool) long-term credits for *Sanierung* and, as a last resort, takes up shares or bonds (as with AEG in 1980) or encourages amalgamation with a larger, more successful firm that it will help to identify. Like government the banks have been at pains to remain as inconspicuous as possible and act on the basis of consent, in part to avoid greater controversy about their role. Their policy style has, in fact, been similar to that of government. For instance, in the 1960s the Deutsche Bank played a major role through its representatives on the supervisory boards of steel companies in bringing about a voluntary self-limitation agreement among steel producers to deal with the problem of oversupply and falling profits. Major industrial rescues like that of Krupp in 1967 and AEG in the 1970s were master-minded by the banks and kept away from the door of government. In 1967 Herman Abs, president of the Deutsche Bank, was elected chairman of Krupp; in 1980 Hans Friderichs, president of the Dresdener Bank, emerged as chairman of AEG in the wake of a new rationalisation programme. This private, efficient system of 'early warning' and control takes much of the political and administrative burden of designing a policy of industrial intervention from government. At the same time banks are powerful actors in industrial policy, and their private power is a subject of some controversy.

Until the mid-1960s the economic policy community had been relatively simple: the Bundesbank provided economic stability; the government supported stability by a 'good-housekeeping' policy of balanced budgets; the commercial banks were the major source of external, selective intervention in industry to resolve problems of adjustment; and social partnership was confined to the level of the firm in the form of worker participation. The arrival of demand management in the form of Keynesianism made for a more complex policy community. Three new elements were added to the community: deficit budgeting required much greater intellectual sophistication within government; the viability of the government's new enlightened economic policy of projections depended on the responsible collective bargaining of the social partners; structural and technological policies became central to the modernisation of the economy in order to deal with new competitive pressures from within the EEC and later from the Third World. Before 1967, in accordance with prevailing economic doctrine, reliance had been placed on the self-regulating character of the economic policy community and on an authoritative, imposed co-ordination by the Bundesbank's policy for stability. After 1967 these two mechanisms of co-ordination were no longer seen as adequate. Two developments took place. *Konzertierte Aktion* sought to co-ordinate collective bargaining with government's projections; and, notably under Schmidt, the role of the Chancellor was reinforced (indeed, one reason for his replacement of Brandt was the expectation that he could better perform this key function). The collapse of *Konzertierte Aktion* in 1977 simply put further pressure on the Chancellor's role as educator and mediator in economic policy. Two pillars of formal co-ordination emerged; each specialised in a particular problem of economic policy. The one pillar focused on the Chancellor and on *Konzertierte Aktion*, was concerned with the problem of consensus and was characterised by a collaborative style; the other pillar focused on authoritative co-ordination of the Bundesbank, was directed at the specific purpose of economic stability and was imperative in style. The co-ordination of the two pillars depended in part on the skills of the Chancellor, who in 1974 persuaded the Bundesbank to publish annual targets for money supply in order to enlighten the rest of the policy community. Consensus and stability were seen as the twin bases of an economic and industrial policy that could realise the goals of high employment and continuous growth. Maintenance of this consensus was assisted by two factors; first, a rationalised trade union structure in which power was very centralised within the seventeen industrial unions; and secondly, the role of the commercial banks in industrial adjustment, for they reduced the load of industrial issues that had to be faced by government. However, rising unemployment, mounting bankruptcies and greater uncertainty of economic growth created new strains within the policy community in the 1970s. The collaborative style of union leadership was threatened by new grass-roots pressures which manifested themselves in the strikes of 1978-9; and mounting problems of industrial adjustment to more intense overseas competition drew government into industrial crisis management on a new scale (as in the Saar). Despite a threat of increased load in the 1980s, the differentiated economic policy community appeared well adapted to the heavy burden of responsibility that is involved in the management of a complex, advanced industrial society.

Rationality in the West German Policy Process

The pursuit of rationality has been a conspicuous feature of West German public policy. However, there are different perceptions of the appropriate organisational reference point for a political planning of policy. For some actors the appropriate reference point is their policy sector (hence, plans for hospital requirements and financing and for education, transport, agriculture and regional structure); for others a co-ordinated rationality that establishes a wider perspective of resources and/or priorities within which particular sectors, programmes and projects can be examined; and for others the more manageable task of decentralised rationality, which involves comprehensive political planning at the level of the state (*Land*) or local authority. These perspectives of rational political planning coexist, often with great difficulty. Co-ordinated planning by the Federal Chancellor's Office remains the weakest of all these exercises (Dyson, 1973). By contrast, this type of planning is more developed at the *Land* level, where in some instances State Chancellery planning staffs have been able to exert a significant grip on policy formation. Sector planning is, nevertheless, the most developed and has proved notably resistant to co-ordinated political planning whether at federal or state level. Indeed, sector planning in fields like education, regional structure, or agriculture embraces both federal and state levels; and identification with, and loyalty to, the policy sector tends to prove stronger than to co-ordinated political planning at either level of government. A major problem for co-ordinated political planning at the federal level has been the existence of different joint federal-state planning committees for regional structure, agriculture and coastal protection, and higher education investment; their priorities and projects cannot be determined autonomously by the federal government.

As in other West European countries, sector planning has been in part a response to functional requirements; it is useful to look ahead, particularly when considering competing projects, and to relate priorities to resources. However, in West Germany organisational and intellectual factors have encouraged its emergence and shaped its rationalistic form. At the federal level ministries are comparatively small and neatly organised; administration is decentralised either to special federal authorities or, more typically, to the state governments. At the state level administration is decentralised to special authorities or to the regional administration, the *Bezirksregierung*. The justification of this organisational pattern is that ministries are concerned with government rather than administration; and planning is readily accepted as a function of government. Hence, federal and state ministries have inclination and time to plan. The commonsense character of sectoral (and even co-ordinated) planning is further suggested by a Roman-law conception of coherence in administration; and by an emphasis on the 'steering capacity of the state' that derives from the integrative values of the state tradition of thought.

The fact that policy sectors like education and transport have become independent-minded and increasingly politicised policy communities has contributed to the difficulties of co-ordinated political planning. At the federal level there has been a transition from a long-term, goal-oriented functional planning of government business in 1969–72 to a more pragmatic election-oriented planning under the Chancellery planner and election expert Albrecht Müller. The political planning after 1969 had involved a complex series of exercises which varied from construction of a computer-based 'early-warning' information system to plan government business to an esoteric and politically problematic long-term task planning involving federal-state planning teams. They were never integrated. Schmidt's election as Chancellor in 1974 confirmed a more limited conception of comprehensive planning and a preference for concentration and crisis management at the political centre (Dyson, 1973). Comprehensive planning was able to establish a firmer grip at the state (*Land*) level. In Hesse the pioneer of political planning, the SPD, established a planning model: a long-term development plan (1970-85) that integrated spatial and sectoral planning, more detailed and flexible implementation plans for each four-year legislative period, and an assessment report every four years. In Lower Saxony the SPD/FDP created a system of medium-term planning that integrated the functional and programme categories of the long-term development programme with financial planning in order to guarantee resources for the programme and to provide greater detail and responsiveness to changing economic, financial and demographic changes. These models were both systematic and flexible; they attempted to reconcile long-term spatial planning, sectoral planning and medium-term financial planning with changing prognoses. In Hamburg the SPD developed a different system of investment programmes which established priorities among programmes and projects and provided finance for them. With the possible exceptions of Hamburg and Lower Saxony a major problem was the rivalry of different types of co-ordinated planning, notably of financial and development planning (for instance, in Hesse). This rivalry, and the rivalry with sectoral planning, intensified with the restrictive financial climate and the uncertainty of financial planning. Co-ordinated planning was also subjected to growing criticism of inadequate attention to public participation in the stage of formulation; and to the effects of tension between coalition partners that sought distinctive profiles. Despite this difficult political and economic context, and despite the autonomy of policy sectors, the disposition to plan comprehensively remained strong, and stronger at the state than at the federal level.

The disposition to plan both sectorally and comprehensively was closely related to, but not to be identified with, SPD participation in government. Quite simply, the SPD favoured an activist and anticipatory conception of policy, according to which the function of government is to identify needs, establish ranked goals and integrate the provision of services. Hence, planning euphoria was identifiable with one-party SPD government of 'model Hesse' in the 1960s and with the Brandt government of 1969–72. By contrast the CDU, for instance, in Baden-Würtemberg, has often resisted comprehensive planning on ideological grounds; it implied an extension of the role of government beyond the provision of a framework of order for society. In this view planning was only justifiable as a technical requirement of certain policy sectors. Nevertheless, other strains of thought supported the idea of comprehensive planning in the CDU: for example, managerialism and a German tradition of orderly administration that suggested at least the wisdom of 'early-warning' information systems that have become typical of state governments.

Conclusion

West German policy style exhibits and reflects various political ideas that live in a state of complex tension and, at the same time, lend a certain adaptability to the policy process. A rationalistic style finds its expression and support in the idea of *Sachlichkeit*, of an objective and thorough examination of all policy options; and in the idea of the *Rechtsstaat*, of relating policy proposals in a rationalistic manner to basic constitutional principles which are sometimes interpreted as a mandate for certain policies. A collaborative style is implicit in the idea of the *Sozialstaat*, which emphasises the need to accommodate group pressures in order to maintain social peace. The prevalence and cultural significance of these three ideas is to be explained against a background of historical experience that places a premium on inconspicuous, deliberative and calculable (*berechenbar*) government. Emphasis on self-restraint of those with power is, of course, functional to the power-sharing of concerted action or social partnership. Hence, governments bend over backwards to avoid the appearance of imposing the nuclear programme even in the name of a comprehensive, objective rationality; government's attempts to regulate the road haulage industry have been impeded by that interest's appeal not just to economic interest, but also to the competitive principle of the market (Braunthal, 1972); government has depended on concerted action in industrial policy; and major government intervention in health policy has been prevented by the appeal of the doctors; organisations to basic political principles of freedom and individual responsibility.

While the West German policy process has displayed a greater faith in objective rationality than its British counterpart, political conditions of coalition and federal politics have combined to prevent or frustrate the language of radicalism in policy presentation. 1969 was the year of the famous 'change of power' in Bonn, of the end of CDU/CSU ascendancy and the commitment of Brandt's new social-liberal coalition to 'dare more democracy'. However, with the possible exception of Eastern policy (which was, in fact, initiated before 1969), 1969 was not a sharp break. The FDP vetoed radical policy postures in social, economic and industrial policies. The party political framework of policy-making implied continuity and a politics of centrality that was mediated by the FDP as the agent of coalition change (Smith, 1976). In addition, the federal system and the key role of the Bundesrat in the federal policy process placed a great political premium on carefully negotiated policy. Policy sectors tend to involve an interlocking of levels of government – federal, state, district administration and local authority – and depend for their stable functioning on a careful and laborious political clearance at formulation and implementation stages. The idea of a sphere of 'non-negotiable' policy has, therefore, been less apparent than in Britain. Currency management is an exceptional and important instance of imposed change in the name of objective rationality, although it is wise to remember that this sphere of policy is taken out of the field of action of elected government and partisan politics. One important product of the negotiability of issues is a politics of status preservation in policy sectors like health and agriculture. In these sectors past government intervention has created institutions with vested interests, in particular public-law corporations whose policy views acquire a special prestige. In the sector of economic and industrial policy, where a similar emphasis on negotiation and consensus is to be found, the same conservatism is avoided by the subordination to market principles and the willingness to anticipate and to adapt to change that this subordination implies.

Sectorisation is another important characteristic of the policy process. It is promoted and protected by the departmental principle that is enshrined in Article 65 of the Basic Law and most state constitutions: according to Article 65, 'each minister directs his own area of business independently and on his own responsibility'. Sector policy tends, moreover, to depend on political clearance through the complex network of federal-state and inter-state committees and through the Bundesrat. Hence a federal or state ministry can claim not to be master in its own house. Sectorisation in the form of departmental autonomy and close bureaucratic links between federal and state ministries creates powerful centrifugal forces that central planners have found difficult to contain. Some limitation is provided by the cabinet principle and by the Chancellor principle (the Chancellor shall determine the guidelines of policy). Comprehensive planning has been constructed on the basis of these two principles. However, the Cabinet principle has proved weak; and the Chancellor's role is a function of personality, executive skills and coalition politics. The political support for comprehensive planning has proved fragile and unstable.

In the 1960s and 1970s West German public policy has been presided over by two generations of politicians and administrators: the 'Weimar' generation whose formative political experience was the radicalism of the 1920s and 1930s and the collapse of democracy; and the 'war' generation that remembered the deprivations of the 1940s and sought to protect the hard-won material achievements of the Federal Republic. These two generations have shaped the values that have informed the policy process: the concern with economic stability, with *Sachlichkeit* and with calcu-lability. From the late 1960s onwards a critique of this 'technocratic', 'dehumanised' policy style began to emerge from postwar generations.

'Post-material' values found their first expression in the student movement, and in the 1970s the nuclear issue revealed their wide dissemination in German society. Nuclear policy was a dramatic illustration of changes that were affecting other policy sectors like housing, education and transport and that were threatening to exacerbate the problem of negotiation and consensus in these sectors. One aspect of the problem was the entry of new citizen action groups on a large and proliferating scale; another aspect was the new values that were being voiced in policy communities. The questions arose of whether the 'war' generation of Schmidt and Strauss could effectively respond to and manage these changes; and of what sort of political leadership was best able to replace them.

References: Chapter 2

Ackermann, P., *Der Deutsche Bauernverband im politischen Kräftespiel der Bundesrepublik* (Tubingen: Mohr, 1970).

Braunthal, G., *The West German Legislative Process* (Ithaca, NY: Cornell University Press, 1972).

Dyson, K., 'Planning and the Federal Chancellor's Office in West German federal government', *Political Studies*, vol. 21, no. 3 (1973), pp. 348–62.

Dyson, K., *Party, State, and Bureaucracy in West Germany* (Beverly Hills, Calif.: Sage, 1977).

Dyson, K., *The State Tradition in Western Europe* (Oxford: Robertson, 1980).

Dyson, K., 'The politics of economic recession in West Germany', in A. Cox (ed.), *Policy, Politics and Economic Recession in Western Europe* (London: Macmillan, 1981).

Esser, J. *et al, Konfliktregulierung durch Kartellbildung – Die Stahlkrise an der Saar*, International Institute of Management Discussion Paper, Berlin (1979).

Kitschelt, H., *Kernenergiepolitik* (Frankfurt: Campus, 1980).

Naschold, F., *Kassenärzte und Krankenversicherungsreform. Zu einer Theorie der Statuspolitik* (Freiburg: Rombach, 1967).

Rauskolb, C., *Lobby in Weiss. Stuktur und Politik der Ärzteverbände* (Frankfurt: EVA, 1971).

Safran, W., *Veto-Group Politics. The Case of Health Insurance Reform in West Germany* (New York: Chandler, 1967).

Smith, G., 'The politics of centrality: the case of West Germany', *Government and Opposition*, vol. 11, no. 4 (Autumn 1976), pp. 387–407.

3

Norway: Still Peaceful Coexistence and Revolution in Slow Motion?

JOHAN OLSEN, PAUL RONESS and
HARALD SÆTREN, University of Bergen

Introduction

The predominant policy styles in Norway since 1945 have been problem-solving, bargaining and self-governance. Crucial to these routine policy-making styles is that most elements are predetermined: (*a*) *who* will be making a decision; each feasible choice set involving only a few people; (*b*) *what* the agenda is and the relevant problems, goals and solutions; (*c*) *how* the decisions should be made; and (*d*) *why* outcomes should be accepted and considered legitimate. Within such constraints, outcomes will seldom deviate significantly from earlier results. The image is one of order, incrementalism and compromise. A modern welfare state has been built without agonising conflicts. Norway has moved from being one of the poorest to one of the richest countries in Europe – a 'revolution in slow motion' (Larssen, 1973) – while retaining peaceful coexistence between major groups.

There are, however, deviations from the routine policy-making styles; mobilisation and confrontation occasionally occur. These styles involve many, and sometimes unexpected, participants; conflicting definitions of problems, goals and solutions; disagreement on pertinent procedures and arenas; absence of legitimacy; and sometimes the imposition of significant policy changes.

This chapter discusses some of the conditions for the use of the different styles. First, policy style characteristics are specified in more detail, and we present some theoretical ideas about how policy styles may be linked to societal cleavages, the political organisation of social groups and the organisation of policy-making institutions. Secondly, we specify the Norwegian setting in terms of major cleavages and the resources mobilised by different politically organised interests. Thirdly, we describe the apparatus for routine policy-making and compare it with more 'irregular' policy-making in terms of participants, issues, values, procedures, results and legitimacy. Finally, we discuss some of the possibilities and constraints for managing the use of policy-making styles.

Policy Styles: Causes and Motives

Political systems have to make a variety of decisions, each calling for a different strategy and organisational structure. Over time policy styles develop: the process by which policies are formulated and implemented acquire certain characteristics, reflecting to some extent typical problems and issues (Thompson and Tuden, 1959). Specifically, we would expect political organisation and policy styles to be influenced by societal cleavages (how people are divided into long-lasting factions), and by the resources mobilised. The structure and standard operating procedures of the state reflect the outcomes of previous political struggles.

We should not, however, expect a simple causal structure. There is the usual inertia: the longer certain cleavages have dominated a system and been 'frozen' into the political-administrative structure, the more likely that they will remain important even after 'obsolescence'. Organising always implies selecting. Some conflicts, issues and groups are organised *into* politics, while others are 'organised out' (Schattschneider, 1960). The ways in which a political system copes with cleavages influence the bases of the cleavages and the development of conflicts. This impact is twofold: through substantive outputs – or the imposing of burdens and awarding of benefits to various interests; and through the procedures and styles employed.

The emphasis on style has always been an important aspect of political governance. We often assume that people accept a policy because they accept the legitimacy of the preceding political process. Hence, we may challenge the idea that styles and processes should be linked primarily to substantive outputs – in other words, who gets what. Styles should also be related to *social outcomes* like (*a*) who thinks and feels what as a result of the process (redistribution of trust, friendship, alienation, distribution of credit or blame, redefinition of interests and truth); (*b*) who is competent for what as a result of the experience, information and so on, gained through the process; and (*c*) who does what as a result of the process (for example, mobilisation, apathy, joining or leaving parties, interest organisations, forming action groups or revolutionary armies, and so on), and potential effects of such actions on the pattern of cleavages and conflicts in society (Cohen *et al.*, 1972; March and Olsen, 1976).

Anticipated social outcomes may provide motives for choice between policy styles, supplementing motives stemming from anticipated substantive outputs and causal factors related to cleavage structures. And they suggest important dimensions for a typology of policy styles. A typology of policy styles should indicate who the participants are – the role of the citizens, elected representatives and experts – as well as their agendas, the level of conflict, their strategies, and the substantive outputs and the social outcomes.

Organising means providing arenas and choice opportunities, and regulating the access of participants, problems and solutions to these arenas and choices. The decision structure indicates which participants may attend an arena or a choice. We are interested in the number and stability of participants – whether choices are made by a few representatives and experts, or whether there is mass mobilisation and unconventional participation. Likewise, the access structure indicates which problems and solutions may attend an arena or a choice opportunity. We are interested in the number and stability of goals and causal theories, and the extent of any conflicts. The level of conflict is often related to attempts by groups to redress the power balance by changing the decision and access structures, and thus the activation patterns and the definition of issues. We are interested in when such strategies are used, as compared with when choices are made through analysis and search behaviour, 'sounding out' and attempts to achieve a compromise (Thompson and McEwan, 1958; Schattschneider, 1960; Olsen, 1972a). Finally, a typology of policy styles should consider results. Substantive outputs may be discussed in terms of whether there are clearcut winners/losers, or a sharing of benefits and costs, as well as whether policies are incrementalistic or constitute basic changes. Social outcomes may be related to legitimacy, and the unifying or polarising effects on people's attitudes and behaviour as well as the development of citizens' political potential and to gains in their effectiveness, knowledge and policy understanding. Table 3.1 summarises some of the main characteristics and hypothesised correlates of five policy styles.[1]

The comparatively limited use of styles like mobilisation and confrontation may be linked to factors such as size, homogeneity and history. Norway is a small and fairly homogeneous country. In modern Norwegian history consensus and peaceful coexistence, rather than dissensus, have prevailed (Torgersen, 1970). Here, however, we are primarily interested in variations in policy styles *within* this general framework. In the section below we indicate the setting of Norwegian public policy-making in terms of the cleavage structure and the politically organised resources behind various interests.

Cleavages and Politically Organised Groups

Cleavages

The best specified model of the Norwegian cleavage structure has been developed by students of the party system and electoral behaviour (Valen

Table 3.1 *Policy Styles – Characteristics and Correlates*

	Structure				Results	
Style	*Decision*	*Access*	*Level of conflict*	*Strategy*	*Substantive output*	*Social outcome*
Problem-Solving (entrepreneurial)	Single decision-maker or a few experts	Agenda given with a few well-defined goals, well-understood means–ends connections	Consensus – objectives, norms, or standards shared, at least at some level; differences over subgoals can be mediated by reference to common goals by testing subgoals for consistency with other objectives	Analysis, identify a solution that satisfies shared criteria; enlarge resources; search for new alternatives; rationalistic and empirical; study problems carefully; reduce uncertainty about causal structures	All winners, no losers; incrementalism	Integration, goodwill and trust building; little competence building, except for the few participants; legitimacy related to cost–benefit analysis, and to beliefs in professional competence
Bargaining	A few recognised spokesmen for well-defined interests	Few, well-defined and stable interests, goals and causal theories	Agreement without persuasion; live with conflicts; disagreement about goals, but goals are bargainable within established rules of the game (arenas and procedural rules)	Pragmatic compromises and 'contacts'; gamesmanship and use of resources; sanctions, threats, offers and promises; no participant can unilaterally force through a decision; coalition building	Sharing more than winners/losers; distributional quantitative outputs; incrementalism	Some strain on the power and status system, but a possibility for long-term trust building; little competence building except for the few participants; legitimacy related to pareto-optimal solutions or from widespread acceptance of both the postulates of politics, and the distribution of power within the system
Self-Governance	Several separated and autonomous decision-making centres with different participants; geographic or functional groups with self-governance; within each arena a few participants	Different definition of problems, goals and solutions; within each a few well-defined and stable interests, goals and causal theories	Implicit or explicit contracts of mutual non-interference and adherence to common rules of peaceful coexistence; different rules and processes within each unit	Conflict avoidance through local rationality and low degree of non-agreement between units; spontaneous adaptation between units	Different solutions in different units; each choice supposedly affects a limited part of the population	Little strain in the power and status system; acceptance of cultural variation at the expense of national standards; more people are trained, and competence such as local knowledge is used; legitimacy related to axioms of self-governance

Table 3.1 (*Continued*)

Style	Structure		Level of conflict	Strategy	Results		Social outcome
	Decision	Access			Substantive output		
Mobilisation	The arena of bargaining is not considered fixed; new participants are mobilised or activate themselves during a policy process	The agenda is not considered fixed; new problems, goals and solutions introduced during a policy process	Fairly high level of conflict; disagreement over goals and causal theories as well as over procedural rules of the game	Power struggle; activate followers; redefine issues; attacks on the management and legitimacy of the process; little agreement about who are experts	Winners or losers – all or nothing; potential for significant changes and renewal		Strong strains on power and status system; reduced trust between groups; increased trust within each group; more people get political experience and training; legitimacy related to direct democracy and people's right to self-governance
Confrontation	The arena of bargaining is not considered fixed; new participants are mobilised or activate themselves during a policy process	The agenda is not considered fixed; new problems, goals, and solutions introduced during a policy process	Very high level of conflict; total disagreement over goals and causal theories as well as over procedural rules of the game	Power struggle; protests; civil disobedience; use of physical power in open, violent confrontations	Winners or losers – all or nothing; potential for very significant changes and renewal		Extreme stress on the power and status system; alienation; lack of trust between groups; increased trust within groups; many people get experience and training; potential for changed 'consciousness' and level of activation; legitimisation related to basic personal or group norms concerning the operation and structure of the polity

and Rokkan, 1974). They describe cleavages as a product of complex historical processes and a sequence of conflicts triggered by waves of mobilisation since the 1880s (Figure 3.1).

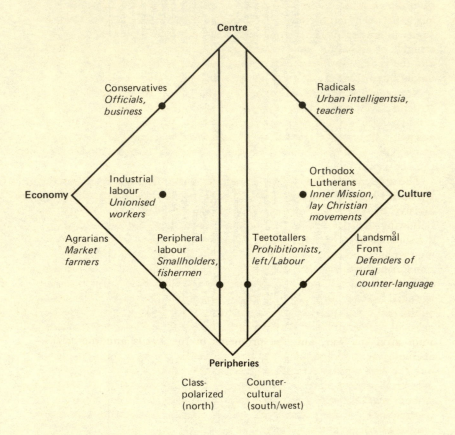

Figure 3.1   *The Valen–Rokkan model (1974) of the Norwegian cleavage structure.*

First, *geography*, a territorial conflict where two distinct peripheries (the south-west and the north) mobilised against the centre. Secondly, *culture*, where three dimensions have dominated: (*a*) the conflict about linguistic policy, between the defenders of the established central standard (*riksmål*) and the protagonists of the rural counter-language (*nynorsk*); (*b*) the conflict about moral legislation, particularly the control with the production and consumption of alcohol; and (c) the struggle for the control of the church, now basically a contrast between the active Christians, mostly orthodox Lutherans closely attached to lay religious bodies, and the great majority of religiously indifferent citizens.[2] Thirdly, *economy*, also with three dimensions: (a) the rural-urban conflict in the commodity market – a battle between market-oriented farmers and the various urban and consumer interests, for the control of prices and subsidies; (b) the rural class struggle of labourers, smallholders and fishermen against local notables and the urban establishment; and (c) the industrial class struggle of the unionised working class against owners and employers.

Norwegian policy-making takes place within this established cleavage structure. New issues have evoked shifting cleavages, but in the twentieth century there is a distinct trend. One aspect is the increasing salience of economic cleavages, especially between unionised industrial workers and employers. Another aspect is the transformation of class conflict into class co-operation.

The sequence of cleavages is important, and so is the level of conflict. Up until 1918 traditional issues on cultural policy proved distinctly more divisive than the new issues of class conflict (Rokkan, 1966, p. 79). Following the electoral success of the socialists in 1927, the principal division has been between socialists and non-socialists, with an increasing emphasis on economic issues. But gradually class confrontation was transformed into class co-operation (Seim, 1972). 1945–(approximately) 1965 is a distinctive period in Norwegian political history, characterised by social change, political stability and an unusual degree of consensus on public tasks and goals (Bergh and Pharo, 1977; Bull, 1979). In 1945 all political parties presented a joint programme: the country was to be rebuilt after the war, and the problems of the 1920s and the 1930s – unemployment and poverty – had to be solved. Economic modernisation was the key word – a belief in solving the problems through growth, industrialisation and mass education. Growth presupposed peace in the labour market, and explicit and implicit contracts of peaceful co-existence – if not consensus – among the major interests contrasted the class struggle of the 1920s and 1930s.

The emphasis on economics, modernisation and class co-operation has affected the saliency of other cleavages. It was widely believed that the rational use of the country's resources presupposed industrialisation, urbanisation, formal education and geographic mobility. Regional differences became less relevant. And with labour and employers as the major poles, cultural conflicts lost some of their saliency. Institutional arrangements for resolving such conflicts developed, and there were comparatively few confrontations over issues like religion, alcohol, or language.

Thus, styles of confrontation and mobilisation may be preferred by groups who are concerned with other cleavages than the dominant one, and by groups who believe more in class conflict than class co-operation. First, we consider which cleavages and issues concern ordinary people. Is the Valen-Rokkan model adequate when extending the analysis from the development of the party system to other political structures and behaviour? Has the welfare state itself caused new divisions in society (Kuhnle, 1980; Valen, 1981)?

Table 3.2 indicates that in the mid-1970s most ordinary people still perceived economic cleavages and issues as the most important. Some use class terminology, others refer to tension between employers and employees, and still others use party terminology – socialists/non-socialists. At the same time the increase in the number of pensioned people and the costs of the welfare state, as well as the growing expectations of pensioners, cause 14 per cent to cite tensions between the working and the non-working parts of the population. The conservationist movement and its criticisms of the economic growth ideology, as well as the local/central conflict, are reflected even stronger in the data.

The traditional cultural cleavages still prevail for 11–18 per cent. In addition comes tension between the sexes and between generations – groups that did not count directly in the structuring of the party system (Valen and Rokkan, 1974, p. 364). Also, large groups are concerned with divisions linked to meritocracy: experts, bureaucrats and people with high formal education, on the one hand; ordinary people and the clients of public bureaucracies, on the other. These are potential cleavages made more conspicuous by the growth of the welfare state.

Table 3.2   *Evaluation of the Importance of Various Cleavages and Divisions; by the Population, Elected Officials and Employees in Economic-Producer Organisations, and Civil Servants in the Ministries 1975–6 (Percentages)*

Type of cleavage/ divisions between:	Population	Economic-producer organisations Elected officials	Economic-producer organisations Employees	Civil servants in the ministries
Economy:				
Social classes	35	39	35	44
Employers/employees	30	71	66	62
Blue- and white-collar workers	11 76	32 92	21 91	20 86
Employed–pensioned	14	36	28	26
Socialists/non-socialists	39	74	73	59

Table 3.2 *(Continued)*

Type of cleavage/ divisions between:	Population	Economic-producer organisations Elected officials	Employees	Civil servants in the ministries
Ecology:				
Economic growth vs environmentalism	25	71	63	54
Geography:				
Centre/periphery	28 ⎫	64 ⎫	56 ⎫	64 ⎫
Rural/urban residents	13 ⎬ 41	39 ⎬ 75	40 ⎬ 67	44 ⎬ 73
Different regions	11 ⎭	32 ⎭	22 ⎭	23 ⎭
Culture:				
Religious people/others	17 ⎫	22 ⎫	14 ⎫	21 ⎫
Teetotallers/others	18 ⎬ 33	19 ⎬ 36	19 ⎬ 27	14 ⎬ 32
Different language groups (*bokmål–nynorsk*)	11 ⎭	14 ⎭	13 ⎭	15 ⎭
Demography:				
Women/men	13 ⎫ 31	35 ⎫ 61	25 ⎫ 51	27 ⎫ 61
Young/middle-aged	23 ⎭	48 ⎭	40 ⎭	50 ⎭
Meritocracy:				
Groups with different levels of education	25 ⎫	47 ⎫	44 ⎫	50 ⎫
Experts – common people	21 ⎬ 45	58 ⎬ 82	53 ⎬ 69	49 ⎬ 70
Public employees – clients	14 ⎭	53 ⎭	39 ⎭	29 ⎭
No. of respondents	(2,084)	(444)	(509)	(756)
No. of non-respondents	(119)	(31)	(27)	(28)

Note: The questions differed somewhat from the population to the three elite groups. Thus, the ranking of cleavages/divisions is more important than the percentage responding to each. The question to the population was: 'In discussions of society and politics we often hear different statements as to the most important divisions or cleavages in this country. This card lists several such cleavages/divisions. Which of these do you consider the most significant one, that is, the one which creates the most important conflicts in our society today?' The next question was: 'If you were to cite some other important cleavages/divisions in today's society, which then would you mention? Are there any you feel are important and of great significance?' The table reports those who have answered one of these two questions. (The respondents were also asked to mention cleavages/divisions of little significance.) For the three elite groups the introduction was identical to the one for the population, but they were asked to evaluate each cleavage/division on a five-point scale – very important, somewhat important, so-so, somewhat unimportant and very unimportant. The table reports those who say a cleavage/division is very or somewhat important. These differences are due to the economic costs of using the latter technique in the survey of the population.

We conclude that the economic divisions have a dominating position, but that Norway – as perceived by the man in the street – clearly has a pluralistic cleavage structure. The likelihood that some of these divisions should provide a basis for mobilisation and confrontation, depends on the politically organised resources linked to the various groups, and on the responsiveness of political institutions – their ability and willingness to accommodate the concerns of various groups in terms of effective problem-solving and conflict resolution.

Politically Organised Resources

The present emphasis on economic issues is reflected in the mobilisation of resources behind various interests. Around 1920 the prohibitionists could, for instance, claim by far the largest organised membership in the country, about twice that of the trade unions (Sparre Nilson, 1978, p. 179). And several political parties were in many ways instruments of the temperance movements.

The Norwegian party system, like the (perceived) cleavage structure, is pluralistic. But since 1945 the Labour Party and the Conservatives have been the most important parties in terms of votes, members, economic resources and seats in the *Storting* (Parliament). The main tendency has been that the Labour Party and the Conservatives are at opposite poles on issues within the advanced corporate urban economy, while they tend to take the same side in territorial-cultural conflicts. Their positions are very similar on the level of support for the primary economy, and they do not differ much in their reactions to the religious activism of the Christian People's Party. Territorial-cultural variables seem to prevail in differentiating the parties of the middle from those of the left and the right, while a set of functional-economic variables helps contrast the socialists from the conservatives (Rokkan, 1966, p. 103; Valen and Rokkan, 1974, p. 335).

The resource concentration around economic cleavages is strengthened because economic interest groups today control more politically relevant resources than any other type of interest group – as well as more resources than the political parties. Approximately 70 per cent of the Norwegian population (15 years and older) are members of one or more interest organisations. Only humanitarian and recreational associations can compete with economic interest organisations in terms of membership, and the former are rarely involved in politics. Cultural associations today mobilise relatively few citizens (Table 3.3). Religious associations may be an exception – but even their membership is modest given that 95 per cent of the population belongs to the state church. The importance of economic organisations also emerges when people with multiple organisational memberships are asked to judge which one is the most important (Table 3.3).

Table 3.3 *Support for Various Types of Organisations in the Norwegian Population in 1975; Percentages (Number of respondents = 2,203)*

Type of organisation	Total membership as a proportion of adult population (15 years and above)	Proportion of members who regard an organisation the most important one*	Proportion of the population who think the influence of an organisation is/should be:			
			big	small	bigger	smaller
Federation of Trade Unions (LO)	18	64	60	2	6	16
Unions and professional associations outside LO	9	73	13	11	5	2
Organisations for people employed in agriculture, forestry, fisheries	5	59	26	11	14	4
Employers' associations and organisations in industry, commerce and shipping	5†	24	50	11	6	18
Housewives' associations	4	31	–	–	–	–
Pensioners' associations	3	43	3	30	22	1
Students' associations	4	12	9	14	4	7
Consumer groups	9	10	17	9	4	4
Environmental associations	–	–	9	13	24	3
Humanitarian associations	17	28	7	13	20	1
Religious associations	9	57	16	19	8	7
Teetotallers' associations	2	19	9	24	9	6
Language associations	2	3	3	27	2	4
Youth associations	5	39	7	14	10	1
Women's liberation associations	2	50	7	16	11	5
Sports clubs	17	37				
Hobby clubs and recreational associations	14	27	4	20	11	1
Automobile associations	12	15	–	–	–	–
Neighbourhood associations	10	20	4	14	14	1

* This question was asked of those with multiple memberships. The numbers represent the percentage of those with multiple memberships who say the organisation in focus is most important for themselves.

† This number is too high. The correct number is about 2 per cent. The question is probably misunderstood by some respondents, and this explains why only 24 per cent say this membership is the most important for them.

– = question not asked.

The tendency is reinforced when the administrative resources of different organised interests are considered (Table 3.4). It is primarily economic interests which have administrative staffs of a size that make them a potential counterweight to public bureaucracies. The size of the staffs is strongly correlated with economic and other resources (Moren *et al.*, 1976; Hallenstvedt, 1979), and the ability of such organisations to disrupt the economic system is a significant political resource.

Table 3.4   *Number of Organisations and their Administrative Resources at the Central Offices at the National Level, by Type of Organisation in 1976.*

Type of organisation:	Number of organisations	Percentage with own secretariat	Number of employees
Economic-producer organisations			
Primary sector	56	61	810
Industry	118	37	305
Norwegian Confederation of Industries	57	24	170
Norwegian Federation of Crafts	25	44	50
Others	36	50	85
Trade	107	29	320
Federation of Norwegian Commercial Associations	61	33	150
Others	46	29	170
Banking, insurance and transportation	61	49	715
Employers' associations	59	25	550
Norwegian Employers' Association	40	40	290
Others	19	27	260
Employees	206	45	990
Federation of Trade Unions	42	81	550
Others	164	38	440
Other organisations	369	47	1,245
Students'	8	87	25
Pensioners'	3	0	0
Youth	9	89	80
Women	4	75	10
Language	7	43	10
Teetotallers'	18	61	50
Religious	58	64	260
Environmentalists'	7	57	20
Humanitarian	64	53	345
Athletics and recreational	85	47	355
International co-operation, culture and professional associations not focused on employee interests	106	24	90

Note: The categorisation used involves several problems both in terms of what should constitute 'interest organisations', and how each organisation should be classified. We have made use of the stated objective of an organisation. Fifty-six organisations in 'productivity and technical affairs' and sixty-one in research and services are excluded, because their primary goal is not interest mediation. Some economic-producer organisations are members both of the Norwegian Employers' Association, and of industrial or trade associations. These are double-counted, which gives six organisations and ten employees too many in the industry category, three and ten respectively, too many in the trade category and nineteen and 115 too many in the employers' category, compared to the categories used by Moren *et al.* (1976). The figure for religious organisation employees is somewhat too small, because we do not have exact numbers for the Salvation Army, the Norwegian Mission Alliance and the Norwegian Lutheran Inner Mission Society. However, none of these discrepancies should change any of the trends in the material or the conclusions.

Source: Moren *et al.* (1976).

A somewhat different pattern is seen in the responses to questions about which organised groups should have more or less influence upon the development of Norwegian society. While a majority of the population has no opinion about this question, or they are satisfied with the present distribution of power, those who do want changes have a clear idea of how influence should be redistributed. The most resourceful and (perceived) influential organisations – economic interests in the secondary and tertiary economies – should have less power. Likewise, there is a tendency to want more influence for those who are considered less powerful (Table 3.3).

The conclusion is that most politically relevant resources are linked to economic cleavages. Still, the pluralism of the cleavage structure is reflected in a multiparty system and in a well-developed system of interest organisations. While the resources of parties and organisations emphasising non-economic tensions are modest, some of them have a significant number of 'identifiers' in the population. These identifiers may be mobilised under certain circumstances, for example, if political institutions do not respond to and accommodate such interests.

Political Institutions and Routine Policy-Making

Since the Second World War there have been important changes in the macropolitical systems of Western societies. The patterns of power, responsibility and accountability have modified in significant ways, and sheer numbers of votes have lost value as political resources. These modifications are closely related to changes in the interaction between governments and organised interests. One central feature has been the extensive and complex interpenetration of governmental agencies and organised interests.

The vast network of organised interests make it unrealistic to base

governance on majorities of votes only. Governments and organised interests are both partners, and competitors for power. A result is that political
parties have been deprived of their hegemony as the intermediary link
between the people and the government, while the locus of public policy-
making has moved from the parliamentary arena to a bureaucratic-
corporative arena (Rokkan, 1966; Olsen, 1981a). Heisler and Kvavik (1974)
argue that Norway is the archetype of the 'European polity' model. Modern
welfare states have institutionalised a stable political process which (using
the categories of Table 3.1) are characterised by:

(a)   *a decision structure*, where the influence of the general public can be
      said to have been effectively removed from decision-making; a decline
      in the role of the parliaments, ideological parties and elections; the co-
      optation of organised groups – so that virtually all have access to
      government. Administrative agencies have come into focus – the co-
      optation of organised groups has been accompanied by the develop-
      ment of a new type of policy-making structure, essentially a network
      of committees, as an extension of the formal governmental
      bureaucracy; a delegation to administrative subsystems where highly
      organised sectors enjoy substantial self-governance, with the groups
      most affected by public policies wielding considerable control over
      distinctive issue areas.

(b)   *an access structure*, where broad ideological issués have vanished and
      the agenda is dominated by more technical issues; high task and goal
      consensus; and causal theories provided by recognised experts, and
      thus –

(c)   *a low level of conflict.*

(d)   *strategies* characterised by analysis, rational argumentation, com-
      promises and bargaining, and little emphasis on politisation and mass
      appeals based on clashing socioeconomic ideologies; lack of com-
      petition and emphasis on security and the avoidance of uncertainty –
      in general strategies presupposing trust rather than hostility and
      suspicion, and emphasising the need to reach decisions by consensus
      rather than one actor imposing a solution on the rest.

(e)   *substantive outcomes*, where all interests are accommodated to some
      extent – the substantive result of policy-making is to produce
      'sharers' more than winners and losers. The test of a good decision is
      not so much some objective rationality, but that as many as possible
      (of the significant parties) agree to it. The *social outcome* is that the
      trust among the elites is preserved and developed. The elites have a
      vested interest in the continued successful operation of the structure,
      while ordinary people are primarily interested in who gets what – not
      in participation and how things are done. Thus, they receive little
      political training and education. The lack of public debate tends to

deprive the political process of the renewal generated by disputation and competition. The political system does not receive inputs from groups not represented in the bureaucratic-corporative policy-making structure, and it is less able to adjust swiftly to environmental changes. Intra (political) systemic phenomena provide better clues for understanding the political process than do environmental factors.

Many of the features emphasised by Heisler and Kvavik are well documented in the literature. In Norway organisations have legitimate and institutionalised rights to participate in all phases of governmental policy-making as representatives of specific interests (Moren, 1974; Kvavik, 1976; Christensen and Egeberg, 1979; Gaasemyr, 1979; Smith, 1980; Egeberg et al., 1978; Olsen, 1981a). There are more than 1,000 governmental committees, the majority permanent ones at the national level. Organisations are represented in approximately 50 per cent of these committees, by around 2,000 representatives. There are group–government interactions like delegation of public authority to interest organisations; the remiss system, whereby interested organisations are invited to comment on public policies before they are presented to the Storting or implemented; and the well-developed informal, day-to-day consultations between organised interests and groups. The self-governance of functional groups and sectors is reflected in the concept of Norway as a segmented state (Egeberg et al., 1978; Olsen, 1980). The level of conflict is low. And both participants and citizens report a fairly widespread satisfaction with the outcomes of public policy-making processes.[3]

There are, however, variations in policy-making styles across issue areas. In ministries organised around economic interests, like the Ministries of Industry, Fisheries, Trade and Agriculture, along with the Ministries of Local Government and Labour, Consumer Affairs and Governmental Administration, and Church and Education, a large majority of the committees at the national level have representatives of organised interests. The Ministry of Petroleum and Energy ranks lowest, with organisational representatives on only 15 per cent of the committees, but this may be due to the fact that this is a new ministry, and a new industry in Norway. Others with few representatives are the Ministries of Defence (33 per cent), Foreign Affairs (33 per cent) and the Environment (38 per cent).

The general tendency in Norway is clearly that ministries concerned with economic policy-making are most likely to develop a co-optive structure. The fact is even more evident in the selectivity of the system concerning which groups are co-opted. Civil servants and the leaders of the economic-producer organisations perceive a pluralistic cleavage structure (Table 3.2), but the bureaucratic-corporate system does not accommodate or permit participation for all interests – not even for all organised interests. Thus, we need to study whether interests not participating in this arena are active in other arenas, and if they in this way make the policy-making more dynamic. The bureaucratic-corporate system is in certain respects *status quo* oriented. However, it is not isolated from other policy-making arenas. In order to understand the dynamics of the system and the use of mobilisation and confrontation, we have to consider the selectivity of different policy arenas and the ways in which the arenas are interconnected.

Selectivity

Economic-producer interests, especially large, powerful business and employers' associations, along with organisations in agriculture and fisheries, labour unions, and the associations of various professions, dominate the committee structure – with more than 90 per cent of the representatives from organised interests. Looking at the distribution of 1,893 committee representatives among some major types of organisations, we find that five organisations have more than fifty representatives, eighteen have more than twenty representatives. These are consistently economic-producer organisations (Brautaset and Dovland, 1974).

In 1979 the Federation of Trade Unions, together with its component unions, was represented in 270 committees. Likewise, the Confederation of Industries participated in approximately 100, and the Norwegian Employers' Association in seventy committees. In contrast, promotional interests – cultural, humanitarian, and the like – were represented on only sixty-seven committees, that is 8 per cent of the total at the national level. Religious interests were represented in six committees; youth, sports and recreational interests in fourteen; and humanitarian interests in twenty-eight committees (St meld. no. 7, 1979–80).

While a majority of the national organisations have contacts with the ministeries, the great majority is *not* directly represented in the committee system (Christensen and Egeberg, 1979). Neither are all such organisations represented through established peak organisations. Table 3.4 indicates that a large number of national economic-producer organisations are not members of the major peak organisations in their sector.

The economic-producer organisations' dominance is also found in the workings of the remiss system, where economic organisations receive five times as many remisses as non-economic organisations (Egeberg, 1981); in contacts with policy-making centres like the Cabinet and the ministries; as well as the judgements of civil servants on the influence of various organised interests (Olsen, 1980; Lægreid and Olsen, 1981).

The conclusion is that the bureaucratic-corporative policy-making system is primarily centred on economic cleavages, and that access is provided mainly to resourceful economic-producer groups. Other groups and cleavages may be absent because they are excluded, or because they choose not to participate. Integrated organisational participation in public policy-making has costs as well as benefits, and sometimes the costs may exceed the benefits to the interest organisations (Olsen, 1981a).

The bureaucratic-corporative arena is also selective in terms of problems that can be solved and conflicts that can be coped with. Economic-producer groups have steadily expanded their spheres of interest, and the Federation of Trade Unions, for instance, today participates in committees connected to all the ministries. But a certain pattern may be observed in this development. The bureaucratic-corporative system is used more often for specific, limited issues than for broad, general issues.

Despite a general acceptance in Norway of organisational participation in policy-making, the major economic organisations have several times resisted governmental attempts to institutionalise participation in economic policy-making. In 1946 fifteen major employers' associations agreed, several of them reluctantly, to send representatives to a Board on Economic Co-Operation. This Board was to set policies concerning post-war reconstruction, price controls, unemployment, currency, wages, consumption and rationing. Only a year later, as it became obvious that the Board's activity involved important principles concerning the structure of the economy, and as the participating organisations were publicly criticised for the policies adopted, the justification for the Board was challenged by the employers' associations. Being in minority, they felt like hostages of the government.

A series of confrontations and crises followed, and in 1952 the employers' associations announced their withdrawal. Two years later the Board was formally dissolved. The employers' associations wanted to interact with government within a less institutionalised framework. Forms of co-operation should be decided in each case. After several new initiatives from the government, the employers' associations agreed to participate in a board on wages and subsidies and a board on general economic policy. The first was explicitly labelled the Contact Committee to signal that its sole purpose was to enable opposing interests to get in touch. The agreement to participate on the other board came after some hesitation, on the condition that the board have an independent position vis-à-vis the government and that there be open exchanges of opinion and information, with no written statements (Moren, 1974; Kvavik, 1976; Bergh and Pharo, 1977).

In 1975 a new attempt to institutionalise integrated participation was thwarted. The issues were prices and wages, and this time the Federation of Trade Unions refused to participate, while the employers' associations consented. The labour unions agreed that a bargaining structure like the one suggested, involving the major organisations and public officials, be used for one year to set wages and salaries, in an attempt to reduce inflation. But the unions refused to institutionalise such a structure, and they declared their right to reconsider the structure from year to year.

Since 1976 the experience with a centrally negotiated incomes policy has also cooled governmental enthusiasm. The government has paid a high price for its participation – a bill that has to be honoured by oil still beneath the North Sea (Schwerin, 1980).

The reluctance to accept permanent integrated participation where general principles – like the structuring of the economy, and especially the right of private ownership and the 'free bargaining rights' of the economic organisations – are at stake, contrasts with the widespread willingness of Norwegian organisations to participate on committees dealing with specific, limited problems. Whether the selectivity of the bureaucratic-corporative arena – in terms of participants, issues, styles, strategies and outcomes – produces tension and in turn mobilisation and confrontation, depends on the interaction of several policy-making arenas. The dynamics of the Norwegian system cannot be understood within the bureaucratic-corporative framework alone.

Arena Interaction

The description of the bureaucratic-corporative arena contrasts with descriptions of other phases of Norwegian political history where the contest for power has generated mass mobilisation into politics; where the conditions for political activity has changed and set the scene for new alignments and new cleavages. These have been periods where the system has lost its equilibrium, and each party has pressed to bring in new allies and tried out new alliances (Rokkan, 1966, p. 76). In comparison descriptions of the bureaucratic-corporative system are static, often it is assumed that bureaucratic-corporative policy-making processes also dominate other arenas and blunt the edges of ideological conflict. This may, however, be to generalise from a very special period (1945–65) in Norwegian political history and to underestimate the extent to which the workings of the bureaucratic-corporative arena depend on a larger configuration of political forces.

The period following the Second World War brought a new wave of committees, but since the 1960s the expansion has been modest. Since the mid-1950s, when postwar reconstruction was drawing to an end, there has been a levelling off in the number of governmental committees with organisational representatives.

The development of this system was not opposed by political parties. On the contrary, the idea of 'democratic corporatism' – economic planning based on a corporate structure – was launched before the Second World War and developed in London and Stockholm during the war on the initiative of leaders of the Labour Party and the Federation of Trade Unions. The new policy-making structure was to co-operate closely with political parties and other democratic institutions (Bergh and Pharo, 1977, p. 38). While the original plans were never implemented, the history of the bureaucratic-corporative policy-making system illustrates the strong links between political parties and economic-producer groups in Norway, and the integrating role of the political parties.

A study of 475 elected leaders and 536 administrators in national economic-producer organisations shows that more than half of the former and nearly half of the latter have held office in a political party or represented a political party in public office. The study also shows that specific parties dominate different organisations: the Labour party in the Federation of Trade Unions, the Conservatives in the employers' organisations, and the Centre Party (former Agrarians) in the farm organisations (Gaasemyr, 1979). The Labour Party and the Federation of Trade Unions have more formalised co-operation than do other parties and economic-producer organisations. However, there is no doubt that the same specific interests and causes are argued both by parties, and organisations.

The bureaucratic-corporative policy-making system also operates within a context where the majority of Cabinet members have held party membership (and most often party office) for decades; where the press traditionally has been strongly linked to political parties; and where political parties spend a lot of time and effort developing their platforms.

Thus, one characteristic of the Norwegian policy-making system is that there is a considerable interaction and overlap in terms of leadership in the bureaucratic-corporative and the territorial-electoral channel. In addition, the law of anticipated reactions is a prime form of co-ordination. The influence of the Storting is often manifested not by active participation in policy processes, but by how its interests and views are taken into account in advance by other participants in the policy process. Neither bureaucrats nor economic-producer organisations view the Storting as a rubber-stamp institution, or view the political parties as insignificant (Olsen, 1980; Lægreid and Olsen, 1981).

In certain respects political parties, elected bodies and the public have recently improved their position *vis-à-vis* the bureaucratic-corporate policy-making system. The change in 1961 from one-party, majority governments to coalition or minority governments enhanced the importance of the Storting in coalition building and bargaining in the policy process. During the 1970s the tensions between the political parties increased, new parties were founded, and in the Storting the number of dissenting votes in committees more than doubled from 1972–3 to 1974–7 (Rommetvedt, 1980). At the same time, public funds were used to strengthen the political parties, and the new instability of voters (Valen, 1981) required the parties to take heed of public opinion. More policy-making functions are delegated to elected bodies at the regional or local level (where bureaucratic-corporative networks are just starting to develop), rather than to administrative and thus bureaucratic-corporate units. More critical mass media, backed by the Right to Information Act on

Administrative Affairs 1970, has reduced the possibility for the bureaucratic-corporate elite to operate 'without the constraints of constant public
surveillançe' (Kvavik, 1976, p. 95).

These tendencies illustrate the limitations of the bureaucratic-corporate
system and its policy styles. They are reflected in a number of significant
policy-making decisions: the Norwegian decision not to join the European
Common market; the democratisation of business banks; the introduction
of free abortion; energy policy-making, such as the decision not to develop
nuclear power, and the decision to build a hydroelectric power plant on the
Alta River; the introduction of the principle that farmers' incomes should
equal that of industrial workers; decentralisation of policy-making functions to regional and local authorities; the decision to store military
equipment for marines in Norway; the introduction of a fifteen-month-long
price and income freeze in 1978.

None of these policy decisions was launched and settled within the
bureaucratic-corporate arena alone. Some were handled completely outside
this arena. Others involved a complex interaction between several policy
arenas and a mobilisation of a large number of citizens. In general, the
implementation of public policies has become more politicised. The real
test of power is whether or not public authorities can get their policies
implemented, and increasingly the task of the policy-makers is to discover
the limits set by those who will implement a policy and those who are
affected by it (Richardson and Jordan, 1979, pp. 137, 141).

What, then, are the conditions under which the standard operating
procedures of the policy-making system break down and citizens refuse to
accept policies arrived at through this system? We try to shed some light
upon such conditions by focusing on ad hoc actions and movements. These
are collective political initiatives channelled outside the political parties
and the interest organisations. They are organised around a specific policy
decision and, thus, they have a limited time horizon. Who are the participants? What is their agenda – what are the protests about? What is the level
of conflict? What are the strategies? What are the results – substantive outputs as well as social outcomes?

Irregular Policy-making: Mobilisation and Confrontation

The standard operating procedures of a polity reflect certain stable
interests, goals and cleavages; causal theories; power and alliances. Are
those trying to transform the institutional context, within which policies are
made, citizens who are excluded from routine policy-making; citizens who
generally do not achieve satisfactory outcomes, and who believe they will be
better off by bringing in new participants, issues, definitions and rules of
the game?

In Norway 48 per cent of the population (15 years of age and above) reported participation in at least one ad hoc action; 13 per cent are actively involved in a wide variety of issues (Olsen and Sætren, 1980). With few exceptions, these initiatives are reactions against public policies, which sometimes change the policy process through styles of mobilisation and confrontation.

Popular movements and ad hoc actions are not tools for the politically disadvantaged – those far removed from the centres of routine politics and with few social resources – to offset their powerlessness. In most cases, participation coincides with one of two types of resources: either administrative experience from public office, parties, or organisations, or with social resources such as high formal education, or high-status occupation. Citizens who are not members of interest organisations and political parties are not very active in ad hoc actions. Pensioners, housewives and manual workers are least active. Two important aspects of ad hoc actions do, however, contribute to an equalisation of the imbalances in other channels: women are as active as men, and young people engage as frequently as the middle-aged. Moreover, ad hoc action is used the most by those political parties with the weakest position in economic-producer organisations and the bureaucratic-corporate channel. Economic-producer organisations are dominated by people from the Labour Party, the Conservatives and the Centre Party (farmers' party), while supporters of the Left Socialists' Party, the Christian People's Party and the Liberal Party resort most frequently to ad hoc action. Organisational and administrative elites are not unfamiliar with ad hoc actions. The rate of participation is somewhat lower among civil servants in the ministries than among the population as a whole. But the rate is higher than average for employees in economic-producer organisations, however, and higher still among the elected officials, and among participants in the committees of the bureaucratic-corporate system.[4]

For the majority the level of commitment in ad hoc actions is low – mostly limited to signing petitions. The elites – those who initiate actions, recruit members, write letters to the editor and give speeches – amount to 8 per cent of the population. The high resource requirement for such activities is illustrated by the fact that the percentage of civil servants in positions of leadership in ad hoc actions is almost twice as high, and almost three times as high among employees and elected officials of economic-producer organisations.

What goals and programmes do activists have, which causes or issues move citizens to become involved? Are actions organised on the basis of non-economic interests? Are action groups primarily change-oriented, in opposition to the *status quo* orientation of routine policy-making? Do activists want confrontation rather than co-operation and peaceful coexistence?

The difference between ad hoc actions and other means of political expression is more pronounced in relation to which issues motivate action, than in relation to which groups are motivated. Economic and industrial policies, and economic cleavages, are of little significance. Issues related to morals, life style and principles in general, are the main motivating factors – along with issues that affect individuals and their families personally.

A more detailed analysis of the different types of actions indicates considerable variation as to programmes and goals. Nevertheless, a trend is discernible. While each action is an ad hoc phenomenon, some of the broad causes are well known from Norwegian political history. On the one hand, there are movements linked to the traditional 'counter-cultures' (religion, teetotalism and rural language). These are not change-oriented, but mobilise for the protection of traditional values; in defence of the nationalism and populism of the countryside, and in opposition to the urbanised and secularised bureaucratic-corporate elites. On the other hand, there are radical movements, recruiting from the left wing of and the parties to the left of the Labour Party, and among eastern liberals. This group has also traditionally reacted against foreign influence in Norway, and since 1945 especially against Western integration of military and economic affairs. Parts of this movement have also preferred less class co-operation and have put more emphasis upon class conflict.

Sometimes these groups take opposite stands (abortion). Sometimes they act together, like in the EEC decision, where they were able to win the referendum and defeat the bureaucratic/corporate/party 'establishment', including the leaders of the Labour and the Conservative parties, employers' and business associations, trade unions and most of the Norwegian press (Gleditsch and Hellevik 1977). Likewise, movements arguing for environmental protection against the forces of economic growth, and those fighting for sexual equality, frequently define themselves in opposition to this 'establishment'. And community groups react against the deprivation of the local environments, and in general, movements often attack changes initiated within the bureaucratic-corporate arena, incremental changes that in the long run add up to major changes in the everyday life of ordinary citizens.

In Norway the level of conflict is low in irregular policy-making, as it is in routine policy-making (see Table 3.5). Most actions and movements appeal to public opinion. The strategy is to gain sympathy among ordinary citizens by evoking their sense of fairness, equity and justice. Civil disobedience is infrequent, and physical violence is extremely rare (Olsen, 1981b). In modern times Norway has never experienced guerilla warfare, civil war, and the like.[5] For most participants in ad hoc actions the goal is to achieve a specific outcome on a specific policy, not to achieve major transformation of the polity, the socioeconomic system, or changes in the territory of the state.

Table 3.5 *Rates of Participation in Various Types of Ad Hoc Actions, by the Population, Elected Officials and Employees in Economic-Producer Organisations, Civil Servants in the Ministries and Representatives in Public Committees (Percentages)*

Type of civic actions	Population (1975)	Economic-producer organisations: elected officials (1976)	employees	Civil servants in the ministries (1976)	Representatives in public committees (1977)
Local environment/ community well being	10	18	17	15	25
School/education	13	15	9	5	16
Environmental protection	8	14	10	10	13
Public funding for local development	7	14	7	2	7
Language issues	5	3	2	3	7
For joining the EEC	8	23	26	–	} 33
Against joining the EEC	15	21	16	–	
Against free abortion	13	7	3	2	6
Wages, price and taxes	4	13	5	3	7
Fishing limits	3	5	2	1	4
Women's liberation, equal rights	4	6	5	6	12
For free abortion	6	5	5	6	9
People's Peace Prize	3	7	3	2	5
Foreign policy issues	4	11	8	9	12
Percentages participating in at least one ad hoc action	48	65	58	33	60
Total number of respondents	(2,203)	(476)	(536)	(784)	(2,142)

–=question not asked.
Sources: Olsen and Sætren (1980) and Hernes and Voje (1980) (the latter provides numbers for representatives on public committees).

Thus, there is little general hostility to actions and movements. Only 10 per cent of the population considers the occurrence of actions outside political parties and organisations a disadvantage. Almost half considers it an advantage. More scepticism towards ad hoc actions exists among the elite groups.

The Alta Case

Although ad hoc actions have been well regulated and tolerated, the struggle over the hydroelectric power construction in Alta (in northern Norway) may mark a new tendency. The issue has not yet proved to be of the same magnitude as conflicts over nuclear energy in other countries, for example, West Germany. But the question has been raised whether the very irregular policy-making style in the Alta case, characterised by much unconventional participation, could have effects – by example – in other hitherto well-regulated and 'peaceful' issues areas.

Policy-making concerning hydroelectric power has long traditions in Norway. Multiple interests are involved, and these have been regulated through a complicated, but relatively specified and well-tested process (Burns and Midttun, 1980). Still, built-in selective mechanisms exist in the system. It is primarily designed to accommodate economic interests and cleavages.

The Alta decision has taken more than ten years. The Storting has three times, by a large majority, decided to commence construction. However, in the summer/autumn of 1979 civil disobedience occurred when local residents and environmentalists blocked the construction of a road to the site of the planned power plant. Police were called in and arrests made, without succeeding to clear the way. The process culminated temporarily with a demonstration and a hunger strike by a group of Lapps in the front of the Storting – an event which received extensive media coverage. The result was that the government decided to postpone the implementation of the Storting decision.

When the construction started in 1981, the demonstrations were also escalated. A new hunger strike took place. Fourteen female Lapps occupied the office of the Prime Minister. Delegations were sent to the Pope in Rome and to the United Nations in New York. And the blocking of the construction road provoked the largest police operation ever in Norway. Several hundred policemen from all over the country were sent to Alta, and they had few problems removing 744 non-violent demonstrators.

In March, in a very tense situation, where the lives of some of the hunger-striking Lapps were in danger, a new postponement took place. It became clear that the government had not adequately observed its duty to clarify whether there were traces of old Lappish settlements in the construction road area. Archaeologists were given an opportunity to undertake such studies (which cannot be done during the winter). But the government declared that the construction will be implemented.

The Alta case illustrates the interaction of several institutionalised spheres or arenas – how a conflict unfolds differently within each arena and between them. There have been conflicts within the central administration between environmental authorities and power construction authorities, and in the Storting between the 'green' parties and the Labour and the Conservative parties. There have been conflicts in local governments – where a majority opposed construction, and at the regional level – where a majority was in favour. The court system has been involved in significant ways. And irregular politics have had a major influence upon the policy process, backed by massive media debates.[6]

In this case the institutional mechanisms for resolving conflicts have broken down. Financial compensation to those adversely affected by the construction has not been effective in resolving the conflict. The calculations and forecasts on which the decisions in the Storting was based, as well as the fundamental constitutional aspects, have been challenged. New participants and new definitions have been introduced. The industrial and economic growth oriented logics of the construction interests have been confronted with the logic of environmentalists, and with a logic based on the traditional rights of the Lapp population. Government has raised the issue of protecting representative democracy and the rule of law. The decision has also developed an international dimension. Environmentalists have mobilised their international organisations, and the Lapps have been supported by defenders of the rights of aborigines all over the world.

Yet even this situation has a touch of 'Norwegian style'. A few days before the police action was to start, TV was able to get the leader of the police operations and the leader of the demonstrators together. Over a cup of coffee and some cookies the two spoke calmly about the future prospects. Both hoped the other party would give in. They promised to do their best to prevent violence, and expressed their understanding for the other party.

Political Effectiveness

In the Alta case the opponents of the majority decision in the Storting have so far had some success. The construction has stopped, and public attention has been drawn to both environmentalists' and Lapp interests. It is more difficult to evaluate the political effectiveness of ad hoc actions in general – in terms of their immediate impact upon policy-makers and the implementation of policies, as well as their long-term social effects.

A striking observation is that few civil servants in the ministries and few leaders of the economic-producer organisations attach much political significance to ad hoc actions. They are ranked well below the constitutional organs, economic-producer organisations, the media and so on (Olsen and Sætren, 1980). This is surprising, given the seeming impact of action groups in areas like energy policy. Does this indicate a certain strategy on the part of the elite groups – are they deliberately playing down the importance of actions? There is no reason to believe that this would be rational tactics. Were ad hoc actions generally considered a threat, one would expect their impact to be exaggerated. One interpretation may be that actions are of considerable importance within certain public policy areas, while the aggregate impact is considerably less.

A study of specific actions supports this conclusion. Also the tendency is that government has been more willing to compromise when civil disobedience has been used than when actions are based only upon appeal to policy-makers and the public through rallies, demonstrations, or petitions (Olsen, 1981b). The defeat of the 'establishment' in the EEC decision is the major victory based on mass mobilisation in Norway since 1945. In many other decisions the policy outputs seem to be less important than social effects like political training, a feeling of solidarity and belonging, and a feeling of participating in meaningful activities. Still, the long-term social impacts are uncertain. The effects upon political loyalties of the EEC mobilisation seemed to disappear within a few years (Valen, 1976).

In sum, we may say that participation in irregular policy-making is highly resource-dependent. Mobilisation is most often linked to *increased* resources, that is, where groups have improved their power, in terms of their own resources and consciousness as well as new alliances. The exclusion argument is most relevant for issues and cleavages. Ad hoc actions in several respects represent an opposition to the 'establishment' organised around economic cleavages, superior in organisational and political party resources, and with an institutionalised right to participate in public policy-making. But it is a split opposition. Irregular policy-making is based on issue-oriented, unstable coalitions. Usually, most of the participants look less for revolutionary change than for the 'good old days', and the style of irregular policy-making is mobilisation more than confrontation. Compromises are achieved fairly often, and the social effects of such actions have so far not changed feelings shared by most Norwegians – a common sense of identity, a fairly high legitimacy of policy-making institutions and of the present distribution of burdens and benefits.

Does, then, the Alta case mark a change in Norwegian policy-making, away from peaceful coexistence and revolution in slow motion? Have the bureaucratic-corporate policy-making styles – based on the co-operation between stable power blocs organised around economic cleavages – been a finite phase? Have they been an institutional solution to the economic problems of the 1920s and 1930s, and the experiences with styles of confrontation and class conflict in this period? Will Norway experience a shift in power and new stable coalitions around other cleavages than the economic ones? Will there be a new equilibrium through changed participation rights for groups and access rights for issues and cleavages? Or will the future bring confrontations between issue-oriented, unstable coalitions?

Among the many factors affecting future trends, we focus upon the role of political design: the degree to which policy-makers can affect future policy styles through a choice of institutional solutions.

Design or Development

The more the public agenda grows in size and complexity, the more the most important role for political leaders will be to manage the policy process, not to make specific policy choices. Political leaders have to become organisers. They may try to affect the access structures, that is, to manage the agenda of various policy-making bodies, the issues, problems and solutions given access. They may try to affect the decision structure, that is, which participants are allowed to take part as well as the interaction between them by influencing the 'rules of the game'. They may try to manage the timing of policy decisions and thus the context (in terms of participants and issues) in which a choice is made. And they may try to create new policy-making arenas or to dismantle established ones. The policy styles used will depend on their ability to control the ways in which streams of participants, problems, solutions and choice opportunities flow together or are kept apart through organisational means.

It is not obvious that political leaders have much freedom to design and manage the policy-making structures and process. Today many groups have the capacity to hurt or halt the political as well as the social and economic system. Governments have to strike a balance between a more complex matrix of competing interests than hitherto (Richardson and Jordan, 1979). Often they try to stick to old policy styles even when many new groups demand participation and policy areas become overcrowded. It is possible that policy styles are the outcome of such a complex set of interactions that they may be difficult to change in a desired fashion (see Chapter 1).

To some degree studies of administrative reorganisation in Norway support such a pessimistic conclusion. We are left with the impression that considerable structural change has occurred since 1945, but largely unrelated to any consistent design on the part of the leadership. Political leaders are not very interested in governing by organisational means, their objectives are often ambiguous or conflicting and means—ends relations are not well understood. In addition, the chances of a successful implementation are limited by the interests of civil servants as well as by organised clients (Roness, 1979; Sætren, 1981).

Administrative issues are directed by the heterogeneous Ministry of Consumer Affairs and Government Administration, where the political leaders usually take most interest in issues like prices, salaries and problems related to sexual equality, families and children. In 1979 a new Ministry of Co-ordination and Planning was established. However, the resources of this ministry are very modest; its leaders are advocating planning as a pedagogical exercise rather than governance, and this ministry will quite likely be abolished by a new non-socialist government.

Thus, we should not look for a 'master-designer'. But neither should we conclude that adaptation and design do not take place. Three possible strategies should be mentioned: *ejection of issues from the agenda, co-optation of groups* and *co-optation of causes or interests*. Political leaders may try to get rid of problems and conflicts they cannot cope with through routine policy-making processes and styles. Or they may try to co-opt the groups, causes, or interests which make routine processes break down and initiate the use of styles like mobilisation and confrontation.

Ejection

Decentralisation is (among other things) a technique for getting rid of difficult policy choices. Central authorities avoid a dilemma when they transfer to local authorities problems like how kindergartens should be organised and what role Christian values should have.

In Norway decentralisation has for some time been a highly valued goal, but opinions differ as to the degree to which such goals have been success-fully implemented. Decentralisation creates a resource problem for the authorities to whom the decisions are decentralised. There are strong norms for equal treatment wherever one lives in the country, and whenever local policy-makers adopt different solutions, it is fairly easy for minorities to appeal to national authorities through questions in the Storting, delega-tions to the ministries, or through the mass media. Thus, we may expect problems and decisions to bounce up and down the system (Gustafsson and Richardson, 1979).

An alternative to decentralisation is to give functional groups more self-governance. Such groups may prefer self-governance, sometimes sup-ported by public money, rather than pursuing their aims in the political system. An example is religious groups which want to reduce state inter-ference in the affairs of the state church, or to dissolve the state church. The state monopoly on TV and radio broadcasting is under attack. And the planning vs market debate has been revived, with a demand for letting market forces operate more independent of public, selective intervention. As public funds have become more scarce, economic-producer groups have also advocated less state interference in negotiations on wages and salaries. However, there are no signs that such groups want to reduce their partici-pation in public policy-making (Lægreid and Olsen, 1981).

While it has become more accepted that many problems cannot be solved through government, no major party wants drastic changes in the public agenda. The Conservatives argue for less public interference, but they have voted for most elements in the present welfare state. In general, the main tendency is a more complex public agenda aiming at 'a qualitatively better society', rather than the ejection of problems and conflicts (Bratbak, 1981). It is unlikely that policy styles will be affected in major ways through trans-ferring decisions from the public to the private sector. Decentralisation to local public policy-makers is more likely, but we expect co-optation to be more significant than ejection.

Co-optation of Groups

Norwegian government has done more to increase participation rights than to reduce the public agenda. For instance, it has been explicit policy to increase the proportion of women on public committees. In 1967 only 7 per cent of the participants were females. In 1975 the number had increased to 11 per cent; and in 1978, 17 per cent. Counting both representatives and substitutes the number was 20 per cent in 1978, 22 per cent in 1979 and 30 per cent of those appointed in 1979 were females (St.meld. no. 7, 1979–80). In the same way females have increased their participation in political parties, the Storting and local councils, and more women are recruited to higher positions in the civil service.

The tendency is that groups who so far have been absent from, or marginal in, the bureaucratic-corporate system are co-opted artists, pensioned people, Lapps, the handicapped, and so on – sometimes not without problems. The new law on public administration (*Forvaltnings-loven*) also states that affected groups should be heard before policies are set, and a proposed law on public planning provides for wider participation by affected neighbourhood groups (NOU 1977:1). Experiments with such participation has taken place within highway planning (Baldersheim, 1979). And the establishing of neighbourhood councils (*bydelsutvalg*) also tends to co-opt and accommodate groups which earlier have sorted to irregular politics (Stokkeland, 1976).

Civil servants in the ministries view the committee network as manageable. They report that they generally control when committees should be established and how the agenda should be determined. They have less control of who should be recruited to such committees (Egeberg, 1981).

Co-Optation of Causes

The political-administrative leadership also has the option of co-opting causes and interests without co-opting representatives of these interests. Causes and interests are built into the administrative structure. Sometimes institutions articulate interests, even if those affected do not participate. Other times administrative agencies supplement and form coalitions with co-opted groups.

One solution is ombudsmen. The ombudsmen for civil affairs, military personnel and consumer affairs have been supplemented with one for sexual equality, and one for children. It may also be argued that the Consumer Council in many ways functions like an ombuds institution. And the civil servants in the Ministry of Environment may give more political leverage to the environmentalists than do their own participation in the bureaucratic-corporate structure or through the remiss institution. Civil servants often defend the interests of strongly organised groups, but they may also be the defenders of weak, unorganised groups unable to represent themselves (Hoem, 1976). Generally, 'new' interests related (and often created by) public services, credit arrangements and so on, are weakly organised and their interests are primarily protected by the professions and institutions providing the services.

The Limits of Co-optation

Co-optation is no miracle cure. For organisations, integrated participation in government has costs in terms of loss of freedom to act spontaneously, loss of ideological identity, responsibility for public policies and loss of control of organisational leaders by members (Olsen, 1981a). Likewise, there are costs for government. Government may find itself responding to social conflicts by incorporating interests and cleavages in its own policy-making structure, and the accumulation of mutually cancelling obligations may paralyse it from taking action (Schwerin, 1980). Policy sectors may become overcrowded, but in Norway the government has tried to counteract this tendency by linking participation rights to mergers of interest organisations, or to the formation of new peak organisations. The result has been a 'structural rationalisation' of interest organisations (Egeberg et al., 1978).

The willingness of organised interests to become co-opted and the ability of government to co-opt relevant interests without becoming immobilised is linked to the level of conflict in society, the political organisations of interests, the resources available and the design of political institutions. Our interpretation of the present Norwegian situations is that styles of mobilisation and confrontation will also be used in the future, but styles of problem-solving, bargaining and self-governance will dominate. The main tendency will still be peaceful co-existence and revolution in slow motion. The Norwegian situation will be influenced by a long tradition of political compromises; by the fact that most (but not all) interests are organised; by the willingness of ad hoc groups to avoid violence; and by a certain ability to adapt political institutions to new circumstances. Certainly, there are limits to what can be achieved through organisational means, but those limits are not given. They may be stretched through more knowledge about the actual effects of various organisational forms in public policy-making.

Notes: Chapter 3

The authors want to thank Morten Egeberg, Martin Heisler, Jeremy J. Richardson, Lars Svåsand, Ulf Torgersen, Reidun Tvedt and Mariann Vågenes for advice and help.

1 The purpose of Table 3.1 is only to illustrate some dimensions (March and Simon, 1958; March and Olsen, 1976; Olsen, 1972b; 1978). Majority decisions through voting procedures have elements of several styles, for instance, the decision and the access structures are often highly regulated. There are conflicts over substance but not procedures. Strategies depend (among other things) on the availability of stable, organised parties. Majority decisions may to some degree take into consideration the interests of the minority, and thus affect the social outcome of the process.

2 Commenting on an earlier draft of this chapter, both Lars Svåsand and Ulf Torgersen suggested alternative ways of categorising the actors in religious conflicts.

3 These tendencies are documented in more detail in the forthcoming final report from the project 'Power in Norway' (spring 1981).

4 Space does not allow a thorough discussion of these patterns. However, the most active in the ministries are young people in low-ranking positions. In the economic organisations those in central positions are most active. Generally, they are more 'exposed' to actions and are activated even when they want the issue to be solved within the routine policy-making institutions. The EEC issue activated many organisational leaders who had never before (or after) participated in ad hoc actions (Olsen and Sætren, 1980).

5 The first draft of this chapter said that Norway had never experienced political murders in peacetime. Since then a nazi-inspired organisation has been uncovered, following the murder of two young men by their colleagues. The public support for any extremist group or party is, however, very small (Hernes and Martinussen, 1980, p. 107).

6 However, as late as May 1980 only 17 per cent of the population said they are very interested in the Alta case, and less than 3 per cent described themselves as well informed about the issue; 37 per cent said the decision did not interest them very much; 35 per cent favoured construction, 27 per cent were against and 38 per cent had no opinion (*Dagbladet*), May 1980). Another poll showed that a majority agreed that the policy should remove activists who blocked the construction decided upon by the Storting (*Aftenposten*, 10 October 1980).

References: Chapter 3

Baldersheim, Harald, *Organisasjonsformer i offentlig planlegging*, Report to the Ministry of Consumer Affairs and Government Administration, Bergen, 1979.

Bergh, Trond, and Pharo, Helge (eds), *Vekst og velstand* (Oslo: NKS-forlaget, 1977).

Bratbak, Berit, 'Fra gjenreising til "et kvalitativt bedre samfunn"', Institute of Public Administration and Organisation Theory, Working Paper, University of Bergen, 1981.

Brautaset, Tarald O., and Dovland, Tor-Inge, 'Organisasjonenes formelle representasjon, litt om omfang og forutsetninger', in Jorolv Moren (ed.), *Den kollegiale forvaltning* (Oslo: NKS-forlaget, 1974).

Bull, Edvard, *Norge i den rike verden* (Oslo: Cappelen, 1979).

Burns, Tom R. and Midttun, Atle, 'The study of complex societal decision-making. Actor-oriented systems theory applied to an analysis of hydro-power construction in Alta', Energy and Society Project Working Paper, Oslo, 1980.

Christensen, Tom and Egeberg, Morten, 'Organized group–government relations in Norway: on the structured selection of participants, problems, solutions and choice opportunities', *Scandinavian Political Studies*, vol. 2 (new series), no. 3 (1979), pp. 239–60.

Cohen, Michael D., March, James G. and Olsen, Johan P., 'A garbage can model of organizational choice', *Administrative Science Quarterly*, vol. 17, no. 1 (1972), pp. 1–25.

Egeberg, Morten, *Stat og organisasjoner* (Oslo: NKS-forlaget, 1981); forthcoming.

Egeberg, Morten, Olsen, Johan P. and Sætren, Harald, 'Organisasjonssamfunnet og den segmenterte stat', in J. P. Olsen (ed.), *Politisk organisering* (Oslo: NKS-forlaget, 1978), pp. 115–42.

Gaasemyr, Jostein, *Organisasjonsbyråkrati og korporativisme* (Oslo: NKS-forlaget, 1979).

Gleditsch, Nils Petter, and Hellevik, Ottar, *Kampen om EF* (Oslo: Pax, 1977).

Gustafsson, Gunnel, and Richardson, Jeremy J., 'Concepts of rationality and the policy process', *European Journal of Political Research*, vol. 7, no. 4 (1979), pp. 415–36.

Hallenstvedt, Abraham, *Organisasjoner og sektorsamordning* (Tromsø: Institutt for fiskerifag, University of Tromsø, 1979).

Heisler, Martin O., with the collaboration of Robert B. Kvavik, 'Patterns in European politics: the "European polity"-model', in M. O. Heisler (ed.), *Politics in Europe: Structures and Processes in Some Post-Industrial Democracies* (New York: McKay, 1974), pp. 27–89.

Hernes, Gudmund and Martinussen, Willy, *Demokrati og politiske ressurser* (Oslo: NOU 1980:7).

Hernes, Helga Maria, and Voje, Kirsten, 'Women in the corporate channel in Norway: a process of natural exclusion?', *Scandinavian Political Studies*, vol. 3, no. 2 (1980), pp. 163–86.

Hoem, Ragnhild, 'Undersøkelse av høringsbehandlingen ved utferdigelse av forskrifter', Report to the Ministry of Justice, Oslo, 1976.

Kuhnle, Stein, *A Crisis of the Norwegian Welfare State?* (Bergen: Institute of Sociology, University of Bergen, 1980); mimeo.

Kvavik, Robert B., 'Interest groups in a "cooptive" political system', in Martin O. Heisler (ed.), *Politics in Europe*, op. cit., pp. 27–89.

Kvavik, Robert B., *Interest Groups in Norwegian Politics* (Oslo: NKS-forlaget, 1976).

Lægreid, Per and Olsen, Johan P., *Top Civil Servants in Norway: Key Actors – on Different Teams* (Bergen: Institute for Public Administration and Organisation Theory, University of Bergen, 1981); mimeo. (chapter in forthcoming book).

Larssen, Olav, *Den langsomme revolusjonen* (Oslo: Aschehoug, 1973).

March, James G. and Olsen, Johan P. (eds), *Ambiguity and Choice in Organizations* (Oslo: NKS-forlaget, 1976).

March, James G. and Simon, Herbert A., *Organizations* (New York: Wiley, 1958).

Moren, Jorolv (ed.), *Den kollegiale forvaltning* (Oslo: NKS-forlaget, 1974).

Moren, Jorolv, Hallenstvedt, Abraham, Brautaset, Tarald and Døvland, Tor-Inge, *Norske organisasjoner* (Oslo: Tanum, 1972).

Moren, Jorolv, Hallenstvedt, Abraham and Christensen, Tom, *Norske organisasjoner* (Oslo: Tanum, 1976).

Olsen, Johan P., ' "Voting", "Sounding out", and "The governance of modern organizations" ', *Acta Sociologica*, vol. 15 no. 3 (1972a), pp. 267–83.

Olsen, Johan P., 'Public policy making and theories of organizational choice', *Scandinavian Political Studies*, vol. 7 (1972b), pp. 45–62.

Olsen, Johan P., 'Folkestyre, byråkrati og korporativisme', in J. P. Olsen (ed.), *Politisk organisering* (Oslo: NKS-forlaget, 1978), pp. 13–114.

Olsen, Johan P., 'Governing Norway', in Richard Rose and Ezra Suleiman (eds), *Presidents and Prime Ministers* (Washington, DC: American Enterprise Institute, 1980).

Olsen, Johan P., 'Integrated organizational participation in government', in Paul Nystrom and William Starbuck (eds), *Handbook of Organizational Design*, Vol. 2 (Oxford: Oxford University Press, 1981a).

Olsen, Johan P., 'Sivil ulydighet og politisk organisering', in Bernt Hagtvedt (ed.), *Den vanskelige lydigheten* (Oslo: Pax, 1981b).

Olsen, Johan P. and Sætren, Harald, *Aksjoner og demokrati* (Oslo: NKS-forlaget, 1980).

Richardson, Jeremy J. and Jordan, A. G., *Governing under Pressure* (Oxford: Robertson, 1979).

Rokkan, Stein, 'Norway: numerical democracy and corporate pluralism', in Robert A. Dahl (ed.), *Political Oppositions in Western Democracies* (New Haven, Conn.: Yale University Press, 1966).

Rommetvedt, Hilmar, 'Sprikende staur eller laftet tømmer? En analyse av partiavstander i Stortinget som grunnlag for borgerlig samarbeid 1945–77', unpublished dissertation, Institute of Political Science, University of Oslo, 1980.

Roness, Paul G., *Reorganisering av departementa* (Oslo: NKS-forlaget, 1979).

Sætren, Harald, *Utflytting av statsinstitusjoner fra Oslo* (Oslo: NKS-forlaget, 1981).

Schattschneider, Elmer E., *The Semisovereign People* (New York: Holt, Rinehart & Winston, 1960).

Schwerin, Don S., 'The limits of organization as a response to wage-price problems', in Richard Rose (ed.), *Challenge to Governance* (Beverly Hills, Calif.: Sage, 1980), pp. 71–104.

Seim, Jardar, *Hvordan Hovedavtalen av 1935 ble til. Staten, organisasjonene og arbeidsfreden, 1930–35* (Oslo: Tiden, 1972).

Smith, Eivind, 'Organisasjoner som virkemidler i forvaltningen', *Nordisk Administrativt Tidsskrift*, vol. 61, no. 1 (1980), pp. 14–42.

Sparre Nilson, Sten, 'Scandinavia', in David Butler and Austin Ranney (eds), *Referendums: A Comparative Study of Practice and Theory* (Washington, DC: American Enterprise Institute, 1978).

Stokkeland, Harald, 'Etablering av bydelsutvalg i Oslo', dissertation, Institute for Political Science, University of Oslo, 1976.

Thompson, James D. and McEwan, W. J. 'Organizational goals and environment: goal setting as an interaction process', *American Sociological Review*, vol. 23, no. 1 (1958), pp. 23–31.

Thompson, James D. and Tuden, Arthur, 'Strategies, structure, and processes of organizational decision', in James D. Thompson, Peter W. Hawkes, Buford H. Junker and Arthur Tuden (eds), *Comparative Studies in Administration* (Pittsburgh, Pa: University of Pittsburgh Press, 1959).

Torgersen, Ulf, 'The trend towards political consensus', in Erik Allardt and Stein Rokkan (eds), *Mass Politics* (New York/London: The Free Press/Collier-MacMillan, 1970), pp. 93–104.

Valen, Henry, 'Norway: the local elections of September 1975', *Scandinavian Political Studies*, vol. 11 (1976), pp. 168–84.

Valen, Henry, 'Valg og politikk: et samfunn i endring' (Oslo: NKS-forlaget, 1981); mimeo. (forthcoming).

Valen, Henry, and Rokkan, Stein, 'Conflict structure and mass politics in a European periphery', in Richard Rose (ed.), *Electoral Behavior: A Comparative Handbook* (New York/London: The Free Press/Collier-MacMillan, 1974), pp. 315–70.

4 The British Policy Style or the Logic of Negotiation?

GRANT JORDAN, University of Aberdeen and
JEREMY RICHARDSON, University of Strathclyde

As regards the way government is conducted, this is always changing without anyone noticing it ... the more central government seeks to intervene in the economy, the less powerful it will become, because it will have to rely on an ever-increasing number of bodies and individuals to do what it wants. Those people in this situation will bargain and make terms. If you believe that elections should determine policies, that policy choices should be clear cut alternatives, and that there is, or should be a wide range of possible alternatives, you will not enjoy the general situation I have forecast, because it is one which creates the need for consensus policies, inter-party deals and bargains with pressure groups. Without such arrangement, it will be difficult to put central government majorities together, or get the various levels of government to function. (Lord Croham, 1978)

Introduction

This chapter examines British modes of handling problems. The procedures which exist are many and vary from one policy area to another, from one type of issue to another, to a degree from one government to another and (to a greater degree) according to whether the government has entered office or has experienced the usual 'accommodations to reality' (J. Critchley, MP, 1978) that have marked recent British administrations.

Obviously, the detailed operating procedures for handling (say) nuclear energy will differ from abortion law reform or the regulation of the privately rented housing market. The British 'policy style' cannot be an accurate description of all these (and many other) procedures. What we identify as the *dominant* style is a procedural ambition. There is a preferred type of machinery, reflecting normative values – which is to avoid electoral politics and public conflict in order to reach consensus or 'accommodation' in the labyrinth of consultative machinery which has developed.

These *preferred* operating procedures tend also to be the *standard* operating procedures. The 'normal' policy style that we identify we have labelled as 'bureaucratic accommodation'. This is a system in which the prominent actors are groups and government departments and the mode is bargaining rather than imposition. The pattern of group/departmental relations can depart from 'bureaucratic accommodation' in two broad (conflicting) ways. On the one hand, there is a tendency to highly formalised 'tripartism' where the Trades Union Congress and the Confederation of British Industry are accorded near-equality by the government. On the other hand, there is some tendency for policy-making to be less orderly than the bureaucratic accommodationist style and to involve an unpredictably wide number of groups in rather unstructured relations. There are then conflicting trends towards order and regularisation, and towards fragmentation.

We are conscious that this account of our understanding of the British style becomes, on occasion, an ideal type of 'how to negotiate'. In other words, we suspect that certain practices appear to be likely to develop in any society as a means of abating conflict. Societies cannot, by definition, be solely based on conflict, and the 'logic of negotiation' appears inevitable. The need for social appeasement in order to develop social cohesion is likely to impose similarities on the general policy processes of various states. The *British* style turns out to be the negotiative style – that is, necessarily not peculiarly British.

This chapter describes five (overlapping) features of the British style – sectorisation, clientelism, consultation, institutionalisation of compromise and the development of exchange relationships. In terms of the basic typology in Chapter 1, Britain is best characterised as emphasising consensus and a desire to avoid the imposition of solutions on sections of society. In that there is no particular priority accorded to anticipatory solutions – and the stress on negotiation itself inhibits radical change – the British style is also 'reactive'. Hayward effectively summarised the essence of the style:

Firstly, there are no explicit, over-riding medium or long term objectives. Secondly, unplanned decision-making is incremental. Thirdly, humdrum or unplanned decisions are arrived at by a continuous process of mutual adjustment between a plurality of autonomous policy-makers operating in the context of a highly fragmented multiple flow of influence. Not only is plenty of scope offered to interest group spokesmen to shape the outcome by participation in the advisory process. The aim is to secure through bargaining at least passive acceptance of the decision by the interests affected. (Hayward, 1974, pp. 398–9)

Bureaucratic Accommodation: The British Style

Sectorisation

The priority accorded to conflict avoidance is perhaps a desirable quality in any political system, but it can lead to a lack of reform and the danger of overinstitutionalisation. Political inertia can result from the addiction to conflict avoidance. Hayward (1976) has argued that the danger to societal stability comes from the practice of cultivating stability to excess. Almost by definition, this style will not be evident in case studies which political scientists have selected because of the political controversy of particular issues: bureaucratic accommodation is the pattern of relationships over time which tends to keep issues off the party political agenda and attract little public or indeed academic attention.

Institutions are one technique in the style, but less formal structures perhaps predominate. Accordingly, the first feature is the sectorisation of policy-making. Aldrich (1979, p. 76), writing generally on organisations, had noted that specialisation in subsystems is inevitable. He argued, 'for without the assumption of a loosely coupled world, a theorist's task is hopeless ... Not all possible links between people, departments, or organisations are realised, and many links develop in ways that promote stability'.

Sectorisation is, then, a means of avoiding the intellectual overload of attempting to weigh up all options. In his study of agricultural politics, Wilson reports a system of 'neo-pluralism' by civil servants within the Ministry of Agriculture, Fisheries and Food. He was told, 'we cannot worry about everything, so we leave some functions to other Ministries to worry about. . . . The duty of MAFF is to present the arguments for help for farming. Other Ministers will soon bring forth criticism based on trade policy or implications for public expenditure' (Wilson, 1977, p. 45).

This advocacy also seems *politically* necessary: almost inevitably ministers tend to act as departmental spokesmen. The fact that ministers tend to psychologically identify with 'their' causes is another factor leading towards sectorisation. As Edward Heath has observed, 'what does happen is that Ministers are expected by their departments to fight their own corner and if one Minister is going to get an increase in expenditure, why then others will ask if they cannot have the same thing' (Heath, 1977–8). Richard Marsh's picture of Cabinet life confirms that of Crossman and other ministers:

> Most Ministers tended to find they were out of the picture on the major issues. The method of handling Cabinet business was such that there was normally no way of becoming involved in issues outside your Department brief. If you were Minister of Agriculture, for example, your knowledge of important negotiations on, say, Rhodesia would be confined to a twice-

weekly mention among a whole string of other things at the main Cabinet. The total discussion would probably last no longer than twenty minutes including a report from the Foreign Secretary. (Marsh, 1978, p. 98)

Cabinet does not act as an impartial jury coolly assessing options put to it by departments. Politically it is too difficult to proceed on a 'critical assessment' basis. Instead 'even-handed' treatment of ministries is the norm.

That is not to say that the participants are always content to proceed on this basis. The *Crossman Diaries* record a series of unsuccessful attempts to provide 'central capability' through the institution of some form of inner Cabinet. Devices such as the Ministerial Action Group on Public Expenditure and the Committee of Non-Spending Ministries were set up to provide some mechanism at the centre for discriminating between departmental bids – but they failed because the politically important ministers were too committed to their own departments to be impartial in judging other options. At Cabinet, therefore, ministers, according to Crossman, 'come briefed by our departments to fight for our departmental budgets, not as Cabinet Ministers with a Cabinet view' (Crossman, Vol. 1, 1975, p. 275).

This is not to say that exceptions never occur. The decision in late 1980 to increase spending on the young unemployed saw the Department of Employment receive £250 million while other ministries were cut, but there were rather obvious (electoral) reasons why the Cabinet as a whole should acknowledge this problem. When it comes to the Treasury's attempt to recoup this extra spending, another main characteristic of Cabinet government was revealed. There is an enduring non-identity of aims between the Treasury and spending ministers. As the Chief Secretary to the Treasury, John Biffen, put it in September 1980, 'it has been the experience of all Treasury Ministers through the ages, quite irrespective of party affiliation, that spending departments always have an interest a little different from the necessarily austere view that has to be taken by the Treasury' (Biffen, 1980). The Cabinet meets too seldom, with members too committed to their own interests, too busy for much intradepartmental reflection, with careers bound up in departmental not 'team' prestige, to be an effective mechanism for central choice and co-ordination. A system of competitive sectorisation operates.

In Britain we see the dominant style as consultation (merging with negotiation): policy initiatives/amendments are 'cleared' with other departments and with the client groups outside the bureaucracy. The client groups themselves co-ordinate their responses to problems and are fully aware of each other's case. For example, it is fairly common for submissions to government departments to be privately circulated to fellow-'clients' as standard procedure. At a later stage, department and clients then co-ordinate their activity in pressurising the rest of the government machine. Thus, co-ordination takes place at a number of levels within the relevant policy community until a common policy emerges which the community 'sells' to the rest of the system. This system of sectorisation and policy communities has policy implications. For example, when poverty came on to the political agenda in the 1960s, only a narrow range of activities were discussed within the Ministry of Social Security: more radical approaches involved functions outwith departmental boundaries (Banting, 1979, p. 87).

Habermas (1976, p. 62) has identified a 'rationality deficit' as a consequence of this general pattern of group–department relations, because 'authorities, with little informational and planning capacity ... are dependent on the flow of information from their clients. They are thus unable to preserve the distance from them necessary for independent decisions. Individual sectors of the economy can, as it were, privatise parts of the public administration'. Sectorisation of policy-making can, then, easily become what we have called the private management of public business (Richardson and Jordan, 1979).

Clientelism

To view departments themselves as bureaucratic interests in competition with each other prepares the way for an essentially clientelistic (La Palombara, 1964) conception of relations between departments and so-called pressure groups. Writing specifically about Britain J. B. Christoph has suggested:

> The vast majority of Whitehall departments manage policies affecting identifiable clienteles, organized or otherwise. While part of the job of civil servants is to analyse, verify, and cost the claim of such groups, and forward them to higher centres of decision, it would be unnatural if officials did not identify in some way with the interests of their clienteles, and within the overall framework of current government policy advance claims finding favor in the department. (Christoph, 1975, p. 47)

Lord Armstrong, former head of the Home Civil Service, appears to have viewed wartime co-operation as an important development towards current practices. His argument was based on the system of industrial sponsorship, but other groups have their 'parent' civil service division:

> The system developed a life of its own, (after the war) so that there is now almost certainly somewhere in the government a little unit of people whose job it is to acquaint themselves with what is happening in each industry, and as far as they can, watch over its interests. . . . I suppose the best known example of this is the Ministry of Agriculture, Fisheries and Food, whose sponsorship of the farming and fisheries is so powerful, close and persuasive that they have frequently appeared to other departments, such as the Treasury, as the official spokesman for these

industries in the counsels of Whitehall. But they are only the most obvious case and there can be found somewhere in Whitehall sponsors for almost every economic activity. (Armstrong, 1976)

It is important to note that Armstrong was discussing economic groups. The practice of clientelistic relations – while perhaps originating in such areas – has spilled over to be the norm in both economic and non-economic areas.

It follows from this line of argument that not only is the department not an unwelcome recipient of group 'pressure', but the department will itself attempt to mobilise activity by groups. For example, in the reorganisation of the water industry in the 1970s, the Ministry of Agriculture, Fisheries and Food attempted to persuade 'its groups' to completely reject the Department of the Environment's proposals – but the groups thought this stance was unlikely to succeed (Richardson *et al.*, 1978, p. 55). In the same case there were similar examples of 'pseudo-pressure'. Thus, when the presidents of the National Farmers' Union and the Country Landowners' Association wrote a joint letter to *The Times*, a draft was shown to the MAFF Minister the previous week! In other words, it was useful for the minister to be able to demonstrate to his colleagues that he was under 'pressure'. In one of the department–group meetings, the Permanent Secretary of the MAFF was minuted as saying that, 'the ministry would need all the help it could get'. Group–department relations tend to produce treaties of mutual advantage.

Consultation/Negotiation

The third major facet of the British style is consultation. There appear to be two principal forces supporting the practice: (*a*) cultural bias containing normative values which emphasises the need to legitimise decisions through consultation; (*b*) functional necessity. Underlying the consultative/negotiative practice is a broad cultural norm that the governing should govern by consent. In Britain according to Lord Rothschild (1976) there is a 'beatification' accorded to compromise. There is the complementary belief that participation ultimately enhances the legitimacy of a policy.

Consultation appears to have become the bureaucratic norm more so than in other countries. Eldersveld *et al.* (1975, p. 149) in their study of bureaucrats' perceptions of interest groups show that (of the five West European countries they discuss) British civil servants were least likely to view the clash of particularistic groups as a serious problem. Only 4 per cent of British respondents saw the close collaboration between a ministry and the groups or sectors most affected by its activity as improper or unnecessary (quoted in Hayward and Berki, 1979).

The 'standard operating procedures' for processing policy problems are based in, and nourished by, normative values of 'legitimate' action. The existence of these enduring values is one of the limitations on change in policy style. Attempts in Britain, such as under the Conservatives, in 1970–4, to move to a more anticipatory, deliberative, information-based method of decision-making undervalued the strong tradition of bargaining and consent (Richardson and Jordan, 1979, p. 37). The proponents of the 'New Style of Government' also underestimated the extent to which government had to react to events (Howell, 1974, p. 62).

A series of mutually reinforcing ideas can be advanced to argue that what we identify as the British style comes not only from board cultural values, but from purely functional requirements. There is a *functional logic* to consultation and negotiation. Consultation contributes to system maintenance not only because it imparts a sense of involvement, but also because it should produce more acceptable policies. Only the wearer knows where the shoe pinches and, arguably, in giving access to interested groups and individuals the system is more effective in supplying public needs than a dirigiste system. Thus, problem definition might be improved as a result of the wider participation by those most directly affected even if the effort and time needed to reach a decision are increased (Gustafsson and Richardson, 1979). With decisions that are specific, technical, complex, managerial, then awareness of particular circumstances is all-important. An interventionist state tends towards a functionally differentiated and fragmented bureaucracy and the relations between department and sectoral interests tend to become closer (see also Beer, 1967, p. 85).

The legitimacy of civil servants in imposing change is less than that of politicians. Civil servants have little recourse to arguments such as 'the government must govern' or 'the electoral mandate'. As politics has become more specific (matched by a tendency for groups to become more particularistic and greater in number) the tendency has been for civil servants to be obliged to carry a larger and larger part of the policy-making load. Given that the civil servants lack legitimacy derived from the 'democratic process', they are ill-placed to impose solutions and conflict avoidance is likely to result. British civil servants, compared with French, generally lack the confidence to operate an imposition relationship with groups (or, indeed, with other public agencies). They, too, are the prisoners of the same values which often lead their political masters to see consensus as *the* goal of policy making.

Consultation and negotiation are, of course, not exclusive categories. Consultation can be purely cosmetic, but it indicates something of the normative values of the society in that it is even in such circumstances considered worthwhile. Our major interest is in the area where consultation turns into negotiation. In such areas the government is probably dependent on the groups for assistance in that specific matter (or the group is so important in some other matter they cannot be needlessly antagonised). In many areas groups wield some kind of veto, which in the last resort the government might be able to overrule – but it would be politically too expensive to override groups on too many issues. Thus, the police have some kind of veto on interrogation methods; teachers' unions have been able to stop the abolition of corporal punishment despite considerable other group pressure in that direction; prison staff effectively control many aspects of the regulation of prisons (see D. Leigh, 1980). Wolfe's term 'the franchising of public policy' quite neatly describes (originally in the USA) the way in which sectors enjoy some degree of self-regulation (Wolfe, 1977), but the metaphor perhaps wrongly implies that the centre has always been keen to allow the sectorisation. The position is more that it has been unable to do much about it.

One study has claimed that the direct contact between civil servants and groups started between the wars and grew rapidly under the pressure of the wartime emergency and became established after 1945 (PEP 1974, p. 80). Before that the convention was that it was quite improper for civil servants to see pressure-group spokesmen; communication between officials and such people should be by correspondence only. After the war, PEP states:

> The official guide to civil servants' duties came to include a section on their obligation to consult all recognised interest groups. The criteria by which a group became accepted and put on the list of bodies to be consulted were fairly simple. The group had to represent the bulk of persons or companies or organisations in the area of activity and had to accept that all negotiations were to be confidential, even from its own members. In return, the leaders of these groups were consulted before any government plans were published and they could thus make their representation at a formative stage when plans were still open to argument and when no loss of face were involved in making changes. Those groups which wanted new laws . . . would go to Whitehall if what was wanted arose out of existing policies: that is if the matter was not highly controversial. On the other hand, if the proposal was in this [controversial] category then the pressure group could not deal with government departments. . . . Those groups whose sole or main objective was a 'cause' requiring legislation clearly still had to try and influence Parliament. . . . But these groups constitute a small minority. The majority are interested in the development and execution of accepted policies and they are on the consultation list and deal directly with government.

The importance of consultation with groups was confirmed by civil servants in a range of departments we contacted in preparing this chapter. Indeed, so uniform are the replies that we quote a range not to make the point – adequately made by the first – but to underline the fact that there is rather a more positive flavour to the replies than (say) received by Suleiman in his survey of French equivalents (Suleiman, 1974). For example, one respondent replied:

> You are quite right to stress its [consultation] importance. Sounding out opinion in advance of potential changes in policy or subjecting possible proposals to informed comment is something which is done in this country whenever possible. Consultation between Departments with a common interest in a particular policy area takes place as a matter of course, both formally and informally, at meetings or on the telephone. The ways in which interested public opinion is tested can range in formality from Royal Commission and Departmental Committees of Inquiry through Green Papers to individual groups and general invitations to express views. (Ministry of Agriculture, Fisheries and Food)

> You are correct in assuming that consultation between Government Departments is an essential part of arriving at decisions . . . consultation between Government Departments and groups outside Government is also an important part of arriving at decisions although the scale and way in which this is done will depend on the type of decision being made. (Scottish Development Department)

> Certainly . . . [one must] attach importance to the process of consultation both within the Civil Service and between Whitehall and other organisations. This is clearly an intrinsic part of the democratic government process. (Department of the Environment)

> If you don't consult them [the groups] they will only try and block the proposal in Parliament. Not consulting them is not worth the risk. (Health and Safety Executive)

It is, in fact, difficult to establish that this stress on consultation is new. It is not easy to find comparable issues in past years. One civil servant replied to our inquiries that it was difficult to 'prove' a growth in the scale of consultation, because in the not too distant past there was no governmental interest in his own policy area. He went on to distinguish between matters put only to the 'regular' consultees in his policy area and areas of wider implications when a consultative document would seek to attract all interested opinion.

It is, therefore, perhaps more realistic to see a 'policy community' existing at the level of detail covered by a civil service assistant or undersecretary – rather than at departmental level. Each policy sector may contain several policy communities (Table 4.1).

Thus, there will be many linkages between the various policy communities in each sector (for example, between branches of medicine, social services and social policy), and no doubt overlapping memberships. But

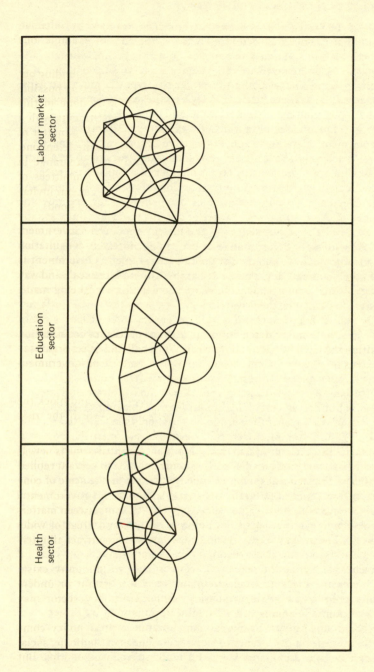

Figure 4.1 *Policy sectors and policy communities*

there will also be some linkages between sectors (for example, between the health and higher education sector and between the education and labour market sectors). Consultation with non-governmental groups will naturally depend on the issue involved. What evidence we have suggests that it is reasonable to claim that consultation of various types is more extensive than formerly. It *may* reflect a change in style by the departments, but it also reflects the greater number of organisations and interests involved.

In the environmental sector in which, for example, the Scottish Development Department operates, it appears to have become more 'congested'. New issues (such as oil) have arisen, and older issues seem to affect a wider geographical range – and hence a larger number of groups. New agencies have been created, such as the Countryside Commission for Scotland, and other agencies have developed new roles or positions – for example, the Department of Agriculture and Fisheries for Scotland has increasingly become aware of the consequences of the loss of good agricultural land. They are now unlikely to let 'change of use' go uncontested. New groups outwith government have entered the policy arena – such as Friends of the Earth and the Scottish Campaign to Resist the Atomic Menace (SCRAM). Older, established groups have taken to participating in the planning processing – for example, the Royal Society for the Protection of Birds now appears at public inquiries in order to represent its 'interest' in the policy process. Thus, both old and new interests are more active in demanding a say in policy-making.

The extension of government responsibility into a new area itself creates a number of specialised interests. As an ex-minister, Edmund Dell has argued 'British governments have created not just aircraft and nuclear power plants but deeply entrenched interests that demand more and ever more by way of resources if they are to be satisfied' (see Dell, 1973, p. 30; Heclo, 1978). For example, over 1,200 groups and organisations gave evidence to the Royal Commission on the National Health Service: many of these bodies are the product of the NHS and, hence, the decision to re-organise in the 1970s meant that government operated in a more congested environment than when the NHS was created. Similarly, the Manpower Services Commission, once established, created its own group network. This makes change in that particular policy area that much more difficult than hitherto. The cause of the 'crowded policy environment' (Heclo, 1975; see also Gustafsson and Richardson, 1979) is partly, then, government action itself as much as the clamorous constituency of groups. Equally, there is increasing pressure from groups who see the benefits of 'policy community politics' and want to share in them. There are, thus, many examples of policy sectors which were hitherto inhabited by rather small numbers of groups but which now accommodate new groups claiming a legitimate interest. As government intervention becomes more specific it requires, encourages (and even begets) a more specialist kind of group.

Thus, while the agriculture arena is dominated by the so-called 'holy trinity' of the National Farmers' Union of England and Wales and the Scottish and Ulster equivalents, there is a range of bodies of more specialist nature. For example, ninety-two bodies commented on the policy review of 'Food from our own resources'.

A distinction is, of course, required between consultation on a universal basis (for example, the Green Paper on *Income during Initial Sickness*) and consultation on a more informal basis. Even where a consultation exercise is very broad, it is often the case that the departments have a very clear view of 'who counts'. Thus, in the departmental consultations following the Finniston Report on Engineering, during the summer and autumn of 1980, over 500 groups and individuals were consulted. Yet the sixteen chartered associations in the engineering industry were clearly the key groups whose support was necessary before change could take place.

In fact, there are considerable advantages in pursuing policy-making in relatively closed arrangements. There is a common language and understanding of what is at issue (even if there is disagreement over policy preferences). By developing understandings, uncertainty is reduced for both department and group, and societal conflict is reduced. The style in the sectors is of inner-circle negotiation (see Devons, 1970). The emphasis is on the integration and accommodation of groups at all stages in the policy process. The 'rule' is that affected interests have the right to be consulted.

It is, however, possible to find examples of this system breaking down, even in areas where consultation and negotiation are the norm. Thus, in the area of relations between central and local government where links are normally rather close, and where permanent consultative machinery exists, there are occasions when the relationship is quite different – for example, the passage of Local Government Planning and Land (No. 2) Bill in 1980. In essence, an important element in the new government's strategy to control public expenditure, the Bill provoked considerable opposition from the local authority associations. Their opposition was not only to the contents of the Bill, but also to the process of 'consultation' which had been used. Thus, the *Financial Times* reported that the clauses dealing with block grants to the local authorities

were introduced on the understanding that they would be subject to meaningful consultation, implying negotiation with local authorities. But consultation on block grants [size] has been used only to the advantage of the consultors, and local authorities say they have not been consulted in a way which would allow them to influence the operational details of the scheme. ... Mr King [the responsible minister] insisted that he wanted quick progress but in the spirit of consultation with local authorities.

By mid-1981, with the government planning to introduce measures to restrict the freedom of local authorities to increase rates, the central/local relationship had become severely strained.

The need to consult and negotiate with a specific set of groups concerned with each policy problem, of course, has a direct bearing on the nature of policy outcomes. Essentially, it normally leads to incremental policy change, irrespective of the party forming the government at any one time. Thus, we may see the 'group constellation' surrounding a particular policy as acting like a magnetic field, holding the policy in place. It *is* possible, under certain unusual circumstances, to induce policy change (to change the 'magnetic field') but there is a natural predisposition for the field to hold the policy in place. Moreover, departments have little desire or incentive to disturb a magnetic field once it has been established. The bureaucratic preoccupation tends to be the minimisation of disturbance, the securing of a stable environment or negotiated order, rather than significant policy change (Richardson and Jordan, 1979). To pursue an anticipatory or active approach to problem-solving, is to risk disturbing an equilibrium (expressed in policy outcomes) which has been carefully negotiated over a period of years. Policy maintenance is, thus, a more common phenomenon than policy change.

The Institutionalisation and Regularisation of Compromise

Despite the attempted 'quangocide' by the Thatcher government (the almost total failure of the exercise is itself instructive) (see Hood, 1980), the outstanding feature of the British policy process is the committee. The extensive system of advisory committees is a way of institutionalising group contact with departments. So extensive is the system, it is difficult to produce a measure of the use of the device. However, the Report on Non-Departmental Public Bodies in January 1980 (Cmnd 7797, p. 1), listed some 1,561 advisory bodies in British government. Indeed, the report itself used the term '*networks* of advisory bodies'. Typical examples would be Advisory Committee on Animal Experiments (Home Office); Committee on Medical Aspects of Food Policy (Department of Health and Social Security); Advisory Committee on Development Education (Foreign and Common-wealth Office); Committee to Review the Functioning of Financial Institutions (Treasury). The 1979 Conservative government's difficulty in 'culling' such bodies (the report recommended winding up 211 such bodies) suggests that the system did not develop by accident (though clearly it was not *planned*). It fulfils the important purpose of co-opting specialised knowledge into the policy process. As the above report admitted, the case in principle for the advisory bodies, is that '... the Departments' own staff cannot provide the necessary advice by themselves, or that it may be desirable to enlist the participation of outside interests in order to formulate publicly acceptable proposals' (Cmnd 7799, p. 2).

It would, in fact, harm both government and groups to seriously curtail the practice. Committees can, of course, be permanent or ad hoc. Our general proposition would be that the atmosphere in a standing body is likely to be more fruitful than an ad hoc body. In a standing body the norms of behaviour – with the longer-term perspective – will be more conducive to settlement, the possibilities for trade-offs on timing more obvious. The possible combinations of the nature of the problem and the type of forum are presented in Table 4.1.

Table 4.1   *Internalised Processing of Problems*

Type of forum	Nature of problem	
	'One-off'	*Recurring*
Regularised	(1) e.g. Central Advisory Water Committee	(2) e.g. Joint Advisory Committee on Mortgage Finance
Ad hoc	(3) e.g. Fulton Committee on the Civil Service	(4) e.g. pay conflict

The regularised arrangements represent the preferred pattern. They are convenient for dealing with recurring problems and as they tend to be imbued with consensual-corporative norms. To bureaucratise the problem, is to make it negotiable. This is caught by Dempster and Wildavsky's (1979) observation on budgeting, that 'an incremental process is also one in which the relationships between actors are regular over a period of years'.

In part, the British system of 'administrative conventions' or 'administrative process' (Henderson, 1977) are risk-sharing procedures. Henderson describes (p. 189) the temptation for the official to protect himself '. . . by making sure that, at every stage of the policy process, the right chairs have been warmed at the right committee tables by the appropriate institutions, everything possible has been done and no one could possibly be blamed if things go wrong'. Again, institutionalisation can be seen as a means of risk and conflict avoidance.

The Development of Exchange Relationships

The improvised British system appears to be predictable from certain basic assumptions. It seems to be a logical response to a set of widely shared ambitions/norms. There has been a professionalisation of policy-making and a preparedness to settle individual policies without complete agreement about ends. The logic of negotiation also suggests that policy-makers in both government and groups will share an interest in the avoidance of sudden policy change. Working together they will learn what kind of change is feasible and what would so embarrass other members of the 'system' as to be unproductive. Members of the system will begin to debate in the same language (if not with the same values), and arguments will be treated seriously only if discussed in these common criteria. There is role diffusion in that all members – government officials, academic experts and group officials – become policy professionals. Wildavsky observed that the British style is one of absorption, '. . . the British accommodate conflict through anticipatory adjustment. No one is expected to deny differences, but these are carried on within the overall expectation that each actor will work out his position so as to take account of the vital interests of others. Consultation is the mechanism to allow anticipatory adjustment: it allows a subtle exchange of desired and acceptable positions' (Wildavsky, 1975, p. 14).

Within the general setting of the departmental sectors, there is a tendency for policy communities to emerge. The policy community in any area is an imprecise structure likely to alter from time to time and from particular issue to issue, yet it is worth identifying as a *community*: in other words, it has continuity, implicit authority structures. The 'community' term stems from Heclo and Wildavsky's telling presentation of British bureaucracy as 'village life' (Heclo and Wildavsky, 1974). More generally, M. Webber (in Worsley, 1970, p. 30) finds it useful to widen the use of the community term from its original geographical context. He distinguishes the idea of community from locality and views it instead as interaction. He argues 'specialised professionals, particularly, now maintain webs of intimate contact with other professionals, wherever they may be. . . . Spatial distribution is not the crucial determinant of membership in these professional societies, but interaction is. . . . Communities compromise people with common interests who communicate with each other'. Not only do these specialised professionals play a central role in the processing of issues – they are also an important source of policy initiatives. Thus, the development of 'professional concern' can be an important stimulus to policy change.

It has been widely argued that the basis of the policy community is exchange for mutual benefits (see, for example, Mackenzie, 1975, p. 73). A system of exchange supplies several very necessary requirements. It provides a longer-term framework in which any one problem can be resolved by acknowledging that 'returns' will be made in later exercises. It aids risk avoidance – which is desired by the professionals on both 'sides' of the game. Heclo (1978, p. 103) quotes a representative of one trade association moving to Washington as follows, 'we didn't come here to change the world; we came to minimize our surprises'. Departments and groups share an interest in warning each other of their next moves. The professionals on both sides could be seriously embarrassed by moves which are not pre-signalled. 'Warning' allows the officials on both sides to preserve their reputations within their own organisations.

Wildavsky (1975, p. 20) argues that the executive arm of British government can be imagined as a system of reputations, 'reputation in general is always likely to be more important to participants than is any particular issue. British central government recognises mutual dependence areas'. This system of reputations which exists within Whitehall also extends to relations with outside groups. The reputation factor limits the acceptable range of options in group–department relations. Given that the department ultimately has the power to recognise 'legitimate' interests, groups cannot with impunity indulge in behaviours which would undermine reputation. The bureaucratisation of problems means that bargains can be struck between professionals who respect the limitation on resources. National leaders of interest groups are socialised into recognising the pressures under which their fellows negotiate.

The most contested of issues is, of course, resource allocation and the sectoral policy-making pattern does not so obviously apply in what is a cross-sectoral problem. Resources are allocated to sectors in accord with a basic incrementalism. Policies with major financial implications (say) 'poverty' are by their nature less suitable for 'in sector' treatment than (say) industrial relations reform. In a sense, all resource allocation is 'an imposition' on departments and groups, but as Heclo and Wildavsky (1974) suggest:

> Ultimately, British Treasury men know that their desires cannot prevail unless they maintain a community to support them ... coercion has its uses and is not to be despised. Far better, however, to create a nexus of interests so that co-operation flows from a sense of mutual advantage.... You go along with the Treasury then, because you must, because you expect to gain, and ultimately, because you are part of a civil service society that wants to do so.

In his volume *Budgeting* (1975) Wildavsky significantly entitles his chapter on Britain 'Budgeting as trust', and emphasised the recognition of mutual dependence even in the midst of conflict.

There is not, then, discontinuity of style between the clientelistic relations of groups and departments and Treasury–department relations. Part of the similarity in style and mood stems from the fact that when the Treasury is bargaining with departments, it is indirectly bargaining with the department's clients – who ultimately can be mobilised (for instance, farmers) in the resource allocation battle.

Dell has described how while the Treasury is intended to be part of the nation's protective apparatus against the excesses of departmental vested interests,

The Treasury is not a technical department. It consists, certainly, of very able men. But there is nobody in the Treasury equipped to argue against a department that one technological project rather than another is more or less likely to succeed, more or less likely to overrun its estimates. . . . No doubt there would be even less control without the professional scepticism of the Treasury. . . . But if the spending department itself does not provide an adequate check, the Treasury will not be able to fill the gap. (Dell, 1973, p. 206)

Elsewhere, Dell has drawn attention to the weakness at the centre of British governments:

I know that popular mythology suggests that the Treasury is too strong. In fact it is too weak . . . there is always a temptation to compromise with the demands of Ministers representing the great public-spending Departments. Even when the country faces such a crisis as that in the autumn of 1976 it can be an exhausting battle crowned only with limited success to secure recognition from a Cabinet of spending Ministers that the party is over. (Dell, 1980, p. 24)

Trends within the 'Policy Community' Pattern

Tripartism

The pattern of relatively predictable policy communities as the means to achieving consensus and avoiding the need to enforce decisions is subject to three rather different, but important, modifications. The first major amendment is *tripartism*. Whereas detail is the currency of the policy community, tripartism is designed to cope with more substantial matters. Tripartism is a technique of policy-making which recognises the potential veto capacity of major actors: it is a means of 'partnership' policy-making in which a limited number of other participants are granted near-equality with government. Thus, in 1972 the then Prime Minister, Edward Heath, stated that he had 'made an offer to employers and unions to share fully with the government the benefits and obligations involved in running the country'. Tripartism proper is manifested in bodies such as the National Economic Development Council (NEDC) in which government, TUC and CBI have been granted formal equality of numerical representation. With near-mathematical accuracy, unions and business also have representation on the boards of executive agencies such as the Manpower Services Commission (MSC), Health and Safety Commission and the Arbitration and Conciliation Service (ACAS). One should see tripartism not as a type of policy-making discrete from policy communities, but policy communities developed to a very formal degree with exceptionally clear acceptance of the group veto power. It is a frank acceptance of the need for concertation (consensus building).

The tripartite device has encouraged discussion of Britain as a corporate state (Pahl and Winkler, 1975; Cawson, 1975; Middlemas, 1979), but tripartism has not been a very stable development and has not developed as commentators perhaps expected in the early 1970s. Moreover, 'tripartism', as it appears in practice, is much removed from traditional catholic and current Marxist connotations of corporatism. Whereas corporatism involves command decisions, consensus over goals and a strong government, 'tripartism' involves bargaining, strong groups and self-interested behaviour. We would not dissent from Marsh and Grant's (1977) argument that tripartism has not always been effective, but it does represent a recurrent tendency.

Even when rhetoric suggested otherwise in Britain, in the period 1980–1, the tripartite trend was still clearly evident. For example, the MSC, ACAS and the NEDC sector working parties continued to function. Similarly, the Department of Employment Tripartite Steering Group on Job Satisfaction operated quite successfully, notwithstanding hostility between government and TUC on other issues. Even very 'big' and potentially very divisive issues, such as the impact of new technology, were subject to attempts at a tripartite solution, though on that occasion without success (Richardson, 1982).

One area where formal concertation/tripartism was proposed, but not implemented, was in control of the nationalised industries. The National Economic Development Office (NEDO) report (1976) suggested a policy council which would be aimed at remedying an absence of 'common purpose, trust and understanding' between government and the nationalised industries. NEDO recommended a 'concerted approach' by which Policy Councils for each industry would be established. These would be representative of the main interests where co-operation was needed if policy was to be effective. The non-implementation of the Policy Council concepts owes much to a British reluctance to acknowledge (formally) the degree to which policy-making has to be conducted subject to the consent of powerful interests. This reluctance to formalise matters is equally evident on the trades union side – whose leaders were very wary at becoming involved in the 'planning agreements' of the Industry Act. This preference for informality does not, however, detract from the preference (and, indeed, necessity) for bureaucratic accommodation.

Internalised Policy-Making

Though we have emphasised the central role of consultation, and its variants, there is a further class of problems which are currently thought not to be appropriate to treatment in this consultative machinery – for example, decisions about the Minimum Lending Rate, British policy towards Zimbabwe, the decision to adopt the new Trident nuclear weapon system, and so on. Such decisions (often extremely important) do not emerge from group–department machinery (though it is interesting to note that the Ministry of Defence had some thirty-one advisory committees in 1978–9), but are evolved by competition inside government. Leaks will be made by sectors of Whitehall to mobilise interested parties outwith the government on their behalf. But the process is perhaps best characterised as 'feedback policy-making'. In other words, policy will tend to be issued without much organised group deliberation (there may be a cacophony of special pleading at the margins). Even so, policy has to be adapted in the light of experience and reaction. Thus, groups do not have insider access to influence all kinds of policy – but even where policy is evolved internally, in the longer term it will only be tenable if it can be 'sold' to an influential constituency. This constituency may be a very tightly knit policy community (say) compared to a field such as industrial training policy, but it may nevertheless be capable of mobilising wider support when necessary. Thus, it is possible to argue that, even in such internalised policy decisions on defence policy, there is a small group of 'professional policy watchers' (Heclo, 1978) drawn from the field of strategic studies, who are policy influentials and who can at least make an input to very private deliberations.

Another variation of 'internalised' policy-making is, of course, policy-making within parties. Moran's study of the 1971 Industrial Relations Act (Moran, 1977) describes an interesting mixture of policy styles. In the unprecedented period of Conservative policy-making in Opposition inaugurated by Edward Heath in 1965, a party committee (with representation of individual businessmen) made policy without a dialogue with major groups. Individual trade unionists and employers were consulted and interested groups responded to published proposals, but this was very different from the sort of 'partnership policy-making' that was eventually required in office. Moran describes how after 1969, 'when the Tories became worried about enforcing their proposals, more serious attempts were made at consultation: there was increased contact with the CBI, some private meetings were held with a number of trade union leaders. . . . This attempt to sell a policy which had already been effectively decided on was, however, very different from the practice of working it out in the first place in consultation with various groups' (Moran, 1977, p. 60). Moran argues that it was this party policy-making – insulated from employer and trade union priorities – that caused problems in office, 'the Tories were, of course, quite aware of the problems of co-operation and enforcement, but their main attempt to secure the consent of interested parties was done by proxy . . . rather than through the detailed negotiation and consultation which usually characterises the relationship between a governing party and the powerful interest groups' (Moran, 1977, p. 76). It is not unreasonable to see the fate of the Industrial Relations Act – one of the most spectacular policy failures since the Second World War – as in large part due to the failure of the Conservatives to recognise the 'logic of negotiation' which we here describe.

Another example where external groups were less important than internal ones is provided in Banting's study of social policy; the options considered owed much to intellectuals and professionals (Banting, 1979, p. 141). The 'experts' put the options on the agenda. He points out, 'the complexity of modern policy problems has increased the uncertainty of policy-makers generally and steadily expanded the role of professionals'. Banting notes, however, that on most issues, 'social scientists raised new issues and prepared innovative policies; but officials and ministers were more confident of their capacity to handle these problems, and the social scientists participated much less in internal deliberations'. None the less, he did conclude that his most striking finding was 'the persuasive influence of intellectuals and professionals' (Banting, 1979, p. 143). In contrast, he found that 'interest groups played a secondary role in the politics of social policy'. While he conceded that the influence of professionals sometimes does flow through group action (for example, the Child Poverty Action Group), the groups had few sanctions to impose on government.

The real contenders on policy-making were, according to Banting, inside government together with those groups who were adjuncts to these forces. Policy-making in the social policy world was interdepartmental with, as in poverty, the DHSS frustrated in its battle for resources by the Treasury. The Banting study highlights the case that the dominant style – group accommodation – is necessary only when there are powerful outside interests to be accommodated. This social policy case is clearly not mainstream pluralism, but it is departmental pluralism – and depends perhaps more on Truman's potential groups than on organised groups (Truman, 1971). The poor might not be organised, but as a potential group they are taken into account to at least some degree.

External Disorder

A further deviation from our description of the predominant style are those occasions when policy-making appears to be conducted between groups – but with no active marshalling role (obviously) made by central government. Rose has used the phrase 'letting the issue stew' (Rose, 1980a), and this effectively conveys the situation where government is waiting for an appropriate moment to intervene (itself, of course, a very reactive policy style). Central government is ultimately involved but it seems reactive to outside events. By 'external disorder' we mean that there is a multiplicity of commercial, technical interests, trade union and other groups where participation has not been regularised.

The growing complexity of the policy-making means that one has some-times to de-emphasise the image of order and compromise implied in the term 'policy community', but it does not detract from the fact that order and compromise are the highly valued qualities of the system – the British style. In this situation of 'group density', the British style is necessarily more difficult to operationalise – but the perceived need for it is, if anything, greater. The gyroscopic effect of the style is very strong and policy partici-pants will naturally search for accommodation (and construct process and structures to achieve it), notwithstanding complexity and overcrowding. Policy-makers will try to play the old game, notwithstanding the fact that there may be too many players and they do not all understand the rules.

Other Styles and Issues

In terms of the simple typology of policy styles in Chapter 1, we have been claiming that the characteristic British style emphasises the development of consensus. In that there is no particular emphasis (unlike, say, West Germany and Sweden) on active/anticipatory problem-solving, Britain normally (by default) indulges in reactive problem-solving – indeed, the stress on consensus might lead to the deliberate non-identification of problems which would de-stabilise agreement.

The characteristic policy style does not, however, operate over all policy issues. It is not the only means of resolving conflict and reaching decisions. Neither is the bureaucratic-group 'arena' (see Chapter 3 on Norway) the *only* arena for solving problems. There are, for example, at least three main types of issue not suited to the standard operating procedures: (1) non-negotiable/manifesto policies; (2) value-changing policies; (3) constitu-tional policies.

All governments come to office with some non-negotiable policies which they have formulated in Opposition. (Though often as a result of interest group influence on them in Opposition.) For example, the Wilson govern-ments of 1964–6 and 1966–70 had firm commitments such as the nationalisation of shipbuilding and aircraft (again as a result of bargains struck in Opposition), and these were not susceptible to negotiation except at the margin. And the Heath government of 1970–4 came to office with its pledge to reform the laws governing industrial relations in the UK, notwith-standing the most bitter opposition from the trade union movement as a whole. All of these policies offered little scope for consultation. When groups do try to play the usual policy style the result is likely to be frustra-tion, bitterness (and sheer bewilderment). For example, when Barbara Castle became Minister of Transport in 1965, she was determined to introduce a system of co-ordinated public transport in certain large connurbations. The so-called Passenger Transport Authorities (PTAs) were non-negotiable, despite opposition from well-organised interests in the bus industry. Nevertheless, 'consultation' had to be gone through and Mrs Castle duly met the opposing groups. At one such meeting Mrs Castle announced that she had only a limited amount of time available: 'After giving a speech on her proposals, she was called out of the room by one of her assistants. When a few minutes had elapsed, the meeting was told that the Minister had been called away on urgent business' (Dudley, 1982). But the number of non-negotiable policies is fewer than is suggested by those who label the British system adversary politics (see Finer, 1975). The 1945–50 Labour government is probably the best example of 'negotiation' over the actual form of quite radical policies. Thus, in road transport, though part of the nationalisation programme, private companies were allowed to retain their own lorries for use on their 'own account'. This concession has had quite fundamental implications for nationalised freight transport since 1947. Similarly, hospital consultants were allowed to continue private practice, notwithstanding the fact that a National Health Service had been introduced. The realities of office ensure that governments must make unwelcome deviations from their intended course. Thus, the Thatcher government demonstrated great flexibility in 1980–1 in amending 'strict' cash limits for various publicly owned industries and at one stage in lowering interest rates, heeding criticism from the CBI and others. The British style/logic of negotiation is so powerful that it can operate in areas where, on first examination, it seems inappropriate.

It is clear that policies such as abortion law reform, or demands for unilateral nuclear disarmament, are not processed in the 'normal' fashion. Such attempts at policy change involving value change cannot use the normal 'insider strategy', because by definition they do not reflect conventional opinion and accordingly are not granted 'legitimate'/consultative status. The policies are, in the main, not suitable for incremental solution and are accordingly marked by a distinctively different style and may enter a different policy-making arena. Thus, these issues may produce a much wider degree of participation than is usually the case through such 'procedures' as the mass lobby of Parliament, public opinion polls (as used by pro-abortionists in the 1960s), public campaigns and mass demonstrations and marches. Such acts of mobilisation can be used in other issue areas (such as support for nurses' pay demands) where regular machinery exists but has failed to 'deliver', but they are more characteristic of value changing policies.

Examination of three major constitutional issues of the past decade – devolution, House of Lords reform and acceptance/retention of EEC membership – demonstrates a domination of the process by Parliamentarians. While over 1,062 amendments were put down to the Scotland and

Wales Bill, with few exceptions – such as those drafted by the Outer-Circle Policy Group – amendments in that instance were produced by MPs or their research help. This is unlike the more normal amendment which will be drafted for the MP by an outside group. For example, when Mr Maxwell-Hyslop, MP, in what is often claimed as an example of backbench influence, successfully objected to the Aircraft and Shipbuilding Industries Bill 1975, he was apparently directed to the drafting flaw by the shareholder of a firm which was to be nationalised. The distinguishing feature of constitutional policies is that they are often a policy area more or less without a population of *directly* affected interests. Outside Parliament, there would not be a great deal of immediate impact on the group world. Industrialists might favour the EEC and oppose devolution and, indeed, help finance the associated public campaigns, but the form of involvement is very different than in (say) the creation of industrial strategy. The *intensity* of interest is nowhere near the same.

Bureaucratic Accommodation and Parliamentary Democracy

In an earlier work (Richardson and Jordan, 1979), we argued that Britain was essentially a post-parliamentary democracy. Significantly, we have paid little attention to Parliament, except in the rather special cases of constitutional policies and value-changing policies. One argument is that the development of sectorisation and the growth of policy communities is itself a cause of the decline in parliamentary influence. Thus, an important factor in the decline of the House of Commons is not simply the growth of executive power, but the 'leakage' of power into the myriad of policy communities surrounding the executive. Also, as Painter suggests, 'Parliament, through its committee system, has found itself inexorably sucked into this system of political specialisation and fragmentation' (Painter, 1980, p. 84).

We do not, of course, mean to suggest that Parliament has no influence in the policy process. Our argument is that one would not see parliamentary influence on policy-making as a *primary* feature of the UK policy style. This is not to say that Parliament *never* influences policy. As Philip Norton's detailed research demonstrates, the incidence of intraparty dissent in the House of Commons has increased considerably since 1970 (Norton, 1980, p. 426). (For example, the Heath government of 1970–4 was defeated six times in the House of Commons. There were more divisions witnessing dissenting votes in the 1974–9 Parliament than in the seven Parliaments during 1945–70. Again, the government suffered several defeats; Norton records that the total number of government defeats in the seven years 1970–9 was sixty-five.) Schwartz suggests (following Polsby's classification) that the House of Commons has moved from an arena or legitimising type of legislature towards a transformative or policy-making legislature over the last decade or so. Thus, he argues that 'during the 1970s, the

House of Commons was a very different place from what it had been. For the first time in decades – generations is perhaps a better term – the Commons began to effectuate policy change by being willing to defeat the government and to compel modifications in the government's policy initiatives; the Commons repeatedly so acted, on a great range of policy issues, some of considerable significance' (Schwartz, 1980, p. 36).

Clearly, then, the House of Commons has increased its policy impact in the last decade. But before we can characterise it as being much nearer Polsby's transformative or policy-making legislature (Polsby, 1975), we need to see the Commons as having a significant impact on the total mass of public policy-making *and implementation* which is such a distinctive feature of the modern state. To what extent did this increased parliamentary activity really change the framework of the majority of public policies in the UK? To what extent is it legitimate to generalise from a period of minority government? And in those policy areas where Parliament *was* active and succeeded in defeating the government of the day, what impact did those defeats have ultimately in those policy areas? The defeats are rather like the reports of parliamentary Select Committees – they may not, and often do not, amount to a row of beans in policy terms. There are, of course, exceptions. Some of those defeats were of major aspects of policies (for example, petrol tax). Our argument is not that they should be dismissed as irrelevant – but that they should be seen against the context of the policy system as a whole. Notwithstanding the increasingly truculent House of Commons, we see Brian Smith's characterisation of the House as mainly a 'constitutional procedural device for legitimising decisions' (Smith, 1976) as still correct in the early 1980s.

While Parliament's set-piece contests give the appearance of adversary politics, Rose's (1980b) analysis indicates that there is little substance to the image of adversary politics as meaning that succeeding governments undo the legislative work of their predecessors. Rose's quantitative data demonstrate that there is a tendency for consensus on Bills – or at least a lack of significant protest in the form of forcing a division. Rose argues, 'a newly installed government repeals little of the legislation enacted by its predecessor. When the Conservatives entered office in 1970, they used their powers of office to reverse only three measures that had been passed in all the two previous sessions of Parliament. . . . Labour [after 1974] did reverse eleven laws adopted by the previous Conservative Parliament. . . . Important as these actions were, they affected only a handful of the total measures passed in the 1970–74 Parliament' (Rose, 1980b, p. 88).

It can be claimed therefore that Parliament, no less than other parts of the political system, operates according to the British style. Wade (1978, p. 24) demonstrates that the 'usual channels' which expedite parliamentary business are based on the acceptance that there is a general assumption that it is mutually desirable that the machinery should work. Normally the

Opposition is permitted to make its ritual opposition without seriously affecting the governmental timetable.

Attempts to Implement Alternative Policy Styles

Having described what we see as the dominant style, it is important to briefly discuss some strategic attempts to change this style. There has, in fact, been a recognition that style is closely linked to incremental outcomes. Where radical policy proposals have been introduced (local government reorganisation and airports policy), we have lacked the necessary determination to carry it through to effective implementation against organised resistance. Thus, on the occasions when Hayward's suggestion that there is a preference for a 'humdrum' (roughly equated with incremental) policy style (Hayward, 1974) does not hold true, it is likely that it will hold true at the *implementation* stage (in other words, groups have three bites of the same cherry. They have a great influence at the issue-emergence stage, they are integrated at the processing stage and often have a veto at the implementation stage).

But governments have, from time to time, come to office seemingly determined to 'buck the system'. The Attlee government of 1945–50 was certainly the most radical and innovative (in policy terms) government since the Second World War (though its programme had strong group origins) and, indeed, managed to introduce the bulk of its policies in the immediate postwar period. Since that government, Britain has seen three governments which seemed set to show a quite different (radical) 'face'—the Wilson government elected in 1964; the Heath government elected in 1970; and the Thatcher government elected in 1979. Each in different ways appeared, at the time of its election, about to change from the dominant policy style. The most innovative Wilson creation was the ill-fated Department of Economic Affairs (DEA). This development reflected Wilson's belief that 'Britain could hope to win economic security only by a fundamental reconstruction and modernisation of industry under the direction of a department at least as powerful as the Treasury' (Wilson, 1971, p. 3). Some five years later, Wilson himself abolished the DEA. Indeed, by the time Wilson left office, he was best known for his pragmatic, incrementalist, 'beer and sandwiches' (late-night negotiations with groups) style of policy-making.

He was succeeded in June 1970 by Edward Heath's government, which had been foreshadowed by much planning relating to possible changes in the machinery of government. It is not unreasonable to see the 1970 White Paper, *The Reorganisation of Central Government* (Cmnd 4504), as a landmark in attempts to make British policy more 'rationalistic'. The main proposals in the White Paper were, first, strengthening of the centre, in terms of fewer, but larger, departments with the new Central Policy Review Staff (CPRS) designed to remedy the fact that governments 'may pay too little attention to the difficult, but criticial task, of evaluating as objectively as possible the alternative policy options and priorities open to them'. Secondly, it was proposed to develop a system of Programme Analysis and Review (PAR) alongside the existing Public Expenditure Survey (PESC) system for monitoring public expenditure. PESC was mainly concerned with the overall departmental budgets, where PAR was to look at the relative value of individual projects. We should thus see the White Paper as a determined attempt 'to do things differently' in the policy sphere – as the introductory paragraph claimed, 'this Administration has pledged itself to introduce a new style of government'. In total, it added up to an alternative system, which in fact presented a real challenge to vested interests both within and outside Whitehall. With hindsight, it is certain that Mr Heath failed to appreciate just how big a challenge this was to the traditional and deeply entrenched pluralist system. The 1970 White Paper was lacking in appreciation of the complex political forces which were at work in the policy process. There is no longer any pretence that a comprehensive pattern of resource allocation through comparison of costed alternatives is to be developed across Whitehall. Yet again we saw the gyroscopic effect of policy style. Any significant deviation being quickly corrected by either pressure from outside groups, or from the Whitehall system itself.

One of the puzzles of British politics is to reconcile the fact that Britain selects its political leaders through a lengthy 'apprenticeship' system and yet new governments appear uniformly optimistic about the amount (and direction) of change that they can exert. A description of the style of the Conservative government, elected in May 1979, is complicated by the fact that by 1981 there was plenty of evidence that it had often shifted from its intended style to the 'normal' style as exemplified by latter-day Wilson, Heath and Callaghan governments. There is an added complication in the fact that for reasons of political machismo, elements of the Thatcher Cabinet believed that there was virtue in pretending that the new management are not running business as usual. When Mrs Thatcher was asked shortly after becoming leader of the party, 'what have you changed?', she replied, 'I have changed everything'. This provides insight into her personal style and aspirations, but does not describe what has taken place.

The intended style was of non-intervention, non-negotiating. Thus, for example, Sir Keith Joseph was reported to have felt that there was a strong case for scrapping his own department (of Industry), and that his civil servants could best reverse the de-industrialisation of Britain by contributing to policy formation in other ministries. Similarly, the Secretary of State for Employment, Michael Heseltine, told the Conservative Party's Local Government Conference in spring 1981, 'I know that we are challenging long-established habits and attitudes. This is what this government was elected to do'. In fact, Heseltine was one of the few ministers whose behaviour bore some resemblance to the rhetoric in that he at least challenged the autonomy of the local rating system.

Generally, the policy-making style proved more resistant to change than ministers expected. In October 1980 *The Economist* drew attention to the 'two faces' of Mrs Thatcher's government. A leader ran:

> The Conservative party which gathers next week for its annual conference in Brighton will see on its platform not one Margaret Thatcher as prime minister but two.
>
> The first is the one it voted for 18 months ago: a Friedmanite believer, radical to the point of revolutionary, committed to a fundamental shift in the character not just of Britain's economy but of its society. This prime minister remains one of the most intriguing ... potentially powerful leaders Britain has had since the war. The second is quite different: a traditional Tory, closer perhaps to Eden than Macmillan, a hesitant though increasingly astute practitioner of the art of compromise, adept at the commons despatch box, obedient to the party's middle-class roots and to the dictates of electoral success in a mixed economy, above all a pragmatist. (*The Economist*, 4 October 1980)

It went on to point out that schizophrenia is to be found in most leaders especially in the early years of office, but that 'the pragmatist soon wins under the pressure of crisis management and the inclination of self-preservation'. *The Economist*'s phrase the 'two faces' deliberately suggests not only that there are two strands to the Conservative style, but that there was conscious hypocrisy in masking one (incrementalist) style with a veneer of the (radical) other. It is possible to catalogue many examples from a broad range of policy sectors – demonstrating that in case after case, the 'rule' was incremental change and that the government was certainly prepared to bargain and negotiate. The episode in 1981 when the government hurriedly accepted tripartite negotiations with the National Coal Board and the National Union of Mineworkers and conceded major concessions on proposed pit closures was only the most prominent case – not an unusual one.

As always, the government had some non-negotiable items. For example, in October 1980 in response to a request from the TUC to the PM that they should meet to discuss the worsening economic situation, Mrs Thatcher kept the TUC waiting nearly a month before a meeting could be arranged. There thus appeared to be a radical shift in policy style in this key policy area with the de-emphasising of consultation and negotiation – though policy was being made with the likely reaction of unions in mind. Yet even here, it is possible to find an opposite, and equally important, case. In the field of trade union and labour relations legislation the Thatcher government was at the same time taking what was essentialy a conciliatory and incremental approach, fully recognising the need to secure the support of rank-and-file trade unionists if not their leaders. The policy pursued by Jim Prior, the Secretary of State for Employment, was in no way radical (though it was opposed by the TUC) or unmindful of the potential veto of which the trade union movement could exercise (and had exercised against the Heath government's attempt to implement industrial relations legislation in 1971). At the 1980 Conservative Conference Mr Prior explicitly asked if the lessons of the 1970–4 government had not been learned? It was necessary to legislate with consent of the unions, otherwise the legislation would be self-defeating. The views of TUC and its constituent unions were thus accorded very considerable weight. Having tried radical policy innovation in 1971, in this field, the Conservatives were in no mood to demonstrate, yet again, that the government/group relationship was much more equal than constitutional theory might suggest. This is, of course, not to argue that the government's policy in 1980 was arrived at by consultation and negotiation with the TUC (although Prior did have private meetings with representatives of the TUC when he was in opposition and continued to have them when in government). Influence can be exerted without periodic meetings.

However, even though the TUC and the government (and of course the government and the CBI, in some respects) were at odds over broad economic strategy, this did not prevent the TUC from participating in other consultative machinery. In fact, a list prepared by the TUC, in September 1980, of government committees and outside bodies to which representatives of the General Council are appointed or nominated by the General Council, ran to over seventy bodies. The list of bodies covered a very wide range of policy areas, typical examples being the Advisory Conciliation and Arbitration Service; Clean Air Council; Commission for Racial Equality; Department of Industry Committee on Tetrotechnology; Advisory Council on Energy Conservation; Offshore Industry Liaison Committee; Equal Opportunities Commission; and so on. The Thatcher government presented a radical face while usually operating an incrementalist style.

The style of conducting public business did not change, nor did the content of public policy match the rhetoric. There was, of course, the intention to reduce the Public Sector Borrowing Requirement to £8,500 million in the year 1980–1, but it had exceeded this after only six months to September 1980 and the eventual out-turn was of the order of £13,500 million. The attempt to limit monetary growth to 7–11 per cent in the period February 1980–April 1981 was meant to include an allowance for the consequence of the removal of the so-called 'corset'. By November the growth for eight months had exceeded 15 per cent and was running at an annual rate of 23·5 per cent. Even making generous allowances for the 'corset effect', it was still a rate of 19 per cent per annum – almost twice the upper ceiling.

The public image of the government (which it itself encouraged) was of a deep commitment to monetary policy, linked to cutting public expenditure. In reality public expenditure rose by 27 per cent in the first half of the financial year 1980–1. Amid heated debate about the government's monetary policy, it seemed to go unremarked that the government was not operating its supposed policy: had the government claimed to be operating Keynsian principles, the actual growth might have seemed excessive! Similarly, the strict cash limits policy did not prevent the government granting extra money or increased borrowing (that is, above the government's stated limits) to BSC, British Leyland, British Shipbuilders, British Airways and the National Coal Board. External financing limits were relaxed in August 1980 after lobbying by the chairmen of twenty-two nationalised industries.

Not only has it been a matter of granting loan facilities, further direct and very considerable assistance was given – to, for example, British Steel, British Rail and British Leyland. By October 1980 the *Sunday Times* was able to report 'on all forms of industrial subsidy, its commitment is larger than that of the Labour government in its later years'. By 1981 'selective intervention' had replaced laissez-faire as a Department of Industry 'now' word. Despite the 'cuts', the share of GDP allocated to the public sector continued to grow.

It is therefore difficult to present the Thatcher government – however much it might have wished it – as breaking the mould of postwar politics. The policy reversals of the government were perhaps part of the explanation for the persistence of the consultative pattern. It was eventually appreciated that if the government was to have much impact on the problems in the real world outwith the Cabinet room, group co-operation was a necessary precondition. The recognition that society must be managed as well as the economy, meant that the urge to govern by fiat had to be tempered. Thus, by February 1981 (after the government's rapid climbdown on pit closures), John Biffen (Secretary of State for Trade) was stressing that the government was 'gradualist', 'pragmatic', sought 'social contact', and that ' a great deal of the job of the society is persuading people not to use the power that they have'. Mrs Thatcher herself seemed to recognise the degree to which the reality had not matched the rhetoric in her government's first two-and-a-half years of office, when she reshuffled her Cabinet in the summer of 1981 in order to strengthen the position of the more radical elements.

We can end as we began with Lord Croham. When addressing a group of civil service trainees in 1978, he warned them that, 'this need to consult and persuade, to secure the support of groups who have the power to block its actions, limits policy options open to government' (Crohan, 1978). This is still how British politics operates. If it is conceded that groups can determine the success of policy, then the necessity for regularised involvement in policy-making becomes clear. The logic of negotiation is difficult to escape.

References: Chapter 4

Aldrich, H. E., *Organisations and Environments* (Englewoods Cliffs, NJ: Prentice-Hall, 1979).

Armstrong, Lord, in D. Lethbridge (ed.), *Government and Industry Relationships* (Oxford: Pergamon, 1976).

Banting, K. G., *Poverty, Politics and Policy* (London: Macmillan, 1979).

Beer, S. H., 'The British legislature and the problem of mobilising consent', in B. Crick (ed.), *Essays in Reform* (London: Oxford University Press, 1967).

Biffen, J., MP, press reports, 15 September 1980.

Boyle, Lord, 'Ministers and the administrative process', *Public Administration*, vol. 58 (spring 1980), pp. 1–12.

Castle, B., 'The loneliness of the short distance runner', *Sunday Times*, 10 June 1973.

Cawson, A., 'Pluralism, corporatism and the role of the state', *Government and Opposition*, vol. 13, no. 2 (1975), pp. 178–98.

Christoph, J. B., 'High civil servants and the politics of consensualism in Great Britain', in M. Dogan (ed.), *The Mandarins of Western Europe* (New York: Halsted, 1975).

Critchley, J., *The Times*, 14 April 1978.

Croham, Lord, 'The developing structure of United Kingdom government', *Management Services in Government*, vol. 33, no. 3 (1978), pp. 105–13.

Crossman, R., *The Diaries of a Cabinet Minister*, Vols 1–3 (London: Hamish Hamilton, 1975–7).

Dell, E., *Political Responsibility and Industry* (London: Allen & Unwin, 1973).

Dell, E., 'Some reflections on Cabinet government by a former practitioner', *Public Administration Bulletin*, no. 32 (April 1980), pp. 12–33.

Dempster, A. H. and Wildavsky, A., 'On change: or, there is no magic size for an increment', *Political Studies*, vol. 27, no. 3 (1979), pp. 371–89.

Devons, E., in Sir A. Cairncross (ed.), *Planning and Economic Management* (Manchester: Manchester University Press, 1970).

Dudley, G., 'Implementation and policy change: aspects of bus passenger transport in the UK', Ph.D. thesis, University of Keele, 1982.

Eldersveld, S., Boonzaaijes, S. Hubée, and Kooiman, Jan, 'Elite perceptions of the political process in the Netherlands', in M. Dogan (ed.), *The Mandarins of Western Europe* (New York: Halsted, 1975).

Finer, S. E. (ed.), *Adversary Politics and Electoral Reform* (London: Wignam, 1975).

Gustafsson, G. and Richardson, J. J., 'Concepts of rationality and the policy process', *European Journal of Political Research*, vol. 7, no. 4 (1979), pp. 415–36.

Habermas, J., *Legitimation Crisis* (London: Heinemann, 1976).

Hayward, J. E. S., 'National aptitudes for planning in Britain, France and Italy', *Government and Opposition*, vol. 9, no. 4 (1974), pp. 397–410.

Hayward, J. E. S., 'Institutional inertia and political impetus in France and Britain', *European Journal of Political Research*, vol. 4, no. 4 (1976), pp. 341–60.

Hayward, J., and Berki, R., *State and Society in Contemporary Europe* (Oxford: Robertson, 1979).

Heath, E., in conversation with A. Barker, 'Heath on Whitehall reform', *Parliamentary Affairs*, vol. XXXI, no. 4 (1978), pp. 363–90.

Heclo, H., 'Frontiers of social policy in Europe and America', *Policy Sciences*, vol. 6, no. 4 (1975), pp. 403–21.

Heclo, H., 'Issue networks and the executive establishment', in A. King (ed.), *The New American Political System* (Washington, DC: American Enterprise Institute, 1978).

Heclo, H. and Wildavsky, A., *The Private Government of Public Money* (London: Macmillan, 1974).

Henderson, P. D., 'Two British errors: their probable size and some possible lessons', *Oxford Economic Papers*, vol. 29, no. 2 (July 1977), pp. 159–205.

Hood, C., 'The politics of quangocide', *Policy and Politics*, vol. 8, no. 3 (1980), pp. 247–66.

Howell, D., 'The rocky road to government reform', *Management Today* (September 1974), pp. 59–62.

Leigh, D., *The Frontiers of Secrecy: Closed Government in Britain* (London: Junction Books, 1980).

Mackenzie, W. J. M., *Power, Violence, Decision* (Harmondsworth: Penguin, 1975).

Marsh, Sir R., *Off the Rails* (London: Weidenfeld & Nicolson, 1978).

Marsh, D. and Grant, W., 'Tripartism; reality or myth?', *Government and Opposition*, vol. 12, no. 2 (1977), pp. 194–211.

Middlemass, R. K., *Politics in Industrial Society: The Experience of the British Society since 1911* (London: Deutsch, 1979).

Moran, M., *The Politics of Industrial Relations* (London: Macmillan, 1977).

Norton, P., *Dissension in the House of Commons, 1974–79* (Oxford: Oxford University Press, 1980).

Pahl, R. E. and Winkler, J. T., 'The coming corporatism', *Challenge*, vol. 18, no. 1 (March–April 1975), pp. 28–35.

Painter, M., 'Whitehall and roads: a case study of sectoral politics', *Policy and Politics*, vol. 8, no. 2 (1980), pp. 163–86.

La Palombara, J., *Interest Groups in Italian Politics* (Princeton, NJ: Princeton University Press, 1964).

PEP, *Reshaping Britain: A Programme of Economic and Social Reform*, vol. XL, no. 548 (1974).

Polsby, N., 'Legislatures', in F. Greenstein and N. Polsby (eds), *Handbook of Political Science*, Vol. 5 (Reading, Mass: Addison-Wesley, 1975).

Richardson, J. J., 'Tripartism and the new technology', *Policy and Politics*, vol. 10, no. 3 (1982).

Richardson, J. J. and Jordan, A. G., *Governing under Pressure: The Policy Process in a Post-Parliamentary Democracy* (Oxford: Robertson, 1979).

Richardson, J. J., Jordan, A. G. and Kimber, R., 'Lobbying, administrative reform and policy styles', *Political Studies*, vol. XXVI, no. 1 (1978).

Rose, R., 'Government against subgovernments', in R. Rose and E. Suleiman (eds), *Presidents and Prime Ministers* (Washington, DC: American Enterprise Institute, 1980a), pp. 284–347.

Rose, R., *Do Parties Make a Difference?* (New Jersey: Chatham House, 1980b).

Rothschild, Lord, *The Best Laid Plans* . . . , Israrel Seiff Memorial Lectures, London, 1976.

Schwartz, J. E., 'Exploring a new role in policy-making: the British House of Commons', *American Political Science Review*, vol. 74, no. 1 (1980), pp. 23–36.

Smith, B., *Policy-Making in British Government* (London: Robertson, 1976).

Suleiman, E., *Politics, Power and Bureaucracy in France: The Administrative Elite* (Princeton, NJ: Princeton University Press, 1974).

Truman, D., *The Governmental Process*, 2nd edn (New York: Knopf, 1971).

Wade, D., *Behind the Speaker's Chair* (Leeds/London: Austicks Publications, 1978).

Webber, M. M., 'Towards a definition of the interest community', in P. Worsley (ed.), *Modern Sociology: Introductory Readings* (Harmondsworth: Penguin, 1970).

Wildavsky, A., *Budgeting: A Comparative Theory of Budgeting Processes* (Boston, Mass./Toronto: Little, Brown, 1975).

Wilson, G. K., *Special Interests and Policy-Making* (London: Wiley, 1977).

Wilson, H., *The Labour Government, 1964–70: A Personal View* (London: Weidenfeld & Nicolson/Michael Joseph, 1971).

Wolfe, A., *The Limits and Legitimacy* (New York: The Free Press, 1977).

5 Mobilising Private Interests in the Service of Public Ambitions: The Salient Element in the Dual French Policy Style?

JACK HAYWARD, University of Hull

Introduction

In seeking to identify a particular national style or styles of policy initiation, making and implementation within a context of cross-national comparison, it is of crucial importance to distinguish from the outset the normative from the behavioural dimension for a number of reasons. There is a vast if variable difference between the principles that are supposed to govern the policy process and the practices that actually occur. This gap is sometimes the result of deliberate deception practised upon the victims and beneficiaries at the receiving end of public policy by those who are responsible for managing the policy process. However, one should not underrate the human capacity for self-deception, particularly when it is necessary to reconcile mundane, day-to-day activities with the legitimising norms enshrined in impressive rhetoric. The most important if obvious first lesson for the academic investigator of the antics of those who have to try to survive the testing pressures of public life is that he must not take either the public or private discourse in which politics and administration are conducted at face-value. Rather, he would do better to suppose that far from what this discourse enunciates being a description of reality, it is permeated by prescriptive values that are intended to shape and authenticate the conduct, both of those who make and expound public policy; those who carry it out; and those who have to live with its consequences. If he is not to be 'taken in', he must distinguish the rhetoric from the reality; but to attain some glimmerings of insight, he should recognise the functional relationship between them. For the peculiar normative rhetoric of each nation will reflect the special cluster of institutional legacies and sociocultural and subcultural characteristics that structure the policy process and infuse it with its special features, built up over time as those that have succeeded in striking a *modus vivendi* with the circumstances obtaining in a particular community.

At a time of rapid change, the relatively stable set of semi-absolutes that constitute the normative framework within which the polity is deemed to operate, may become more or less dysfunctional. The actual behaviour engaged in by those involved in this or that part of the policy process may diverge sharply from the norms that are supposed to govern it, putting them under increasing strain. War (especially defeat in war) and economic crisis are particularly propitious moments for precipitating changes in behaviour of such magnitude and quality that the normative framework may be drastically modified, telescoping into a short period alterations that would otherwise have been extended over time and might well have taken a different form. (It will be argued that such a cataclysm did occur in France during the Second World War, a second shock coming with its full exposure to the international market from the 1960s.) Nevertheless, the sociocultural and institutional peculiarities of a particular polity will survive in a modified form, and when the dust has settled, one is usually surprised at how modest the modifications have in fact been when seen in relation to the practice of the whole society. If one is to try to detect a perennial, predominant policy style in any country, it will be vital to see it as the product of a set of norms that must not be confused with the diversity of the actual behaviour of participants in the policy process. This will vary tremendously over time and as between different issue areas. The contrast with the normative style holds, even though the prevailing norms are not necessarily mutually consistent. If one tries to identify a policy style by engaging in hot pursuit of whatever passing conjuncture of circumstances seems to have provisionally crystallised into a stable stylistic compound, one risks quickly debasing the concept into a flatulent cliché as transient as it is insubstantial. It will make for greater clarity if policy style as a set of enduring norms is distinguished from how people involved in the policy process actually behave. As such, policy style is a higher-order, metapolitical phenomenon to which actual conduct more or less remotely approximates. It is the standard by which actual policy practice is categorised and judged.

If this specification of how the term 'policy style' is to be used is accepted, it is next essential to select the normative categories that appear to have the greatest policy relevance, in the context of a cross-national comparative analysis. In discussing national economic planning in terms of the process by which decisions are taken and implemented, a distinction was drawn between heroic and humdrum decision-making. 'It would be heroic in the dual sense that it would be both an ambitious political exercise in rational decision-making and an ambitious assertion of political will by government leaders' (Hayward, 1974, p. 399). The reference to rationality was relevant to a discussion of certain aspects of planning, as well as being more generally appropriate to an account of policy style at a period (the late 1960s and early 1970s) when PPBS – Planning Programming Budgeting Systems – was all the rage in the USA and its foreign by-products (PAR –

Programme Analysis and Review – in the UK, and RCB –*Rationalisation des Choix Budgétaires* in France) were enjoying ephemeral if absorbed attention by innovative, elite members of the policy community. However, now that the fashion has passed, it can be seen that the 'ambitious assertion of political will' was the more important of the two senses in which decision-making could be said to be heroic. There is no necessary connection between boldness and rationality, appealing as they do to will and reason respectively. In the simple typology distinguishing between national policy styles, used in this book, the problem-solving dimension contrasts policy-makers normatively inclined to be willing to act in an assertive, innovative, unconventional way, with those who are inclined to act in a passive, responsive and traditional way. It is advisable to avoid the term 'incre-mental', because it has become evident that it is by no means clear precisely what is or is not incremental, and because it is customarily regarded as the alternative to a rational style of policy-making which would point us in the wrong direction, even in supposedly Cartesian France.

The other dimension by which policy style should be characterised relates to the process by which policy is elaborated and implemented. Here the appropriate distinction appears to be between those policy-makers who are normatively inclined towards negotiation as the principal way in which the private actors in the policy process can be induced to achieve consensus with the public actors through mutual accommodation and compromise, on the one hand, and those inclined to impose public policy upon the private actors. Consultation is a technique utilised even by policy-makers with an intransigent policy style, who may wish to engage in tactical 'window-dressing' to allay resentment against what might be regarded as high-handed behaviour, while negotiation implies reciprocal give and take rather than a unilateral condescension to consult even when the decision has already been taken and will not be altered. Imposition implies the legitimacy of the *fait accompli*, provided it is accomplished by an appropriate public authority, thanks to its superordinate status. The norms of the particular polity will prescribe which matters of public policy are or are not negotiable in principle. This does not mean that there will not in practice be divergence from the prescribed norms; these norms may even be more honoured in the breach than in the observance. It follows from this that while it might be possible, *in normative terms*, to locate particular countries in relative positions along the dimensions proposed, it is not possible to average out a range of *behavioural* policy styles for each country because these will vary according to subject-matter and circumstances at any particular time, owing to changes in the balance of power between the actors involved in the particular policy issue.

The French Style of Authority

The most searching review of the alternative explanations of the dualist nature of political authority in France identifies three distinct types of two-France theories: (1) the diachronic bimodal conception, which conceives of France as alternatively being subjected to two different types of government: a weak, 'democratic', liberal regime, and a strong, 'authoritarian', personalised one; (2) the segmented-society view, which sees Frenchmen divided into two conflicting ideological groups: there are the red, left, progressive, individualistic, democratic Frenchmen and the black, right, conservative, state-minded, authoritarian Frenchmen; and (3) the schizoid-individual view, which argues that each Frenchman has two distinct sets of dispositions toward political authority: he both fears, dislikes, distrusts, and seeks to avoid submission to authority and concurrently needs, seeks, and depends upon political authority (Schonfeld, 1976, pp. 142, 137 ff.).

Far from being mutually exclusive, these three types of explanation, focusing on the institutional structure of the political regime, the sociological bases of ideological cleavages and the psychological attitudes of insubordination and submissiveness, are mutually consistent and provide support for a dualist interpretation at the level of the individual, group and political community. This approach to the French style of authority can draw upon the writings of such founding-fathers as Alexis de Tocqueville, as well as a leading non-French contemporary political scientist like Stanley Hoffmann.

What the little empirical research that has been undertaken to test the validity of such speculative consensus seems to show is that there is a substantial disparity between both the official and unofficial authority norms and the observed reality. Building on the pioneering work of Michel Crozier's *The Bureaucratic Phenomenon*, which characterised the French 'conception of authority as an absolute that cannot be shared, discussed or compromised' (Crozier, 1964, 1970, 1979), William Schonfeld argues that the routine style of authority relations in France has three salient features. They are:

(1) subordinate behaviour is determined by general rules [written instructions], remembered socialization, observation and imitation of superordinate and peer behaviour, and/or 'advice' solicited from superordinates; (2) subordinates *perceive* their behavioural patterns as being forced upon them by superordinates; and (3) superordinates *in fact* rarely issue directives to subordinates and do not [or cannot] enforce compliance through the use of sanctions. (Schonfeld, 1976, pp. 114, 174–7)

In the terms of our policy-relevant norms, this routine, bureaucratic style of decision-making is reactive in character and finds it difficult to bring about change by negotiation. It is only when the accumulation of serious dysfunctions leads to a crisis and the emergence of an active leadership, capable of asserting its authority and imposing its will, that the breakdown of bureaucratic routine and the threat of disorder can be resolved by a short period of change... or the appearance of change.

Schonfeld's study was based upon empirical investigations into authority in French secondary schools – themselves a vital part of the process of political socialisation by which children acquire their attitudes towards authority – and in the *Ecole Nationale d'Administration*, the institution responsible for training some of the most important wielders of state authority. The latter study was conducted at the time of the May 1968 crisis which, in the educational sphere, was characterised by the appearance of spectacular change rather than its reality. As has been noted in connection with the 1968 events and in contrast to Crozier, 'crises rarely bring in their wake far-reaching reforms because the atmosphere of uncertainty that they generate ... creates timidity, and fear of further dislocation of existing order' (Suleiman, 1978, p. 90). An attempt to challenge the Crozierian model, based upon a case study of the 1968 Act reforming higher education in France, sought to demonstrate that France was far more amenable to a pluralist-cum-incrementalist analysis than is usually allowed. While case studies of decision-making are notoriously likely to impart a pluralist bias by a process of methodological determinism, this study is typically incapable of identifying which elements in the pluralist process were most decisive. It has no way of explaining why in fact so little of importance changed and much of that little has been susequently reversed or vitiated, despite the heroic leadership of De Gaulle's astute Minister of Education in 1968–9, Edgar Faure (Fomerand, 1975, pp. 59–89; Hayward, 1978, pp. 53–5). (We shall hear more of him in another connection.) There will, however, be a place for pluralism in our analysis.

Further support for an amended version of Crozier's conception of the dominant French style of authority is provided by a study of the interaction between political culture and the behaviour of industrial firms in France. Avoiding the circularity that arises from Crozier's isolation of bureaucratic organisations from their environment, John Zysman argues that 'Since many of the conflicts inside an organization will be settled in the political arena outside and the rules imposed on the organization by the state, *the institutionalization of the political struggles of the past, the establishment of particular values in the forms of rules and procedures in organizations, can contribute to the formation of the typical behaviour of a culture*' (Zysman, 1977, p. 170). He goes on to assert, in classical fashion, that the state is 'the only organization with which at least potentially all members of the nation will interact, and thus it provides the one common experience with authority in the society', so that '*national patterns of authority behaviour can be understood as the residue of the political struggles that create the state*' (Zysman, 1977, p. 177). While one should not be taken in by the pious propagandist mythology of the centralising monarchs uniting France over the centuries as retailed in elementary history textbooks, nevertheless it is arguable that France is a country where 'from the beginning the state was an instrument of centralizing power, created apart from society, almost in opposition to it, and thus at least partially autonomous' (Zysman, 1977, p. 194). We shall have occasion to return to the view that even if this assertive, active policy style does not in practice mean integrated or decisive action, it implies a *capacity* for policy initiative, a *potential* for far-sighted planning and a *propensity* to impose its will when this is necessary to obtain public objectives. It will be advanced that although French policy-making may be characterised as having a predominantly reactive short-term and piecemeal approach to problem-solving, at the summit of the French state there is an informal network or nucleus of executive power capable of challenging the routine norms and attempting to impose an active, longer-term and comprehensive style of policy-making and implementation.

The Actors in the French Policy Process

The strength and durability of France's pre-liberal and pre-democratic traditions can be seen operating in the working of the politicoadministrative system but it is especially evident in the jurisprudential norms of French public and administrative law. The enduring significance of the legal fiction of popular sovereignty, the post-Revolutionary source of legitimate political authority, lies in the fact that though it is the politico-administrative elites who decide what the general interest implies in practice, they have to secure the assent of the people expressed through universal suffrage. Elsewhere I have argued that while 'to single out state sovereignty as the salient feature of the French political tradition involves a great oversimplification the attitude of the French elite towards politics has been dominated by a belief in the need for a strong, centralised authority, capable of containing the centrifugal forces that constantly threaten the integrity of the state' (Hayward, 1973, pp. 3–4). It should be reiterated that the official norms must not be confused with the empirical reality, even though these norms are not merely embedded in the formal rules but are assiduously inculcated into the minds of those who wield a portion of public authority and those who are subject to it. However, the French elites are adept at the double-think of what is true 'in principle' not being what is true 'in practice', so frequently are they at variance that one is sometimes tempted to regard them as antithetical, which would be excessive. One has constantly to bear in mind the co-existence of two distinct but interrelated levels of a dual politicoadministrative reality characteristic of policy style in France.

An obvious problem that one faces is how this normative framework can cope with the large tracts of sociopolitical reality inhabited by the private actors in the public process that are such a feature of the contemporary world but of which it did not have to take official cognisance. What is clearly not acceptable is the normatively conditioned, one-sided approach, characteristic of Anglo-American political science in which the multilateral and reciprocal system of influence of public and private actors are seen in terms of unilateral pressure of groups on government, whereas in reality the groups are often as much or more pressured than is the government. The pioneer of both pressure group and technocracy studies in France, Jean Meynaud, curiously enough never brought the two sides of his work together, so much was he intellectually dominated by the ethnocentric assumptions of his Anglo-American paradigm (Meynaud, 1960, 1962, 1965). It was left to an American scholar, Henry Ehrmann, to show that the relationship between public administration and private interests in France was frequently collusive, so that the term 'pressure group', abstracted from the working of the politicoadministrative system, is highly misleading. He demonstrated that not just the societal side, but both sides of the state–society equation, were highly fragmented, despite the pretensions to monolithic unity of hypostasised public power (Ehrmann, 1957, 1961). Detailed studies of French administration have subsequently shown this to be true not merely as between ministries, but as between *directions* in the same ministry and between *bureaux* in the same *directions*. Furthermore, it has become accepted that the regular contact enjoyed by some groups with particular parts of the government apparatus may persuade at least the group leaders to absorb something of the officials' 'general interest' values, while the senior civil servants may come, in terms of practical action, to identify the public interest (as it relates to a particular policy area) with the satisfaction of the claims of one or more private interests.

However, if we are to find policy-relevant pathways through the immense marshland of group activity, we must segregate the types of select groups that Ehrmann identified as worthy of being negotiated with from those that were only fit to have public decisions imposed upon them. At the national level, such a distinction has been adumbrated but not elaborated upon by the foremost American *connaisseur* of France's administrative elite, Ezra Suleiman, while at the local level, the most suggestive work has been done by a perspicacious *connaisseur* of peripheral power in France, Pierre Grémion. However, we must first distinguish private group actors in terms of their policy relationships with the public authorities, rather in the way that Wyn Grant has distinguished between 'insider' and 'outsider' groups in terms of their strategies in seeking to influence public policy, without subscribing to his cautious reservation that this distinction may be 'peculiar to British culture'. Building upon Maurice Kogan's and Jeremy Richardson's identification of those groups that are officially recognised as legitimate spokesmen for a group interest and are consulted on a continuous basis because they adhere to 'an unwritten code of moderate and responsible behaviour', Grant stresses that acceptability to the public authorities is not the sole determinant of their relationship with any particular organised interest: 'Some groups may want insider status and be granted it; others may want it but may not be able to attain it; yet others may wish to avoid becoming enmeshed in the political-administrative system and may therefore prefer to remain as outsider group' (Kogan, 1975, p. 75; Richardson, 1977, pp. 23–4; Grant, 1978, pp. 2–3, 15). The price of rejecting the bureaucratic embrace may be high but the strategy and tactics pursued by such dissentient, outsider groups may preclude their adopting a stance and modes of behaviour necessary for them to acquire the institutionalised status of being *interlocuteurs valables*.

As the self-styled guardians of the general interest, the attitudes and behaviour of the French senior civil service provide excellent guidelines to why some interest groups are regarded as legitimate while others are not. Suleiman has contrasted the attitude of state officials towards the respectable, co-operative, useful and trustworthy 'professional organisations' and the disreputable, unco-operative, disruptive and unrepresentative pressure groups (Suleiman, 1974, pp. 337–41). Whereas contact with the insider groups would not taint the paragons of the public interest with the pitch of particularist demagoguery, the outsider group – labelled in English as 'lobbies', the foreign term persuasively suggesting the further slur of an outlandish import – are dismissed or repressed as irresponsible troublemakers. The major professional organisations are acceptable as 'social partners', though for the more traditional state officials they are clearly regarded as junior partners, who can be expected to provide reliable information and support in intra-administrative conflicts. The spokesmen of such officially recognised organisations acquire the status of being *notables*, while in return they strengthen the position of their official patrons by lending them assistance from outside the public decision-making system. In this way, each bureaucracy's clientele confers an informal 'legitimacy from below' that supplements the formal legitimacy from above and may sometimes partially compensate for the latter's weakness. So insider groups acquire a privileged, institutionalised status, even though France has not gone as far as the EEC Commission in establishing a Bureau of Social Partners.

Such social partner/public policy-maker relationships have long existed at the local level in France. They have been closely analysed by the group of scholars that gravitated around Michel Crozier's Sociology of Organisations Centre, who have stressed the interdependence between local political and administrative leaders:

Research shows that communications are easier between bureaucrats and their partner notables than within the hierarchical pyramid of the

Administration or even between elected representatives of the same local authority. The difference between notables and bureaucrats is much weaker than it seems at first sight. The State bureaucrat is in many ways a local notable; as for the notable, he is often a better expert in 'bureaucracy' than his bureaucratic colleague. A complicity develops between bureaucrats and notables based upon sharing a common experience, complementary interests and identical norms, a sufficiently strong complicity to successfully survive divergences in their roles and interests. Thus both elected representatives and State officials accept as legitimate norms like the general interest and both make full and sympathetic allowance for the electoral preoccupations of the former. This relationship of conflictual complicity between bureaucrats and notables is encountered at various territorial levels: between Mayors and sub-Division heads of the Ministry of Public Works and Housing (*Equipement*), tax collectors and sub-Prefects at the local level, between councillors, Prefects and field service Directors in the *departments*. (Crozier and Thoenig, 1976, pp. 6, 14 ff.; see also Grémion, 1970, 1976)

However, this cosy 'bureaucratic-*notable* system', in which the acquiescent leaders of local communities and groups may achieve the envied status of state-sanctified insiders, while the dissentient leaders are dismissed as utopian and anachronistic obstacles to the working of an advanced industrial society, has become increasingly divorced from social reality. The emergence of new social demands which have not or cannot be institutionalised within the 'bureaucratic-*notable* system' has meant that the leaders of the proliferating protest or outsider movements cannot successfully be ignored as irresponsible activists. The statesmanlike *notables*, who 'understand the realities' and know how far to go too far, cannot be relied upon to manipulate those forces that they do not themselves 'animate'. Their monopoly of mediation between the leading public and private actors at the centre and the peripheral provincial masses has itself become dysfunctional and been challenged by new militant mediators, some of whom have the power to disrupt society and so must either be repressed, or accommodated. The recent history of some trade union, as well as nationalist, regionalist, environmentalist and feminist organisations, exemplify this development in its extreme form (Hayward, 1978, pp. 55-65; Françoise and Jacques Caroux, 1979, pp. 8–9, 15).

The dualistic typology of private and public actors and as between elected and bureaucratic public actors developed so far, when linked with the two dimensions of policy style sketched earlier, help us conflate three of the four models of group–state relations identified by Vincent Wright in an attempt to render the 'infinite variety of situations' more comprehensible (Wright, 1978, pp. 186, 174 ff.). His 'crisis domination' and 'concerted politics' models reflect two aspects of the consensus-centred, bureaucratic-group' *notables*, social-partner relationship with professional organisations. The 'concerted politics' (which, unlike Federal Germany, does not necessarily accord veto power to the 'social partners') variant corresponds to the 'normal', routine, day-to-day relationship characterised by reactive problem-solving, while the 'domination crisis' variant corresponds to a breakdown in the customary relationship, a situation in which one or both sides seek to engage in active imposition. This first pair, appropriate to the Crozierian model, has to be supplemented by a second pair, representing the conflict-centred style of relationship in which the private actors are regarded as irresponsible outsiders. The 'endemic conflict' policy style variant corresponds to the routine situation in which fragmented groups console their supporters with vociferous ideological protest for their inability to resist the *faits accomplis* imposed upon them by contemptuous and intransigent public authorities. Defeatist demagoguery on the part of the private actors operates functionally, their mock-heroics either being tolerated by the public authorities as a safety-valve, or more or less brutally repressed as a nuisance. Wright's fourth model, pluralism, is simply a less organised form of 'concerted politics'. Instead, one needs to substitute for it a model of 'institutional collapse' or anarchy. This would be the crisis situation variant of the reactive problem-solving response to a conflict-centred relationship between groups and public authorities. A good empirical example of this would be the relations between the student organisations and the government in 1968 which moved from 'endemic conflict' to anarchic 'institutional collapse', although in May 1968 the crisis was surmounted, whereas ten years earlier the regime had succumbed to a combination of military and settler revolt in Algeria.

Before examining whether such models of relations between public and private actors are heuristically helpful in interpreting policy practice, we must identify the major types of actors in the policy process and establish identify the major types of actors in the policy process and establish whether they have a particular style of policy-making and implementation. In a country where the traditional norms imply a pyramidal authority structure, with the state institutions superimposed upon society, it is sensible to begin with the public actors, distinguishing them into two categories: those that man the 'horizontal' staff networks, and those that head the 'vertical', line hierarchies. Despite the widely held view – encouraged by the vogue that was enjoyed by the concept of technocracy – that the *grands corps* that made up the French politicoadministrative and public sector elites owed their prestige and power to their *specialist* training and skills, it has become clear that this is misleading in the extreme. Rather, it is the *generalist* capacity not to be confined to a particular policy sector by one's expertise that characterises the French policy-makers and leads them to cultivate an all-rounder style that allows frictionless movement between the summits of the vertical hierarchies that constitute the bulk of the governmental structure. As Suleiman has put it, 'While the elite rationalises its power and privilege on the basis of its training and competence, it must also deny that it is a speclialized elite so that it may maintain and extend its position (Suleiman, 1978, pp. 174–5; see also Birnbaum, 1977; 1978). The quality most required among the small, informal, interministerial elite (who by a process of *pantouflage* fan out to occupy prominent posts in public and private business and in politics) is the capacity to take the broad view, deemed to correspond to the general interest rather than to the special interests, with which the specialist technocrat feels most at home. Because they change their role with the position they occupy, the select few from among the *grands corps* are supposed to have acquired the eagle-eye, detached view through movement between a range of command and *cabinet* posts. However, those that man the high-level horizontal networks are concerned with preserving their corporate power, 'rather than using that power to achieve goals. . . . It is not the policies per se that matter, for policies are judged according to their impact on the power and position of the elite' (Suleiman, 1978, p. 247; also pp. 98, 108, 117, 167, 244–5).

Suleiman argued in a previous book that, far from the *grands corps* providing the agents of change within the bureaucratic system as asserted by Michael Crozier, they reduced the pace of change because the corps networks frequently functioned at cross-purposes, so that 'the formulation of policy . . . is reduced to the lowest common denominator between the rival corps' (Suleiman, 1974, pp. 274). However, he admitted that this hypothesis seemed to be verified in the behaviour of the technical-corps graduates of the Ecole Polytechnique rather than in that of the generalist-corps graduates of the Ecole Nationale d'Administration. Clearly, the logic of corps monopolies over parts of public administration leads to 'ministries that tend to be agglomerations of introverted specialist divisions, each jealously protecting its own assigned area of responsibility', resulting in the need to organise intraministerial and interministerial co-ordination to reconcile or bypass the rivalries that threaten to paralyse action. However, Catherine Grémion has argued that while the traditionalist members of the politicoadministrative elites – characterised by their legal training and the likelihood that they have not moved outside their discipline, their ministry, or their country – may be guilty of a propensity to immobilist compromise, the modernising members of the central decision-making nucleus have an innovative profile associated with the diversity of their experience. Their career socialisation has been marked by their experience of change: they have studied several disciplines, they have been mobile geographically and administratively (serving in several ministries as well as abroad) and having moved out of line administration into staff work in ministerial *cabinets*. On issues of 'high politics', while the President of the Republic, the Prime Minister, or other ministers (albeit often members of the administrative *grand corps*) may identify a policy problem and take policy initiatives, they rarely remain in effective control throughout the whole policy process through to implementation (as we shall see in the Rhine–Rhône waterway case). It is the existence of innovative politicoadministrative networks, such as existed in the 1960s Club Jean Moulin, that enables ministers to introduce new policies. (Chaban-Delmas's 'New Society' programme of 1969 was largely inspired by ideas developed in and by members of the Club Jean Moulin and by Jacques Delors in his club, Citoyens 60. Chaban-Delmas's premiership launched a new style of activism by the Prime Minister's personal staff, working in teams, which remains important in the sphere of industrial relations, even though the President's staff have secured an inconspicuous role in the economic sphere, which is a policy area where the President, the Prime Minister and their personal staffs have to try to work closely together.) So Catherine Grémion concludes that it is often the politicians who provide the necessary backing for the 'administrative members of this central decision making *milieu* that are responsible for taking the initiative, ensuring continuity and giving practical shape to decisions' (Grémion, 1979a, pp. 32, 20 ff.; Kessler, 1979, pp. 36, 43; Grémion, 1979b, pp. 362–5, 383–5, 389, 392–400).

The oft-noted fact that the French use the same word *politique* to cover both 'politics' and 'policy' directs our attention to the interface between 'politics' and 'administration' which provide the focus of policy-making and implementation. It is precisely here that the interaction between the heads of the political executive and their bureaucratic staffs can be observed, as they attempt to overcome the inertia of the government machine in a situation where fewer and fewer policy decisions can be circumscribed in a way that avoids the need to call upon the capacities of the elite old-boy networks. Those concerned are principally the President of the Republic and his personal staff, the Prime Minister, his personal staff and the Government Secretary General (the French equivalent of the British Cabinet Secretary) operating through an elaborate network of interministerial councils (chaired by the President of the Republic), interministerial committees (usually chaired by the Prime Minister)) and interdepartmental committees (chaired by a member of the Prime Minister's personal staff). The formal summit of this network of decision-preparing and decision-taking committees is, of course, the Council of Ministers but this body has become a policy-making body.

Though the personal policy style of particular Presidents of the Republic and Prime Ministers has influenced the frequency with which meetings take place, the Fifth Republic has been characterised by an increase in the number of meetings of interministerial councils and interdepartmental committees. The reason for this change is an increasing concentration of power, going beyond the presidentialisation of the regime, with the President of the Republic and his staff taking over co-ordinating and 'arbitrating' functions previously exercised by the Prime Minister and his staff, who in turn have been encroaching upon the decision-making autonomy of the ministries. Particularly under Giscard d'Estaing, the interministerial councils over which he presided became the place *par excellence* at which decisions were taken. In 1974 he established the Central Planning Council, at whose monthly meetings all economic and social policies were reviewed in turn, while in 1975 he instituted the system of biannually sending a public letter to the Prime Minister (after consultation with him), setting out the programme of government activity for the next six months. This took the form of setting out the general objectives and guidelines of government policy, together with the salient themes and particular issues upon which the interministerial networks would concentrate their attention, with preparatory interdepartmental and interministerial meetings being organised. (There is a special telephone network, called 'interministerial', linking top politicoadministrative policy-makers, who prefer to communicate orally or by brief notes.) Each minister is shadowed (though not in one-to-one proportion) by a member of both the President's and the Prime Minister's staff, so that it is not just derision to describe the Shadow Cabinet as the one nominally in office. The major institutional loser in this modified, de facto decision-making process – in addition to the spending ministers generally – has been the Ministry of Finance, which has additionally been split since 1978 into a separate Ministry of the Economy and Ministry of the Budget. However, it has been asserted, with deliberate exaggeration, that there has been a paradoxical combination of centralisation of power in the hands of the politicoadministrative elite with its diffusion among them. 'The (line) civil servants do the work, the general staff re-do it, the minister's cabinet modifies it and the Prime Minister's cabinet reopens the whole question' (Bodiguel, 1979, pp. 15, 12–14; Delion, 1975, pp. 274, 268–76). So, an institutional device intended to speed up decision-making and make it more consistent may in practice lead to a dysfunctional divorce between the policy-makers and those in direct contact with the problems and to whom will be confided the task of implementing the policies.

   In correcting a tendency to suggest an all-embracing domination of the policy process by a politicoadministrative nucleus at the summit, Bernard Gournay has pointed out that the role of the relevant member of a minister's, Prime Minister's, or President's personal staff is to take charge of a policy issue on their behalf and to steer it past the obstacles that may hold up its resolution:

> From the stage of preliminary contacts and first studies through to the final adoption of the project, the member of his personal staff is responsible. He collects information and advice from the ministries, contacts and seeks to persuade them and other ministerial personal staffs to collaborate, receives delegations (from interested parties), chairs

meetings of officials within the ministry and interdepartmental meetings, deals with correspondence and even drafts the bill relating to the project and so forth. (Gournay, 1979, pp. 19, 8–9; Cohen, 1980)

This is not to be confused with usurping the minister's formal right to take the decision when all that is happening is an implicit or explicit delegation of ministerial power. However, this attempt to reconcile facts with constitutional rectitude should not obscure the need to differentiate certain policy areas or issues that are decided over the heads of the politicoadministrative inner circle, such as foreign, defence and colonial policy (reflected, for example, in the decline in the military budget as a percentage of public expenditure from the 1960s and its increase in the late 1970s), while other issues, like the increasing preoccupation with the environment or decisions on agricultural policy probably owe more to press publicity and pressures from groups than the activities of the elites who are reacting to the initiatives of others.

We should, therefore, turn from the reactions of the public actors to the mediators between them and the private actors, as one moves out of the corridors of power into the political, social and economic marketplace in which the political parties, locally and nationally elected representatives, the elite and mass media become our principal focus. We leave the sedate 'court politics' atmosphere of a President of the Republic, who is partially secluded from the turbulent sociopolitical environment by an entourage that filters the outside pressures, with each collaborator having the task of keeping a part of that environment under surveillance, providing his master with early warning of trouble so that he can react quickly or take the initiative betimes. Certain members of the personal staffs of each minister, of the Prime Minister and of the President, have particular responsibility for dealings with parties, politicians and the media as well as their clientele among the private actors, just as others are concerned primarily with overseeing the government machine. While the personal style of the political leaders may account for the salience of this or that institutional mediator, the Fifth Republic has been characterised by a decline in the importance of political parties and of Parliament, partially counterbalanced by an increase in that of the media, both the mass medium of TV and the elite medium of the daily *Le Monde*. The enormous effort put into domesticating radio and TV into an instrument for projecting the public authorities' view of public policy both in what is publicised, and what is edited out, is as important an indicator of the importance attached to the communication of official truth as the sensitiveness to criticism published by *Le Monde* or by the scurrilous but courageous *Canard Enchaîné*. The latter is the medium to which those – including members of the politicoadministrative elites – leak information that most of the press refuses to publish either out of prudence, or pusillanimity, or simply because those who own and control them support the powers that be. Despite modest improvement in access to the mass media, such as the introduction of *tribunes libres* on the third TV channel for political parties, trade unions and a range of voluntary associations, there has been an upsurge of episodic pirate radio stations, launched by environmentalist groups, trade unions and even political parties, as a means of communicating with a local (though not a national) public, securing the more publicity because of their illegality.

Rather than relying upon press and Parliament as sources of information about public opinion, the French government has turned increasingly to confidential opinion polls, on which large sums are spent particularly by the President and Prime Minister, out of a 'secret fund'. Public attitudes on particular policies are thus tested independently of the views of the political parties which, especially on the right, are regarded as disciplined supporters rather than organisations with their own collective policy views. This corresponds to a general downgrading of representative as compared with a pseudo-direct democracy under the Fifth Republic; 'pseudo' because the people are treated as a manipulable mass, rather than an informed public.

However, an even more distinctive feature of the French policy process is the extent to which the functions of articulating and aggregating interests have been assumed by public officials. At the local level this has been *par excellence* the strength of the prefect, although with the development of large towns, where mayors are also either deputies or senators, as well as presidents of the departmental or regional council, the prefect may lose his capacity to represent the local community's demands on behalf of the *notables*. They may have the capacity to do so directly and the central ministries – even the staffs of President or Prime Minister in certain cases – may welcome the opportunity to deal directly with such intermediaries in preference to bureaucratic competitors within the public administration system. Although Members of Parliament, still less the local *notables*, may not have the capacity collectively to modify public policy through the legislative process, they can often secure more or less significant changes in the way the rules are applied in particular cases, such discretionary flexibility enabling central decision-makers to make concessions to political friends and those it would be unwise to coerce. This tendency for Members of Parliament to concentrate upon defending the particular interests of constituents reinforces the senior civil servants' view that they alone defend the public interest. Because the representative peak organisations are more likely to take a broad view than are parliamentarians, they make more congenial partners than does Parliament. In any case, the constitutional shift in the Fifth Republic of the boundary between law and regulation, in favour of the latter, has meant that senior officials need devote less time to bothering about placating Members of Parliament – in so far as they regard it necessary to consult any others – and switch their attention to the organised interests when preparing regulatory decrees and orders. Their norms and their preference inclines them, as one of their members put it, to 'soliloquise through the rules' (Mayer, 1968, p. 44; Suleiman, 1974, pp. 287–315).

If we switch our focus from the attitudes of members of the central decision-making nucleus to the mass of administered provincial Frenchmen, it is evident that there is a marked contrast between the rural population which continues to enjoy stable and close interpersonal relations and the disoriented urbanised masses. Table 5.1 indicates that far from being parochial in the sense of lacking awareness of and ability to use the political system for their purposes, farmers are more likely to be acquainted with, and to have recourse to, local *notables* than any other socio-occupational category of the population. So, despite the rapid decline in the farm population, the access farm spokesmen have had to political and administrative policy-makers has meant that the remorseless pressures of modernisation have been eased. It is not surprising that managers and big businessmen have impressive acquaintanceship and recourse to local *notables*, but when we consider the bulk of the white-collar employees and manual workers, there are surprisingly high figures on both counts. This may doubtless be a tribute to the survival of a large number of communes, with some 36,000 mayors and nearly half a million councillors ensuring a much greater face-to-face contact between the mass public and their representatives than exists in any other industrialised European country. However, not unlike the farmers, a small minority of the urbanised mass turn to militant action through voluntary associations of local residents, consumers, or environmentalists, which continue to increase in number and activity, even though associated self-help does not usually enable French citizens to reverse a structural situation of powerlessness (Hayward, 1978, pp. 55–8; Scholoff, 1980, pp. 236, 219 ff.).

Table 5.1 *Acquaintance with, and Recourse to, Notables by Socio-Occupational Category (Percentages)*

Socio-Occupational Category	Acquaintance	Recourse
Farmers	94	84
Higher managerial and bigger businessmen	62	70
Small shopkeepers and artisans	60	60
White-collar staff and employees	48	64
Manual workers	55	64
Inactive	57	63
All	62	66

Source: Adapted from Elie Sultan and Clarence Preiss (1979), pp. 92–3.

In turning to the mass of private actors in the policy process, whose behaviour both responds to and in a measure conditions the policy style adopted by the public actors, there are some fundamental preliminary questions that must be raised, even if we can go only a little way towards answering them in our present state of ignorance. The first pair of questions concern how representative these organised private actors are in relation to their potential clienteles and the problem of how inclined French people are to join groups. The statistical information is not very reliable (groups are counted when they come into existence, but not when they disappear), and even if accurate membership figures were available, what significance should be attached to them compared with other indicators of an organisation's capacity to mobilise its constituency? Sometimes there are elections which enable us to measure the support enjoyed by various organisations. This is so in exceptional cases (like trade unions and parents' organisations in state schools) but what about the other groups? What financial and organisational resources do French groups have at their disposal? We seldom know the number and quality of their staff, much less what they have to offer government in terms of information in helping to identify a problem, expertise in devising a solution, political support in carrying the policy into law, or assistance in securing its implementation thereafter. Though we can ascertain fairly easily how stable the group leadership is, it is not easy to establish how centralised authority is in practice. Can the leaders commit their members when they engage in negotiation with the government, or must they confess, like the unfortunate Ledru-Rollin in 1849: 'As I was their leader, I had to follow them.'

What one can state on the basis of existing research is that 70 per cent of the heads of division (*directeurs*) in the central ministries were accustomed to meet interest-group representatives 'very often', while only 11 per cent claimed never to meet them. In the case of two-thirds of the directors, they did not initiate these meetings, while a third sometimes did. The main benefits from such contacts were that they helped in the formulation and (especially) the implementation of policy (28 per cent); provided advance warning of opposition (20 per cent); enabled them to acquire information (15 per cent); secured a reciprocal exchange of information (9 per cent); and explained decisions that had already been taken (10 per cent). Two-thirds of the directors saw no serious disadvantages in meeting interest-group representatives, because few groups could, as a result, leak information that would lead to the mobilisation of opposition and prevent the correct decision being taken. The contacts with the groups are – except in the case of the trustworthy 'insider' groups – carried out so late in the secretive process of policy formulation that it often amounts to a formal gesture rather than a substantive part of decision-making as such. Some groups lobby ministers or their private staff rather than the directors, but these tend to be 'one-off' exercises, there being no reason why groups that have close and continuing ties with a ministry should confine themselves to the more bureaucratic channel of access to policy-makers (Suleiman, 1974, pp. 324–36).

A Case Study: The Rhine–Rhône Waterway

An isolated case study (confined to one case for reasons of space, which draws heavily upon the doctoral theses of Kammerer, 1978, and Schreiber, 1979) cannot do more than highlight some of the features of national policy style. However, the particular case that has been selected allows comparisons over time because it extends over the whole life of the Fifth Republic. It involves a very extensive range of actors: from the President of the Republic to local environmental pressure groups, via large firms, trade unions and both national, regional and local political and functional representative bodies, as well as staff and line administrative officials. It represents a very substantial public investment project, involving transport and regional policy in a major way; as such, it has been closely connected with successive national plans and allows this particular issue to be seen in the context of comprehensive, medium-term policy-making. Finally, the dramatic and grandiose dimensions of the scheme to link up the Mediterranean and North Sea by a waterway improved to accommodate large vessels provides an excellent opportunity to observe what at first sight appears to be a heroic, innovate and far-sighted policy initiative in the toils of a routine decision-making process.

If one is inclined to be impatient with the sluggishness of a process that has all the sedateness of a waterway compared to more modern forms of transport, it is worth bearing in mind the history of the existing small-scale canal linking the Rhine with the Rhône. It was proposed under the *ancien régime* and decided upon during the French Revolution, building commenced during the First Napoleonic Empire, continued during the Restoration and under the July Monarchy and was completed during the Second Empire of Louis Napoleon. It took thirty-nine years to plan (1753–91) and sixty-two years to construct (1792–1853). Given his modernising vision of the resurgent France of the Fifth Republic, it was natural that De Gaulle should embrace the idea of catching up with the Federal German Republic, which had inherited a Rhine–Main–Danube waterway scheme from the Weimar republic. Speaking at Marseille in November 1961 De Gaulle declared:

> Naturally, the Rhine–Rhône link is the keystone of a great reorganisation that is necessary from the national and European standpoints. . . . As far as the Fourth Plan is concerned, I repeat, preliminary studies will get underway and the decision has been taken in principle. Precisely when

work will commence, I cannot say. All I can say is that it will be carried out.

This was merely one of dozens of similar speeches made by successive Presidents of the Republic and Prime Ministers, in which fervent commitment in *principle* was counterbalanced by such evasive vagueness in *practice* about when and how it was to be implemented that they encourage cynicism about the politicians' capacity to promise rather than to perform. As we shall see, the technobureaucrats and budget officials who were overwhelmingly opposed to the scheme, were content to tolerate the rhetorical commitments, provided they could prevent them being implemented in practice. Political decisions were thereby transmuted into administrative non-decisions.

Like other pet-schemes associated with the Fifth Republic, all the essential arguments concerning the Rhine–Rhône waterway had already been mooted during the Fourth Republic. Its initial champion and for long its most eloquent advocate was the Deputy and Mayor of Strasbourg, Pierre Pflimlin (the last Prime Minister of the Fourth Republic before the handover of power to General De Gaulle). Alsace was seeking 'compensation' for the Lorraine steel industry's success in securing the Moselle Canal in 1956 and a consortium for the modernisation of the east and south-eastern waterways bewailed the absence of a Rhine–Rhône element in the Second Plan (1954–7) and claimed that it was a 'national imperative' that it should be included in the Third Plan. However, it was in the period preceding the preparation of the Fourth Plan (1962–5) that the idea was officially launched. In 1959 a political friend of Pflimlin, Pierre Sudreau, then Minister of Housing (who was to become President of the Association Mer du Nord – Méditerranée) requested a waterways report from the Commissioner for Regional Planning, while the Waterways Division of the Ministry of Public Works and Transport decided to prepare a draft scheme. In June 1960 the Prime Minister established an interdepartmental working party to investigate, under the chairmanship of a socialist former minister. After a very thorough investigation on the spot at fifteen hearings, the Boulloche working party proposed the postponement of a decision, reflecting the hostility of officials from the ministries of Finance, Public Works, Industry and the Plan, rather than the views of Housing, Agriculture, Foreign Affairs and the Interior which were favourable. When the matter came before an interministerial committee in August 1961, Prime Minister Debré and four of his ministers wished to postpone any decision pending further study, while four ministers (including Sudreau) were in favour of proceding immediately but were overruled. Despite pressure from a newly formed pro-waterway parliamentary group, including opposition leaders like the socialist Defferre as well as Pflimlin, all the government would agree to do was to continue investigation and start purchasing land. Planning

Commissioner Massé reflected the hostility of the administration in an October 1961 confidential letter to the Prime Minister in which he argued that the Rhine–Rhône waterway was 'more likely to be an extension of the nineteenth century rather than anticipate the twenty-first century'. He went on sagely to warn that 'A [favourable] decision in principle, unaccompanied by any timetable of implementation, will only be eyewash. It is likely both seriously to embarrass future governments and profoundly disillusion the scheme's protagonists'. The Fourth Plan's priorities were firmly in the fields of health and education investment, aimed at reflecting a 'less partial idea of man' rather than materialist economic growth. Though parliamentary support for Rhine–Rhône won a *lettre rectificative* amendment after the 1962 debate, it offered encouraging words but no firm commitment to the lobbyists.

This led them to establish the Association Mer du Nord–Méditerranée in October 1962, with as its first president Wilfrid Baumgartner, who had been the Finance Minister whose officials opposed proceeding with the waterway in the Boulloche working party! Its vice-president was Philippe Lamour president of the Compagnie Nationale du Rhône (of which more later) and chairman of the Planning Commissariat's Regional Planning Commission. It numbered among its supporters three Fourth Republic Prime Ministers (including Edgar Faure) but the main impetus came from the provincial economic *notables*, especially from the chambers of commerce. Unlike earlier champions of Rhine–Rhône (such as the Association des Nautes, which represented the waterways operators, equipment manufacturers, loaders and agents), the new association and its operational offshoot the Société d'Etudes Mer du Nord–Méditerranée (SEMNM) confined itself to public and semi-public bodies, which it was to claim entitled it to be regarded as a public interest group rather than a pressure group. Its claim to 'insider' status came from the prominent political and economic *notables* that headed it and the membership of thirty-five chambers of commerce, twenty-six municipalities and fourteen public investment companies (Sociétés d'équipement or établissements publiques). Despite Planning Commissioner Maseé's hostility to the Rhine–Rhône project, he could not prevent the North Sea–Mediterranean being chosen in 1964 by the government as a long-term (1985) development axis in the guidelines for the Fifth Plan. This was done on the advice of the Commissariat's own Regional Planning Commission chaired by Philippe Lamour (vice-president of both the Association and the SEMNM), whose relevant study group included Raymond Barre, Edgar Faure and Pierre Pflimlin among its members.

Matters appeared to come to a head with the National Assembly debate on the guidelines of the Fifth Plan in November 1965, when – following a particularly well-argued speech by Pflimlin and the reception of a parliamentary delegation by the Prime Minister – Pompidou made a categoric, official commitment that was subsequently frequently quoted as a reminder when there was no official sense of urgency to implement this seemingly irrevocable commitment. Pompidou declared: 'The Government has discussed and settled the matter. It has decided to develop the North Sea–Mediterranean axis, in the form of an uninterrupted network of deep draught waterways' (*Un Dossier*, 1979, p. 195). (One of the key ministers at the time, Edgard Pisani at Equipement, subsequently claimed that he had not been consulted about the Prime Minister's decision.) The type of counter-lobbying from rival interests to which the Prime Minister was subjected is evident from a sarcastic remark he made several days earlier: 'there is no scarcity of economists and engineers, often *polytechniciens*, often from the SNCF, arguing that waterways do not pay.' Inaugurating a lock on the Rhône in July 1967 Pompidou made clear his attitude to cost–benefit calculations, which Pflimlin had undermined in the 1965 debate with the remark 'it suffices to change the experts' initial hypotheses very slightly for a project considered unprofitable to become profitable'. Pompidou declared: 'Naturally, in coming to this decision [reaffirming the priority of Rhine–Rhône] we have not evaluated profitability in terms of the strict calculations of cost, because in addition to this certain [sic] and mathematical profitability there is an imprecise but substantial profitability that results from the attraction which a waterway and its accompanying installations cannot fail to exert.' The marks of the Regional Planning Commission's influence can be seen in his dwelling upon Rhine–Rhône as an unquantifiable counterweight both to Paris and to the Rhineland, rather than judging it purely in terms of transport economics. (The switch in emphasis from counteracting the Paris magnet to the Rhineland–Rotterdam delta had dangerous implications for Rhine–Rhône because it encouraged opposition from those who considered that the main result of the enlarged waterway would be to promote the penetration by exports from rather than to Germany, carried moreover by German transporters.) Similar arguments were used by the Compagnie Nationale du Rhône (CNR) against the Finance Ministry and the Electricity Public Corporation (EDF) assertion that hydroelectric power was uneconomic because of cheap oil; the CNR stressed its subsidiary navigation, irrigation and flood-reduction functions. The May 1968 'events' resulted in a major squeeze upon public investment in the Sixth Plan, slowing down work on the Rhône and further delaying progress on making the axis a reality. The oil 'crisis' of 1973–4 was not to prevent the Rhine–Rhône project from becoming a Seventh Plan Priority Action Programme with an apparently firm financial commitment of 1·5 milliard francs from 1976–80, but it was to help prevent it being spent (Hayward, 1981, forthcoming; Green, 1980, pp. 112 ff.); while 104·4 milliard francs allocated to modernising the French telephone system was cheerfully spent, despite the former Planning Commissioner Massé's attribution of France's poor telephones to 'the politico-industrial coalition in favour of a typically nineteenth century investment, the Rhine–Rhône canal'. At this time half France was said to be waiting to have the telephone installed, and the other half were waiting for the dialling tone!

Rather than continue with the saga of the Rhine–Rhône 'non-decision', the pattern that has emerged will be sketched, before we stand back to evaluate the role of the major actors we have already encountered, as well as some who only became actively involved in the 1970s. With an impressive continuity that indicates certain structural determinants operating during the presidencies of De Gaulle, Pompidou and Giscard, the same cycle is repeated again and again. As the Rhine-Rhône's two historians have put it: 'pressure from certain economic milieux, amplified by a few political leaders, meetings of government committees, summit *arbitrages* during the preparation of the Plan, decline in interest after the Plan's adoption, until it is realised that the funds have not materialised, resulting in renewed pressure from economic and parliamentary quarters' (Kammerer, 1978):

> The process was the same at each Plan: a committee or an expert prepares a so-called complete report but comes to no conclusion or an unfavourable one, which enables the Government to avoid coming to a decision. Under political pressure, the Government is compelled to change some words in the Plan, makes fine declarations of principlê but grants little of substance, this little disappearing when brought face to face with the harsh budgetary realities, as evidenced by the low rates of implementation for the Fourth, Fifth and Sixth Plans. (Schreiber, 1979)

The Seventh Plan effective rate of implementation for Rhine–Rhône was less than 40 per cent, and by the Eighth Plan (1981–5), Rhine–Rhône had been eliminated as a priority. What does this process have to tell us about the way in which the various policy actors operate both in this particular case and more generally?

Let us first consider those who are the protagonists of the waterway, beginning with the industrial firms. Until the 1969 decision to build the steel plant at Fos near Marseille, the Lorraine steel industry had been ardent supporters of Rhine–Rhône, competing with Alsace for the choice of route. However, the decision not to develop the steel industry in Lorraine meant that the way was open for the Alsace link, reinforced by the Thyssen decision that one of the conditions for German participation in SOLMER (the steel joint subsidiary established at Fos) was completion of the Rhine–Rhône waterway via Alsace (Green, 1979; Tarrow, 1978, p. 107 and ch. 4). The main industrial protagonist was probably the Peugeot motor company, whose main plant was at Sochaux-Montbéliard, with a smaller plant at Mulhouse. Because Peugeot had a long-term growth strategy, backed by lots of detailed traffic studies, it was in a better position than most other actors to influence decisions. It hoped to secure the same benefits as its nationalised rival Renault obtained on the Seine for transport between its plants, as well as the ability to ship its cars by containers for export, northward via Rotterdam, southward via Marseille. While Peugeot was definitely more interested in a Montbéliard–Mulhouse motorway than in a waterway, and pressed harder (and successfully) for it, it was discreetly active in promoting the project until it became clear that it would not be able to have four-tier barges on stretches of Rhine–Rhône. In the late 1960s the cabinet of successive Ministers of Transport, in which capacity he had been secretary of the Boulloche working party. As such, he was not only well informed about official views on Rhine–Rhône, but had no problem of access to his former colleagues. He was appointed to the governing bodies of the SEMNM by the Besançon Chamber of Commerce, Peugeot sometimes preferring to act indirectly through chambers of commerce and regional economic development organisations. (It prefers to deal with the big nationalised railway and electricity firms directly but with local administration indirectly. While direct contact was more likely to yield results, too obvious an expression of interest might have prompted a demand from the government that Peugeot share in the cost of the waterway.) Peugeot's main short-term motive seems to have been a desire to have a publicly financed alternative mode of transport, to enable it to beat down rail and road charges, rather than any intention to make major use of the waterway, which in any case would take many years to complete. Such a surmise is reinforced by three examples. The Salzgitter steel company persuaded the Federal German government to build the Elbe Canal and then did not use it because it was able to sign a ten-year contract obtaining a 20 per cent tariff discount from the Bundesbahn. Thus, the German government had not only squandered millions of marks on the canal, but in addition had to subsidise the increased railway deficit! Similarly, in France the SNCF decision to electrify the Dôle–Mulhouse line was partly motivated by a desire to discourage road and waterway competition for freight traffic, while in the Rhône valley SNCF sought to persuade industrial firms to sign five- or ten-year contracts at very low rates to avoid losing customers.

Little support for Rhine–Rhône could be counted upon from most trade associations or the peak business organisation, the CNPF, because of reluctance to upset the powerful road lobby, while the transport-users association was dominated by industrial users that did not favour the project. The waterways profession was very weak and divided, the mass of small shippers not being equipped with large barges and so having more to fear (especially from German competition) than to hope, compared with Strasbourg. (The main waterways journal was published in Strasbourg and was ardently pro-Rhine–Rhône.) It was, in fact, the Strasbourg Port Authority which was – with the help of its president and the town's long-serving deputy and mayor, Pflimlin – the waterway's main proponent.

Unlike the seaport of Marseille – whose port authority, chamber and mayor-deputy, Gaston Defferre, was second only to Strasbourg in its advocacy – it was a riverport, so Rhine–Rhône was a primary rather than a secondary preoccupation. The port authorities linked in the Association des Grands Ports de France, are influential bodies, managed by prestigious Ponts et Chausseés waterways engineers (but not the more numerous and powerful road and rail specialists) responsible both to their local authority, and to the Ministry of the Environment, but representing the interests of their industrial and commercial customers. The Strasbourg Port Authority was not only responsible for the local waterways administration on behalf of the central government, but ran its own industrial estates. It was not only a pivotal protagonist for Rhine–Rhône, but through the Strasbourg Chamber of Commerce was linked with another major cluster of support.

Chambers of commerce are among the most underrated actors in economic decision-making, being epitomes of the 'insider', *notable*-led bodies upon which the central government leans. The Ministry of Industrial Development, having rather weak field services, relies so heavily upon the chambers as sources of information and as policy instruments that in some respects they become virtually a substitute for such deconcentrated administration. The Strasbourg Chamber of Commerce was active not merely through local and regional economic expansion committees, consortia to defend the waterways, as well as through briefing local politicians on economic issues; it also operated nationally through an alliance of the chambers in support of Rhine–Rhône and internationally through a Union of Rhineland Chambers of Commerce. At the centre of this network was the Secretary General of the Strasbourg Chamber, close collaborator of Pflimlin before working with André Bord, the Gaullist who succeeded for a while to Pflimlin's political fiefdom. The political links of the Rhine–Rhône lobby were always closer with the centrists – initially the Christian Democratic MRP, strongly entrenched in Alsace – particularly the local and regional *notables*, who through their representation in local government and in the regional councils traversed by the waterway, were able to create an *illusion of unanimity* on its behalf, amplified by the regional press which reported the activities and speeches of the *notables*. Once the environmentalist opposition develop in the 1970s, the *notable* monopoly of regional views was effectively challenged and the press amplified public opposition to the waterway.

It was a leading centrist, the then President of the National Assembly Edgar Faure, who played a key role in securing a spectacular 'commitment' in November 1975 by President Giscard d'Estaing to the completion of the waterway by what its critics described as a 'political manoeuvre'. Faure had previously been inconspicuous, leaving matters largely to his close friend the senator-mayor of Dôle, vice-president of the Consortium for the Modernisation of the East and South-Eastern Waterways. However, chancing to meet the President of the Republic at the military airport of Villacoublay in September 1975, the superlatively crafty President of the National Assembly presuaded him to attend the Interregional (Six Regions) Conference in favour of the Rhine–Rhône link to be held in the old Burgundian *Parlement* at Dijon in November. Giscard took his decision, faced with two 'technical' reports. One was very hostile. It was prepared in the Ministry of *Equipement* (now Environment) and had the support of the Finance Minister. It sought to establish the wholly uneconomic character of the project as a public investment, dwelling upon its estimate that only 20 per cent of the cost would be covered in fifty years; viability required a traffic of 50 million tonnes of merchandise but only 10 million could be expected by 1990; the 'opportunity cost' of other transport schemes foregone – rail, road and waterway – was intended to clinch an unfavourable decision. The favourable report from the SEMNM argued that 100,000 jobs would be created over fifteen years; 22 milliard francs had already been spent, so why not spend another 6 milliard francs to avoid ending in a cul-de-sac; the annual state subsidy to the SNCF exceeded 6 milliard francs and the unprofitable Paris ring road had cost three times Rhine–Rhône. More important for the politicians was the pyschopolitical argument that the waterway would placate the restive frontier region of Alsace and bind it to France. With the decisive support of the Prime Minister Chirac and the Regional Planning Commissioner Monod, the pro-waterway side won the day, Monod having accepted in 1972, when Guichard was *Equipement* Minister, that the waterway should go ahead with a completion date of 1982! No Cabinet meeting or interministerial meeting discussed the issue; it was ultimately settled by the President of the Republic though there was enough ambiguity about the timing of the work to suggest that, thanks to resistance from the budget officials, it would not get underway until the end of the Seventh Plan, that is, the late 1970s (*Un Dossier*, 1979, pp. 202–6). Giscard was supposed to have told a 10-year-old boy at Dijon: 'You at least will see the Rhine–Rhône waterway!' This is an appropriate point to turn to the influential opponents who have so far been mentioned incidentally.

The main antagonist to the Rhine–Rhône scheme as a source of energy was the French electricity public corporation EDF, which felt particularly threatened by the CNR's desire to follow the German precedent of financing the cost of the Rhine–Main–Danube waterway by slightly increasing the unit charges for hydroelectric power. EDF was in general inclined by its economists to be hostile to the Rhine–Rhône projects, as we saw in connection with Pierre Massé's opposition (*Un Dossier*, 1979, pp. 47–52). The CNR – formally made responsible for building and operating the waterway by a January 1980 Act of Parliament, after long delays – encountered strong resistance not only from EDF (which did not like increasing electricity charges however minimally), but from its sponsor Ministry of Industrial Development. Furthermore, the Ministry of Finance did not like this autonomous quango, with its tendency to overspend. Unlike Ministry of the Environment engineers, who simply stopped work when the funds run out, the CNR pressed on. However, the CNR got the job because its staff was running out of work, so it would not be necessary to recruit new staff. Furthermore, there was the prospect that the work would proceed without a running battle to ensure that the annual budgets respected the undertakings of ministers.

As a means of transport the SNCF rail public corporation competes with roads and waterways for freight and can act as a brake on the CNR from within because like EDF it holds 25 per cent of the shares. It also has the advantage of lobbying from within the state apparatus, based upon its sponsor Transport Ministry helped by the *Polytechnicien* old-boy network. At the same time, through the traditionally important railworkers federation, it influenced the attitudes of trade unions – especially the CFDT – against the Rhine–Rhône waterway. The road lobby has the advantage of being popular with both the politicians and the public, assisted within the administration by a strong Roads Division. (Significantly, whereas a plan for roads was approved by the government, a waterways plan, though drawn up in 1971, was denied official recognition.) Waterways, by contrast, look to two ministries to defend their interests – Transport and Environment – and this is a source of weakness; coupled with the fact that the Waterways Division inside the latter is feeble and not keen on Rhine–Rhône, partly because it threatens to be financed at the expense of other waterway claims out of a declining, diminutive budget. Somewhat unexpectedly, it is the Foreign Affairs Ministry which, because of the 'European' dimension, has sometimes – notably in 1971 – lent the project influential support but attempts to secure EEC funding or financial participation by Germany or Switzerland have come to nothing. Because the ministries, especially the Budget Ministry, are decisive in whether or not policies are actually implemented and at best are highly suspicious of vast schemes that involve long-term financial commitments, it is likely that Rhine–Rhône will, for at least a decade, be a waterway of *tomorrow*, proceeding at waterway speed. Extended argument over what part of the cost will be borne by the interested regional councils provides scope for further delay.

While Rhine–Rhône was little discussed at elections, substantial environmentalist opposition built up in Alsace and Franche–Comté in the 1970s, in which an active part was played by an Anti-Canal Liaison Committee and the splinter socialist party, the PSU, on the spot. The inquiry into whether the scheme was in the public interest provided the occasion and the environmental impact studies the matter for much heated argument from time to time in the regional press in the second half of the 1970s. The national mass media largely ignored the issue. Most of the political parties tended to articulate the views of others; in the case of the non-communist left the views of the trade unions or environmentalists; the centre, those of the *notables*; the right, those of business and the senior civil service. The Communist Party fluctuated between a denunciation of Germany and big business, and complaints about delays in achieving it after all the past promises. Political parties in France, in any case, play a much less important part in the policy process than they do in most of the other countries of Western Europe.

Inconclusive conclusion

It is something of an understatement to infer that what we earlier described circumspectly as 'a *capacity* for policy initiatives, a *potential* for far-sighted planning and a *propensity* to impose its will when this is necessary to attain public objectives' is conspicuously absent in this instance. The waterway case demonstrates that even in France, with its reputedly assertive style of policy-making, the general pluralistic constraints operate, albeit in a distinctive fashion. Even if we discount the notorious fact that the case study approach to decision-making slants the findings in a pluralistic direction, it could be argued, moreover, that had we considered the case of the ambitious French electronuclear programme, we would on the contrary have shown that capacity was abundantly fulfilled, the potential attained and the propensity realised in practice (Lucas, 1979; Gravelaine and O'Dy, 1978). Clearly, the politico-economic-administrative actors involved in the one case were able to keep the issue on the policy agenda without forcing it through to implementation, whereas in the case of the other more central and crucial problem, the political will, backed by support from key industrial and administrative actors, has so far been able to triumph over opposition without undue difficulty. Within the dual style we have argued to be characteristic of France, it can – in the absence of further detailed policy studies – only be speculative to suggest that the mobilisation of private interests in the service of public ambitions is, indeed, the salient element in the French policy style. Yet we have in 1981, with the coming to power of a socialist President of the Republic in the shape of François Mitterrand and of an overall socialist parliamentary majority, an invaluable opportunity to observe both the continuity and change in national policy style of which France is capable. The key political institutions of the Fifth Republic for the first time will all be controlled by the left, which has never heretofore either had the opportunity to carry out its programme, or to challenge the norms of the national policy style. What are some of the public ambitions in whose service the Mauroy government will seek to mobilise private interests as well as the public administration?

The new Prime Minister has argued that the French electors in 1981 voted 'not only for power to be exercised by different people, but in a different way'. He has promised not merely to changes in objectives – restoring full employment has become the salient target – but changes in the way they are to be attained. While public ownership and public investment are to increase, public power is to be reduced in many ways. Local and regional authorities are to have their capacity for autonomous action substantially increased (with drastic curbs on the prefect and treasurer paymaster-general), the executive is to be subject to a more independent judicial scrutiny, the radio and TV are no longer to be sycophantic official propagandists and the recourse to extensive telephone tapping against political opponents is to cease. The capacity for radical policy initiative seems to be intact, though it is too early to know how many of these changes will fully materialise. The potential for medium-term planning will be put to the test, following a two-year interim plan to grapple with the short-term problems. The new President and Prime Minister have stressed their desire to have genuine consultations before imposing their will in matters of public policy. Early examples of this were the decision to suspend the Giscardian electronuclear programme (and the abandonment of the Plogoff site in Brittany, though not of *any* future installation there) pending proper investigations and the encouragement of a negotiated reduction in working hours prior to legislation. After some initial hesitation, the Prime Minister confirmed – in traditional fashion – the decision to complete the Rhine–Rhône waterway but the prospects for rapid completion have receded because the funds will have to be shared with other canal projects. (The Rhine–Main–Danube Canal has been halted because the Bonn government has stopped contributing to the cost owing to current financial cutbacks.) As the pressure of events external to the national policy-making process increases in scale, intensity and tempo, the capacity of national policy styles to retain their distinctiveness can be expected to diminish. In France, however, such a retreat will be bitterly and obstinately resisted.

References: Chapter 5

Birnbaum, P., *Les Sommets de l'état: essai sur l'élite du pouvoir en France* (Paris: Editions du Seuil, 1977).

Birnbaum, P., Baruch, C., Bellaiche, M. and Marié, A., *La Classe dirigeante Française* (Paris: PUF, 1978).

Bodiguel, J. L., 'Les réunions interministérielles', paper to the Conference on 'L'administration et la politique en France sous la Ve République', Paris, November–December 1979.

Caroux, F. and Caroux, J., *Les Associations de cadre de vie: l'émergence de leur projet socio-politique* (Montrouge Centre d'Ethnologie Sociale et Psychologique), vol. 1 (1979).

Cohen, S., *Les Conseillers du Président: de Charles De Gaulle à Valéry Giscard d'Estaing* (Paris: Presses Universitaires de France, 1980).

Crozier, M., *The Bureaucratic Phenomenon* (Chicago: University of Chicago Press, 1964).

Crozier, M., *La Société bloquée* (Paris: Editions du Seuil, 1970).

Crozier, M., *On ne change pas la société par décret* (Paris: Grasset, 1979).

Crozier, M. and Thoenig, J.-C., 'L'importance du système politico-administratif territorial', in A. Peyrefitte, M. Crozier, J.-C. Thöenig, O. Gélinier and E. Sultan, *Décentraliser le responsibilités: pourquoi? comment?* (Paris: La Documentation Française, 1976).

Delion, A., 'Les conseils et comités interministériels', *Actualité juridique. Droit administratif,* vol. XXXI (June 1975).

Ehrmann, H., *Organised Business in France* (Princeton, NJ: Princeton University Press, 1957).

Ehrmann, H., 'French bureaucracy and organised interests', *Administrative Science Quarterly,* vol. V, no. 4 (March 1961).

Fomerand, J., 'Policy formulation and change in Gaullist France; the 1968 Orientation Act of Higher Education', *Comparative Politics,* vol. VIII, no. 1 (October 1975).

Gournay, B., 'L'influence de la haute – administration sur l'action gouvernementale sous la Vᵉ république', paper to the Conference on 'L'administration et la politique en France sous la Vᵉ République', Paris, November–December 1979.

Grant, W., 'Insider groups, outsider groups and interest group strategies in Britain', University of Warwick Department of Politics Working Paper, No. 19 (May 1978).

Gravelaine, F. de and O'Dy, S., *L'Etat EDF* (Paris: Editions Alain Moreau, 1978).

Green, D., *The Fos Maritime Industrial Zone: An Assessment* (London: HMSO, 1979).

Green, D., 'The budget and the plan', in P. G. Cerny and M. A. Schain (eds), *French Politics and Public Policy* (London: Pinter, 1980).

Grémion, C., 'Le milieu décisionnel central', paper to the Paris Conference on 'L'adminstration et la politique en France sous la Vᵉ République', Paris, November–December 1979a.

Grémion, C., *Profession: décideurs: pouvoir des hautes fonctionnaires et réforme de l'état* (Paris: Bordas, 1979b).

Grémion, P., 'Introduction à une étude du système politico-administratif local', *Sociologie du travail,* vol. XXII, no. 1 (January–March 1970).

Grémion, P., *Le Pouvoir périphérique: bureaucrates et notables dans le système politique français* (Paris: Editions du Seuil, 1976).

Hayward, J. E. S., *The One and Indivisible French Republic* (London: Weidenfeld & Nicolson, 1973).

Hayward, J. E. S., 'National aptitudes for planning in Britain, France and Italy', *Government and Opposition,* vol. IX, no. 4 (1974).

Hayward, J. E. S., 'Dissentient France: the counter political culture', *West European Politics,* vol. I, no. 3 (1978).

Hayward, J. E. S., 'From planning the French economy to planning the French state; the priority action programmes of the 1970s', in V. Wright (ed.), *Giscard and the Giscardiens* (London: Allen & Unwin, 1981); forthcoming.

Kammerer, L., *Un Processus de répétition dans l'échec: la non-decision 'Canal Rhine-Rhône',* University of Paris IX, Dauphine, UER of Organisation Sciences (1978).

Kessler, M. C., 'Le cabinet du Premier Ministre et la Secretariat-Général du Gouvernement', paper to the Conference on 'L'Administration et la politique sous la Vᵉ République', Paris, November–December 1979.

Kogan, M., *Educational Policy-Making: A Study of Interest Groups and Parliament* (London: Allen & Unwin, 1975).

Lucas, N. J. D., *Energy in France: Planning, Politics and Policy* (London: Europa, 1979).

Mayer, R., *Féodalité ou démocratie?* (Paris: Arthaud, 1968).

Meynaud, J., *Les Groupes de pression en France* (Paris: Presse Universitaires de France, 1960).

Meynaud, J., *Nouvelles études sur les groupes de pression* (Paris: Colin, 1962).

Meynaud, J., *Technocracy* (London: Faber, 1965).

Richardson, J. J., 'The environmental issue and the public', in *Decision Making in Britain* (Milton Keynes: Open University Press, 1977), block V, 'Pollution and environment'.

Schonfeld, W. R., *Obedience and Revolt: French Behaviour toward Authority* (Beverly Hills, Calif.: Sage, 1976).

Schreiber, M., *L'Axe Mer du Nord–Méditerranée: la régionalisation française et l'Europe* (Paris: University of Paris II, 1979).

Sokoloff, S., 'Rural change and farming politics: a terminal peasantry', in P. G. Cerny and M. A. Schain (eds), *French Politics and Public Policy* (London: Pinter, 1980).

Suleiman, E., *Politics, Power and Bureaucracy in France: The Administrative Elite* (Princeton, NJ: Princeton University Press, 1974).

Suleiman, E., *Elites in French Society: The Politics of Survival* (Princeton, NJ: Princeton University Press, 1978).

Sultan, E., and Preiss, C., 'Les citoyens et l'administration', in A. Peyrefitte *et al.* (eds), *Décentraliser les responsabilités*, op. cit.

Tarrow, S., 'Regional policy, ideology and peripheral defence: the case of Fos-sur-Mer', in S. Tarrow, P. J. Katzenstein and L. Graziano, *Territorial Politics in Industrial Nations* (New York: Praeger, 1978).

Un Dossier: la liaison Rhine–Rhône, Notes et Etudies Documentaires, Nos. 4547–8. (Paris: La Documentation Française, December 1979).

Wright, V., *The Government and Politics of France* (London: Hutchinson, 1978).

Zysman, J., *Political Strategies for Industrial Order: State, Market and Industry in France* (Berkeley, Calif.: University of California Press, 1977).

6

Sweden in the 1970s: Police-Making Becomes More Difficult

OLOF RUIN, University of Stockholm

Introduction

In Sweden, as in other countries, there are fairly well-accepted ideas governing the policy process. These ideas, these norms for action, can be readily fitted into the basic typology of policy styles described in Chapter 1. In practice, this has meant that policy-makers, in their day-to-day political decision-making, should seek agreement among participants and avoid conflict; should try to build large majorities for policies rather than force their standpoint on minorities; and compromise rather than cling rigidly to their own policy preferences. Furthermore, this has meant an emphasis on trying to direct events rather than letting events dictate policy, on being active and innovative rather than reactive.

These norms for political action, although vague, have not been codified into formal statutes or constitutional documents. Nevertheless, the norms can be identified: individual politicians, when articulating fundamental views about the political life of Sweden, have tended to argue in these terms; the same approach can be found in reports from official committees and in government Bills presented to Parliament, and so on. And policy-makers themselves, in discussing policy issues, appear to recognise that such norms are important.

The way in which decisions are actually taken in Sweden – 'the standard operating procedures' – in some degree reflect those normative values. The policy process is divided into different phases, involving a multiplicity of participants and, as a result, is rather cumbersome. Thus, policy-making at the national level can be said to have followed a well-defined pattern. A commission is appointed to investigate the problem and to make recommendations. The commissions are appointed either by the Cabinet or, for lesser problems, by a central government agency. (Swedish central administration is characterised by an organisational distinction between comparatively small ministries and large independent agencies.) The commissions at times can be one-man commissions but usually contain many members. They consist, in varying combinations, of politicians, representatives of different interests, bureaucrats, independent 'experts', and so on. Their investigations usually take a long time – two, three, or occasionally several years. The commission's proposals are submitted to a number of public authorities and relevant interest groups for their comments (under the 'remiss' system). The government then drafts a Bill on the basis of the commission's report and the responses to it. After consideration in a parliamentary committee, Parliament reaches its decision. Finally, on the basis of the parliamentary decision, detailed regulations are often worked out within the administration (Birgersson and Westerståhl, 1979). This process, with all its different stages, is usually very time-consuming; it is not unusual for a period of six to eight years to elapse between the referral of a problem to a commission and the appearance of new regulations in the problem area, which can then be implemented.

It is one thing to hold norms considered important in political life – for instance, 'try to reach agreement', 'try to be innovative' – but it is another to put them into practice. There have, then, been variations, during the post-war period, in the degree to which these norms have been affected, from one policy sector to another and from one period of time to another.

The ability to reach consensus, measured by the lack of outwardly discernible conflict during the decisive phases of the policy process, has been particularly evident within certain policy sectors. This is particularly true in terms of foreign, defence and constitutional policy. The capacity to reach consensus has usually been considerably less with labour market, industrial and tax policies (Elvander, 1969). In other sectors the conflicts have at times been difficult to bridge, at other times they have been fairly small.

The ability to be innovative, to adopt an anticipatory policy style and to plan, has also varied according to policy sector and over time. Two areas which, over the decades, have been characterised to a particularly higher degree by an anticipatory and planning approach to problem-solving have been social policy and education policy. In the area of welfare policy Sweden has gradually built up a system unique in its scope. Virtually all aspects of human life have attracted public finance, and Sweden has been seen as a pioneer in creating a welfare state. Similarly, in education policy, it has gradually built up a system which has been characterised at all levels by the desire for comprehensiveness and broad accessibility of education. Thus, in the early 1950s a decision was taken concerning a uniform nine-year schooling period which would be obligatory for all children. After a decade of experimenting, it was decided that this school system should apply for the whole country. During the 1960s a decision was reached, after exhaustive investigations, concerning high schools. Again, a policy of comprehensiveness and amalgamation of different types of schools and study programmes was adopted. Finally, in 1977 it was decided to radically reform higher education, with great emphasis on co-ordination and, again, comprehensiveness (Premfors, 1980; 1981).

It is, of course, never an easy task to generalise about the degree of consensus and the approach to problem-solving in a country. It does appear, however, that Sweden has become particularly difficult to characterise in the early 1980s. It was easier to formulate generalisations a decade earlier. It was then reasonable to claim that Sweden, despite variations between and within policy areas and over time, was characterised by the norms and values discussed earlier. The normative and behavioural styles were rather close together. Much has happened during the 1970s to make it difficult to match behaviour in the policy field to these generally accepted norms.

It is not my intention in this chapter to discuss the practical application of policy-making norms in Sweden, for among other things, there is a lack of systematic data on the policy process. It is, however, possible to discuss a number of interrelated factors all of which have contributed to making it more difficult to make and implement policy decisions. An already complicated system of decision-making has been made more complicated. This development must, in all likelihood, have consequences for the application of the norms which emphasise consensus and anticipatory problem-solving.

Many of the problems which will be dealt with here are common to most West European societies; others are specifically Swedish. Sweden's development has a certain symbolic character in comparative terms. For a number of decades in the postwar period it was Sweden's turn to serve as a 'model'. Different aspects of Swedish society were held up as examples to be emulated – the everyday Utopia to which others could strive. This was true of industrial life and of the labour market, it was true of the welfare system that was built up and it was also true of certain aspects of the political system as others saw it. These 'images' were often formed by foreign journalists and foreign social scientists. Thus, in perhaps the most-quoted English language description of the Swedish political system, Anton described Swedish policy-making as:

> Extraordinarily *deliberative*, involving long periods of time during which more or less constant attention is given to some problem by well trained specialists. It is *rationalistic*, in that great efforts are made to develop the fullest possible information about any given issue, including a thorough review of historical experiences as well as the range of alternatives suggested by scholars in and out of Sweden. It is *open*, in the sense that all interested parties are consulted before a decision is finally made. And it is *consensual*, in that decisions are seldom made without the agreement of virtually all parties to them. (Anton, 1969; see also Rustow, 1955; Fleischer, 1967; Hancock, 1972; Tomasson, 1978)

In their turn the images served to strengthen the norms concerning consensus and the direction of reform, which were considered to characterise political life. Today, however, it has become less common to hold Sweden up as a model to emulate (Richardson, 1979). This changed image is a reflection of the problems which occurred during the 1970s, and which will be discussed below.

A New Economic and Social Situation

Economic conditions radically altered and deteriorated in Sweden during the 1970s, as was the case in a number of other advanced industrial countries. These changes appeared to be particularly striking in Sweden because of the country's tradition of exceptionally great economic progress.

During the early postwar years Sweden found herself in a uniquely favourable situation. The country had not been involved in a war and her industry was, therefore, intact. Her industrial strength was well suited to the reconstruction situation in Europe. Transport costs to the European market were negligible. Existing production was rationalised and made more efficient. Weak parts of industry were deliberately run down. Government, unions and employers co-operated in furthering the movement of labour from competitively weak sectors to undertakings and businesses which were more competitive and efficient. A great sense of calm prevailed on the labour market.

Sweden's extremely favourable economic position was weakened by degrees. Other countries began, within the framework of rapidly increased world trade, to penetrate into those areas where Sweden had specialised. Newly industrialised countries began, from the mid-1960s, to offer strong competition within certain fields. The textile industry was the first branch of industry to run into serious difficulties. Yet the gross national product continued to increase during the whole of the 1960s and early 1970s.

The difficulties became conspicuous during the 1970s. The type of problem which had earlier affected the textile industry now struck those industrial branches which had traditionally been absolutely central to the Swedish economy: shipbuilding, steel and iron ore. The rate of growth in the country's economy was for many years exceptionally low. Unit wage costs were allowed to rise considerably in comparison with other countries. In addition, the oil crisis hit Sweden particularly hard by virtue of the fact that the country has a very energy-intensive industry, while at the same time it lacks energy sources (other than water and nuclear power). Inflation has increased; during the latter half of the 1970s the rate of inflation in Sweden tended to be above the OECD average.

At the same time the public sector has continued to grow. This has been in part due to increased costs in existing areas of public expenditure, but also because governments have extended their areas of responsibility. Public consumption has therefore continued to increase, notwithstanding an extremely low industrial growth rate. The tax burden has as a consequence been very high. Even so, tax revenues have been insufficient to finance the public sector. The resultant gap has been bridged by foreign loans and the country had incurred an avalanche of foreign debts. The deficiencies in Sweden's economic position are only too obvious at the beginning of the 1980s (SOU, 1980).

The policy style which was long considered to operate in Sweden – that is, consensus and anticipatory problem-solving – was naturally closely coupled to a continuing growth economy. Its aim was to distribute surplus and to draw up plans for a future which, it was believed, would provide ever more resources. In a very short time the situation has radically changed. Instead of distributing surplus, the current aim is to redistribute or cut down. Instead of planning new costly reforms, the aim is to consider economies and reductions.

Social conditions in the country have not changed as radically as economic conditions, but there have been developments there too. For example, relations between different groups within the population were traditionally very good and peaceful. Sweden was characterised by social harmony. That was considered to be a result, among other things, of the population being fairly homogeneous in terms of language, religion and race. That is no longer true. The 1960s saw a large influx of foreign immigration. Today no fewer than 1 million of Sweden's population of just over 8 million are immigrants, or the children of immigrants. Finns comprise the largest immigrant group. The area of Greater Stockholm has a particularly large immigrant sector concentrated in particular areas of the city. Tensions have arisen between immigrants and non-immigrants, although they have as yet not taken on any dramatic form.

Relations on the Swedish labour market used to be considered almost unique among the industrial nations of the West. Few working days were lost as a result of industrial conflict. The explanations for this peaceful state of affairs were seen to lie in strong organisations of employers and unions, in centralised negotiations, in a high degree of independence and a sense of responsibility among the organisations themselves and, of course, in the favourable economic preconditions. The situation became more difficult during the 1970s. The number of 'wild-cat' strikes increased; the most notorious one occurred in the late autumn of 1969 in the mining area of Kiruna. Normal bargaining negotiations between the chief organisations in the labour market were fraught with difficulties in the prevailing economic climate. The risks of further disputes increased. A large dispute broke out in the spring of 1980; it was the largest labour dispute which Sweden had suffered since the great strike of 1909. Almost 700,000 workers were affected by the dispute; a minority had been called out on strike by the unions; a majority was locked out (Forsebäck, 1980). It seemed that the much-vaunted understanding between labour and capital which had contributed to the efficiency of the economy had suffered a very serious blow.

In the mid-1960s it was not unusual for Swedes to see their country as an almost perfect society of prosperity, happiness and peace. The work of reform seemed to have been concluded. Quite soon, however, as new investigations were published, it was realised that many people still lived under difficult social conditions despite the great achievements in creating a welfare state. By the 1970s increasing attention was paid to people who, in a number of ways, had 'dropped out' of ordinary life: those who could not keep up with the tempo of work, who met with misfortune and became disabled, who sank into alcohol and drug abuse, and so on. Protest and criticism became commonplace; new demands were made. The earlier feeling in the country that everything was continuing to improve seemed to be flagging.

The social welfare system which was built up during the postwar period is no longer quite the same as it was. Charges have been introduced to an increasing extent, benefits have decreased in value, and so forth. A dramatic dismantling or rundown of this comprehensive welfare system was, however, not attempted during the 1970s. Neither was a conspicuous increase in unemployment allowed to develop, in spite of the country's economic difficulties. The costs of this social support system have obviously become very high and partly explain the growth in public expenditure. Despite those difficulties, the population's appreciation of, even pride in, this system remains considerable in comparative terms. Thus, in a survey carried out in a number of countries in the winter of 1977–8 people aged 18–24 were asked if they thought that their own country had something to be proud of. Of those who were questioned in Sweden no fewer than 60 per cent listed social welfare (Zetterberg, 1980).

The changes which have occurred in the economic and social milieux have to some extent brought about increased tension in society. Relations between labour and capital have been sharpened; inflation has been high and many groups have experienced a decrease in their living standards; antagonisms have developed within the area of tax legislation between citizens who have succeeded in evading or lessening their tax burden and those who have not been able to do that; the deviant groups within society seem to arouse greater distrust than previously. Opposition has even arisen to the very concept of social progress based on expectations of continued growth and a continued increase in material advantages for different groups. Actions in support of environmental protection have often assumed quite drastic forms – 'unconventional participation' has increased.

How have policy-makers responded to these developments? Over 300 senior civil servants were interviewed in 1971 in order to discover their views of different phenomena in the country. Many of the questions related to the problem of increased tensions in society. Are there conflicts, what are their causes and have they lessened or increased? The interviews took place shortly after two notorious events which were taken by many to be an omen of a more acrimonious social climate. The first event was the 'wild-cat' labour dispute in the orefields in Kiruna in the late autumn of 1969. The second event has become known as the 'battle of the elms'. The issue concerned a park in central Stockholm (Kungsträdgården). In 1971 environmental protesters surrounded a grove of elms which were to be felled to make way for a new underground station. Eventually the police had to be called to protect the workers against the demonstrators. Despite these contemporary events (which, in the context of Sweden, are very dramatic) the survey responses were rather reassuring. Sweden was seen as not without conflicts, but the conflicts were not perceived as fundamental. In general they were not of a class character, they in no way constituted a threat to social harmony. Indeed, almost two-thirds of those interviewed thought that the divisions in society had lessened during the past fifteen to twenty years (Anton, 1980; Mellbourn, 1979).

Unfortunately, there is no corresponding data for the beginning of the 1980s. One can only speculate about how policy-makers see the situation in the country. It seems likely that they would consider the conflicts to be more profound than ten years ago. An opinion poll in the autumn of 1980, based on a sample of the whole population, certainly shows that the average Swede's view of his own country has quite clearly changed during the past decade. For example, one question was concerned with views of life in Sweden. In 1975 68 per cent thought that Sweden was a very good country to live in; by 1980 this proportion had fallen to only 50 per cent. Another question concerned faith in the future. In 1975 28 per cent had considerable confidence in Sweden's future; by 1980 this proportion had fallen to 11 per cent (Törnqvist, 1980, p. 106).

Increased tensions in a society obviously have consequences for a policy style which has placed great emphasis on consensus and anticipatory problem-solving. The impacts are, however, not completely clear. It might be the case, for example, that it can be easier to ultimately reach agreement when the original disagreements are sufficiently large than when they are relatively small, because of the fear that continued dissension might turn into serious social conflict. But as a rule it can be assumed that the very appearance of increased tensions reduces the possibility of reaching agreement and consequently of taking long-term action to solve problems.

Changes at the Parliamentary Level

The parliamentary situation in Sweden underwent a number of radical changes during the 1970s. An essential change lay in the fact that the constitutional framework was altered. In 1975 a completely new constitution replaced the 1809 constitution, which for many years had been the second oldest written constitution in the world. (The 1975 reform was, in fact, preceded five years earlier by a series of basic changes to the 1809 constitution, later incorporated in the new constitution.) Thus, a legislature consisting of two chambers was replaced by a unicameral Parliament of 350 members (later reduced to 349). A change was also made to elections every third year, with parliamentary, county and municipal elections taking place simultaneously. Previously, there were biennial elections resulting from elections every fourth year to the county councils, which in their turn elected the First Chamber and direct elections to the Second Chamber every (other) fourth year. A previous voting system which, although characterised by proportionality, involved some over-representation for the largest party, was replaced by a voting system with two characteristic features: complete proportional representation in the distribution of seats for all parties which receive at least 4 per cent of the votes cast; no representation at all in Parliament for parties which fall below this figure. In several respects the new Swedish constitution, in comparison with the old, promotes greater instability in political life and allows greater scope for sudden change: now there is a single-chamber instead of a two-chamber legislature; the entire legislature is elected at one point in time instead of elections being spread out over several years; the election periods are shorter; and finally, the largest party is no longer over-represented.

Five parties have remained represented in the Parliament (Riksdag): the Conservatives, Liberals, the Centre Party (formerly Agrarians), Social Democrats and Communists. Sweden's multi-party system has ancient roots. Conservatism, liberalism and social democracy as political tendencies were already established at the turn of the century; the predecessors of today's Centre Party and Communist Party date from a somewhat later period. The five established parties are furthermore well integrated and cohesive; they all have a strong organisation. The hurdle of 4 per cent which has applied since 1970 makes it, on the whole, very difficult for new parties to establish themselves in national politics.

Fluctuations in support for the Conservative, Liberal and Centre parties – the three parties generally recognised as the 'bourgeois' parties – have tended to be large in Swedish politics, and these changes persisted during the 1970s. The Conservative Party (*Moderata Samlingspartiet*), which at the beginning of the decade was the smallest of the three, with only 11·5 per cent of votes at the general election in the autumn of 1970, had become, by the end of the decade, the largest 'bourgeois' party, with 20·3 per cent of the votes at the general election in 1979. The Liberals (*Folkpartiet*), who had dominated the 'bourgeois' side during the first postwar decade, recorded considerably lower figures during the 1970s; at the 1973 election they ended up with less than 10 per cent. Finally, the Centre Party

(*Centerpartiet*) recorded the greatest election successes in its history during the 1970s, with an all-time record of 25·1 per cent at the 1973 election, only to see itself overtaken as the largest 'bourgeois' party by the Conservatives.

The *central* event in Swedish party politics during the 1970s was, of course, the defeat of the Social Democrats in the 1976 election. Apart from 100 days during the summer of 1936, the party had enjoyed an unbroken spell in power since 1932 either independently, or in alliance with one or more of the 'bourgeois' parties.

The division into two blocks in Swedish politics – a 'two-party' system rather than a multiparty system – was strengthened during the 1970s. Paradoxically, at the same time, the traditional right–left dimension of Swedish politics was somewhat weakened. Earlier decades, characterised by strong economic growth, had to a great extent been centred on the politics of social reform and the distribution of the country's increasing resources. In this context the political parties had generally aligned themselves within a right–left spectrum, with the conservatives and the communists providing the respective extremes. During the 1970s, however, environmentalism emerged as a central issue. The environmental issue had three important dimensions: protection of the physical environment; the possible hazards of the nuclear energy programme; and the questioning of the desirability of further economic growth. These questions brought to the fore a latent dimension in Swedish politics – the industrial-agrarian dimension. Conservatives and Social Democrats each tended to support continued technical, high industrial development which, in its turn, was considered to presuppose large units and centralised government. The Centre Party, and to a certain extent the Communists, expressed unease about high industrial development and placed considerable emphasis on small units and decentralisation (Petersson, 1977). On the nuclear energy issue, both the Centre Party and the Communists have fought against the continued exploitation of nuclear energy and for a swift dismantling of those nuclear power stations already in existence.

At the parliamentary level the most important development in the 1970s, parallel to the new constitution, was the weakening of the executive. The power of the government is considered to depend on the size of its parliamentary support; upon the degree of unity within the governing majority; and, naturally, upon its general competence and political skill. Strong government is taken to mean an ability to take unpopular decisions, an ability to distance itself from special interests, and an ability to formulate long-term plans (Ruin, 1968).

Government had, since the 1930s, a reasonably secure parliamentary majority within the framework of the two-chamber system. (At certain times this majority was achieved through so-called combined voting – voting including at the same time members of both the First and the Second Chamber – at other times the government had its own majority in both chambers.) In the 1970s, however, the situation was different. During the parliamentary session 1970–3 the Social Democratic government, led by Olof Palme, lacked a majority in its own right but could count on support from a majority block of Social Democrats and Communists combined. During the 1973–6 session the Social Democrats continued in office but their parliamentary support had shrunk to exactly half of the Members of Parliament. Sweden experienced a peculiar period of so-called *lottriksdag* (a pun combining 'lotteri' and 'Riksdag') with a number of tied votes in Parliament. During the first two years of the 1976–9 session the three 'bourgeois' parties formed a majority government under the leadership of the leader of the Centre Party, Thorbjörn Fälldin; for one year a Liberal minority government, under the leadership of Ola Ullsten, held office, notwithstanding the fact that the Liberals were one of the smallest parliamentary parties. The last government of the decade, which came to power after the general election in the autumn of 1979, was once again a 'bourgeois' majority government under the leadership of Thorbjörn Fälldin, but with only a single-seat majority over the Social Democrats and Communists.

The strength of a government is also related to the degree of unity within the government itself. Earlier coalition governments in modern Swedish parliamentary history had either consisted of two parties, or as in wartime, of all the larger parties. The two coalition governments of the 1970s, however, consisted of three parties of reasonably equal strength. As a result there were significant problems of co-ordination. Indeed, Fälldin's first government split after two years over an issue (nuclear energy) on which the government parties had earlier shown that they were deeply divided. In the spring of 1981 Fälldin's second three-party government broke up as well; this time the three 'bourgeois' parties could not agree on the future tax policies to be pursued. A minority government was formed, consisting of the Centre Party and the Liberals.

Swedish parliamentarism, during the past decade, showed itself to be significantly less successful in providing strong government in at least two important dimensions: majoritarian government, and a degree of cohesiveness and integration in the policy field. This adverse development coincided with the country's difficult economic problems. In addition, as we shall see, bureaucracy continued to expand and special interests strengthened their role in the policy process.

The Growth of Bureaucracy and Increased Sectorisation

The growth in the public sector implied both a growth in the number of administrative agencies, and a growth in the number of administrators. This was due to the addition of new public responsibilities and to the demand for increased quality and effectiveness in established areas of public responsibility. Furthermore, the growth itself accelerated the increase; growth in individual sectors caused an increase in the number of those employed in public co-ordination and information roles.

The total number of central administrative agencies was reckoned in 1975 to have reached about 300. Almost one-third of them were less than five years old. Within this multitude of agencies, whether new or old, there was a gradual vertical and horizontal differentiation: new layers were established, new divisions and groups came into being, new co-ordinating mechanisms created, and so on. The number of people employed in central public administration was approximately 50,000 in 1975, in addition to employees at the regional and municipal levels. In particular, the Swedish municipalities have very extensive areas of responsibility. The *total* number of people employed in the public service during the ten-year period 1965–75 rose from 700,000 to 1·2 million, with the most marked increase at the municipal level (Tarschys, 1978, pp. 61–4).

This large public apparatus – large even if one ignores the expansion at the local level – can be seen as an instrument in the hands of a government which is oriented towards anticipatory problem-solving, towards being innovative, and so forth. The central administration's area of responsibility has not only been considered to be one of guaranteeing a competent and just implementation of new social responsibilities, decided by Parliament and government, but also one of active participation in the shaping of society. The central agencies have their independence but have often maintained very close relations with their sponsoring ministries. These relations seem to have been particularly close during the long period of Social Democratic rule. The individual ministers held office for a long time; they often appointed people as heads of central agencies whom they had worked with or whom they knew well; the heads of these agencies and other senior civil servants often regarded politicians not as a 'disturbing' element in their work, but rather as partners co-operating with them (Mellbourn, 1979, p. 135). The close and confidential relations between the central administration and the government seem to have weakened somewhat during the late 1970s.

Over the last decade, even though the central administration was regarded as a valuable and necessary instrument in the effort to continuously and consciously 'drive society forward', it was also the subject of criticism because of its expansion. The administration was so extensive as to be difficult to survey, difficult to manage and difficult to control. It was also felt that parts of this apparatus, with its large resources, had tended to appear less as partners to government and Parliament in the reform process and more as the initiator and driving-force. This was seen as a retrograde step in that it was not elected representatives or indeed interest groups who were making demands, but bureaucrats in dynamic central agencies. Finally, it was also claimed that the administration, through its very size and its extensive network of administrative agencies and organs, tended to paralyse the work of reform rather than force it through. Agreement about new measures and new reforms could be even more difficult to reach when the conflicting bureaucratic interests had to be accommodated.

The size and diversity of the administration, which is a reflection of the general expansion of the public sector, has also contributed to the promotion of a sectorisation of governmental activity. The policy sectors can be rather autonomous, although considerable variations occur. During the 1960s and early 1970s there was a tendency to deliberately encourage this very sector-oriented thinking. It was part of an emphasis given at that time to long-term planning, to reasoning in terms of goals and in terms of means expected to lead to a realisation of these goals. Sectorisation was seen as a way of facilitating and promoting effective social planning (Lindensjö, 1981). This view was also reflected in the amalgamation of separate government agencies into agencies representing coherent sectors. The desire to integrate related agencies in order to facilitate co-ordination can be illustrated by the social and education sectors; these were the two policy areas that, by way of introduction, we suggested were typical of a desire to plan and to be change-oriented rather than being conservative. Today there is one central agency, the National Board of Health and Welfare (*Socialstyrelsen*), which, on a national level, is responsible for both health and social welfare; a single central agency, the National Board of Education (*Skolöverstyrelsen*), is responsible for all education at elementary and secondary level; a single central agency, the National Board of Universities and colleges (*Universitetsoch Högskoleämbetet*), is responsible for all higher education in the country (with the exception of agricultural education).

A sector-consciousness in Swedish administration has also been promoted by the fact that central administrators tend to stay within the same sector during the whole of their professional life. This does not mean, however, that they are necessarily in the same jobs or have the same employer. They can move between ministries, various commissions, central agencies, Parliament, local government and administration, and even in the private sector (for example, working for interest groups). But they do tend to be occupied with the same policy issues. They are sector specialists, not so-called generalists, able to move from one sector to another. There are, of course, sector variations but many policy areas seem very stable in personnel terms. The education bureaucracy, which increased greatly in line with the education 'explosion' of the 1960s, is a good example of a bureaucracy which exhibited great stability. Moreover, many of those who today hold key posts within this bureaucracy were at one time recruited straight from activity in student organisations which had traditionally played an important role in Swedish education policy (Ruin, 1979). It has to be added that Swedish civil servants have no common educational background and have not been through any special institutions (such as the ENA in France) as a preparation for service in public administration.

The problems caused by sectorisation have recently become more apparent. Cross-sectoral conflicts occur as well as delays caused by the need to achieve some co-ordination. In fact, much effort has been spent in trying to find methods for effective and rapid co-ordination. A variety of contacts and institutional arrangements have been tried.

Corporatism

Sweden has a long tradition of a strong centralised interest group system, with very high membership levels. The country has three employee organisations: the Swedish Confederation of Trade Unions (*Landsorganisationen*, LO); the Swedish Confederation of Professional Associations (*Sveriges Akademiska Centralorganisation/Statstjänstemännens Riksförbund*, SACO/ SR), representing salaried staff with an 'academic' training; and the Swedish Central Organisation of Salaried Employees (*Tjänstemännens Centralorganisation*, TCO), representing the remaining white-collar employees. The Swedish Employers' Confederation (*Svenska Arbetsgivarforeningen*, SAF) is the main representation of private employers. The country's municipalities and county councils each have their own central organisation: the Swedish Municipalities' Association (*Kummunförbundet*) and the Swedish County Councils' Association (*Landstingsförbundet*). Farmers have established producer co-operative organisations; over 1 million consumers belong to a consumer co-operative movement, with the Swedish Cooperative Union and Wholesale Society (*Kooperativa Förbundet*, KF) as the central organisation. Temperance organisations and free church organisations also play an important role.

In addition, there has also been a long tradition of close contact between interest groups and government. The groups have been indirectly represented in Parliament in the sense that many parties have been careful to nominate candidates with interest group links. The groups are well represented on government commissions which formulate new policy proposals. They also, within the framework of the 'remiss' system, have the opportunity to comment on these commission proposals. Furthermore, informal contacts are well established between the more important interest organisations and the government. For a few years in the 1960s representatives of the interest groups and members of the government met for informal negotiations at the Prime Minister's official country residence at Harpsund (giving rise to the term 'Harpsund democracy'). By the end of the 1960s, it had also become common practice to give the central interest organisations seats on the central agencies' laymen boards which were set up at that time (Elvander, 1969).

Central policy decisions have traditionally been preceded by extensive and time-consuming negotiations between government and interest groups. Foreign observers of Swedish politics who have characterised the Swedish policy process as 'deliberative', 'rationalistic', 'innovative' and 'radical' have often tended to ignore this dimension of long-drawn-out and often difficult negotiations. The processes of policy-making have instead been represented as being in the main shaped by purely intellectual considerations: the identification of problems, the investigation of correlations, the solving of problems.

Two policy areas from the 1960s, which have been analysed in detail, provide a good illustration of how policy decisions have indeed been preceded by clear negotiations between affected parties. One took place at the beginning of the decade and concerned the financing of higher education. A radical policy change was decided upon: a grant system, which had been gradually built up in earlier years, was replaced by a student loan system. The policy process proved difficult, with Olof Palme, chairman of the government commission proposing the change, playing the central role. A majority, consisting of the two large employees' confederations, LO and TCO, together with the Social Democrats and two 'bourgeois' parties, supported the decision. SACO, the trade union of those with academic training and the National Swedish Union of Students (SFS) remained firmly opposed to it and had parliamentary support from the Conservatives (Ruin, 1979). The other, less controversial, policy decision in the late 1960s concerned air pollution. The Swedish policy process in the air-pollution field has been contrasted with that in the USA. Thus, American air-pollution policy is characterised as being like a hare – sudden quick jumps – while Swedish policy moved gently and deliberately like a tortoise (Lundqvist, 1980). The policy process in Sweden took a long time; great efforts were made to find solutions acceptable to all concerned; significant policy change was achieved. In the area of environment policy it was therefore possible to reach a degree of consensus in contrast to the area of student finance.

The integration of interest organisations in national policy-making, though having a long tradition, was further extended and intensified during the 1970s. Paradoxically, this occurred as a response to the 'grassroots' unrest which hit Swedish society around the turn of the decade (Ruin, 1974). There was a sudden emergence, in many sections of society, of a dissatisfaction with the extent of the individual's influence on events. Members of established organisations, such as interest groups and political parties, demanded greater influence within their organisations; citizens at the local level wanted more participation; workers wanted to take part in the running of businesses; employees in public agencies wanted to have more say in the running of the agencies; students wanted to participate in the administration of universities, and so on. These groups directed their attention either at conditions outside Swedish borders – for example, Vietnam or apartheid – or at conditions within the country. It became extremely common to protest against measures which affected or even directly threatened the environment (Gidlund, 1978). The 'participation movement' also saw the creation of a large number of ad hoc 'action groups'.

From the government's viewpoint, it seemed vital that the demand for greater participation should be accommodated. One method was simply to give the 'discontented' seats on various policy-making bodies. This desire to integrate – and thereby to pacify – was particularly marked in higher education. It was quickly decided that student representatives should be elected to the many bodies of all universities and colleges. These had previously consisted mainly of professors. Participation by students in the governing bodies was soon followed by different employee groups within the universities and colleges: untenured faculty, staff, assistants, and so on (Ruin, 1982).

The long-established organisations also showed themselves to be very anxious both to channel this pressure for participation, and to encourage it. This applied above all to the trade unions. They regarded themselves as having a central role to play in the question of accommodating employees' demands for increased influence in the workplace – either public, or private. Participation issues were looked upon as a central trade union concern. During the 1970s the government reached a decision on employee representation, through local trade union associations, not only on the boards of private business but also on the boards of central agencies. This reform has meant that these boards now have two kinds of trade union representation: through the principle, introduced during the 1960s, of selecting some trade union representatives as lay members of the boards, and under the reform of including direct representation of local trade union branches. In addition, a decision was reached, during the 1970s, introducing a completely new type of relationship between employers and employees. It became incumbent on employers, whether private or public, to take the initiative in discussing important changes in working conditions with the trade unions. An extremely comprehensive negotiation machinery, called MBL, is set in motion when any changes are proposed within organisations (A. Gustafsson, 1979).

The extension of the integration of different groups in policy-making has thus been particularly important in the *implementation* stage of the policy process. Previously, the demand for participation had centred on earlier stages in the policy process (for example, in commissions *formulating* policy proposals, as well as in the opportunity existing thereafter to comment on the proposals). Now this participation has been extended to the implementation stage in that interest groups have been granted representation in the large number of agencies involved in public administration. It has not been considered as sufficient participation merely to be asked for advice and to put forward one's views. One should also be formally part of the decision-making. This development has been seen as increasing the degree of corporatism in Swedish society.

The intensification of participation of interest groups in policy-making has been accompanied by a series of justifying statements. It is considered valuable that representatives of those directly affected by decisions should participate in the different stages of the decision process; points of view can be continuously presented and taken into account; those affected feel, in addition, a responsibility for the decisions which emerge; this very responsibility can in turn contribute to effective implementation. Public policies, even if their achievement takes time, become 'well-anchored' and a sense of legitimacy concerning decisions is hopefully established.

The increased integration of groups in policy-making has, however, created many problems, particularly in terms of reaching decisions. One problem is the 'crowding' which has arisen. Those demanding more participation have still not been private citizens defending common citizens' interests, but simply groups. The number of more or less well-organised groups has increased as new policy problems have emerged. At the same time, many long-established organisations have had their position strengthened. The crowding, a result of both the formation of new groups and the extended activity of existing groups, has made it difficult to accommodate all demands for participation in the various stages of the policy process. Perpetual discussions are conducted, when new commissions are appointed, or various new bureaucratic bodies are being formed, about their size and composition. Negotiations are often long and difficult. Compromises are reached by having the same person represent different sections of society.

Another, considerably more serious, problem is that the increased participation of different interest groups can prolong the decision processes and can present difficulties in reaching agreement at all. The views presented can prove almost incompatible; the representatives of different interests can tend to distrust each other and block each other's proposals; they can be tempted to bring the decision processes to a standstill. In the formulation stage of the policy process it can become difficult to propose any measures at all which can be presented to Parliament for a decision; above all the risk can arise, even when Parliament does make a decision, that it may not be implemented in the way intended because a variety of interests, with different views, are also involved in the interpretation and implementation of decisions.

One result of increased conflict in the policy process, when the pressure to reach *some* agreement is strong, is vagueness and lack of clarity. For example, this can be seen in the comments on commission proposals submitted by various public agencies, as part of the 'remiss' system (Swahn, 1980). Also the amount of work involved in producing 'remiss' answers increased during the 1970s. The bodies which produce the agencies' views on these proposals generally include representatives of a large number of different interests. These representatives can have conflicting views about the commission reports, but instead of giving a clear indication of these different views, they tend, in the name of the agency, to indulge in woolly and imprecise formulations. The value of the submissions, as information about different opinions in society, is therefore reduced. It should also be added that the different interests, which within the framework of different public agencies take part in the shaping of submission answers are often simultaneously submission bodies (*remissinstanser*) in their own right and, therefore, have the opportunity of presenting their views and demands without the need to compromise.

A further consequence of intensified participation is the strengthening of sectorisation. Representatives of particular 'clients' are integrated into the management of agencies in some sectors and they have shown a tendency to form a coalition with agency staff in defence of the interests of their common sector; they also often receive support from the politicians involved in the work of the agencies. The negotiating position of the different sectors tends, therefore, to be strengthened – for example, in the face of the threat of a cut in appropriations – when the sector's spokesmen are no longer merely a number of prominent bureaucrats and politicians, but also representatives of different affected interest organisations.

Decentralisation

Policy-making is, of course, also conducted at a regional and local level. Policy-making at these lower levels (particularly in local government) has traditionally been of great importance for the lives of ordinary citizens. The importance of local government has further increased during the past decade. Efforts have been made to strengthen decision capacity at these levels and to transfer areas of responsibility to them from the national level.

At the regional level there are two public institutions, independent of each other: the county administrations (*länsstyrelserna*), with a governor at their head, and the county councils (*landstingen*). The county administration and governor represent the regional state administration, the county councils are directly elected at the same time as the general and local elections. For a long time the main duty of the county administration and the governor was to implement central laws; the chief duty of the county councils was to organise health care in the country in co-operation with central administrative agencies. The distinction between the two types of regional authority is now less clear and there is some debate about future arrangements. Regional tasks have increased. For example, an extensive planning capacity has been established over the last decade or so; greater efforts are now made at the regional level to pursue anticipatory policies and to improve the co-ordination of different social programmes at this level. A move in this direction was the reform of regional state administration in 1971. A board was established for each regional administration, chaired by the governor, consisting of regional politicians and representatives of different interests (Hagström, 1978).

At the local government level there is a very strong tradition of far-reaching local independence (for example, local authorities have wide taxation powers). In the postwar period there have been periodic amalgamations of local authorities. At the beginning of the 1950s there were over 2,400 municipalities still in existence, but by the beginning of the 1960s the number had dropped to approximately 1,000 and today the country has only 279 municipalities. These amalgamations, spectacular in comparative terms, were based on the belief that large units are necessary if an effective service is to be provided. The decision processes which led to the reorganisations are, in fact, a good example of policy-making which has been substantially characterised by an anticipatory planning approach and a strong desire for change (G. Gustafsson, 1980).

As a part of the conscious effort at decentralisation in society during the 1970s, responsibilities that previously were the task of central agencies have to some extent been handed over to these strengthened local authorities . This has happened, for example, in both social and education policy; duties which had earlier been the responsibility of the central agency for higher education have, however, not been transferred to these lower levels, but to six new regional boards as well as to the individual universities and colleges. The central agencies have to a corresponding degree begun to change character. They are less concerned with detailed administration, within the framework of guidelines laid down by Parliament, and are more concerned with general areas of responsibility such as advising regional and municipal bodies, co-ordination and long-term planning. There has also been an attempt to reduce the numbers employed in these agencies.

The nature of the actual legislation has also changed in line with the goal of decentralisation. Thus, 'framework' legislation has become more common; specific regulations are left to administrative agencies, often on a regional and local level. Also, the criteria which are laid down in the text of the law, for the application of different regulations, have become increasingly vague. Phrases such as 'general interest' and 'existing needs of different kinds' are often applied to the application of the law. Vague formulations of this type naturally give greater flexibility to administrative agencies when they handle problems. And this greater flexibility will increasingly rest with the regional and local authorities, as a result of the decentralisation movement.

There were a number of causes of the decentralist movement in Sweden in the 1970s. An important explanation lies in the increased difficulty of reaching decisions at the national level. Central administration had become too large and difficult to manage and it was thought possible to reduce its size through decentralisation; the adverse effects of sectorisation could be reduced by decentralisation as more effective co-ordination could be achieved at the local level; and people's ability to influence decisions affecting them could be increased when those very decisions are taken at a point closer to them (SOU, 1978). A further advantage of decentralisation was that difficult problems could be exported to a lower level (Gustafsson and Richardson, 1979). The more general the legislation, the more the problem is left to those who are involved in implementation lower down the system. The wish to decentralise during the latter half of the 1970s has to some extent been influenced by the shift in political power and a certain suspicion within the non-socialist majority, of central agencies and the role they have played over the years. Distrust developed, among other things, because social democratic values and attitudes seem to have persisted in many central agencies as a natural consequence of the Social Democrats having held office for more than forty years. Signs of this distrust have been efforts on the part of the ministries, parallel with the efforts of decentralising duties from the central agencies to lower levels of government, to take over duties from the same agencies and to steer them more effectively.

A tendency has also arisen, particularly obvious in recent times, to begin to question the very dominant role that the state has come to play in Swedish reform policy. Voluntary initiatives have not, so many have thought, been sufficiently encouraged. This applies to individual initiatives as well as to initiatives of different groups. The central government, the county councils and the municipalities have assumed too great a responsibility for the welfare of the population.

An important consequence of the efforts in the 1970s to decentralise is that the importance of the implementation process has increased. Important decisions about the solution of social problems are no longer only taken in commissions, in Cabinet and Parliament and in central agencies. What happens when regional and local bodies of different kinds have to carry out centrally shaped regulations has begun to assume almost equal importance. The results are often difficult to calculate. The centrally shaped regulations have tended to become, as suggested earlier, increasingly vague in their formulation; the affected interests are nowadays themselves involved in the implementation process.

One of the prices which has to be paid for decentralisation is greater uncertainty about what is actually happening in society. Future judgements about whether the Swedish policy style remains anticipatory, change-oriented, innovative, increasingly depend upon evaluations of what *de facto* occurred. Monitoring society and the supply of information is likely to assume greater importance.

Monitoring Society and the Supply of Knowledge

There has been a long tradition in Sweden of a close connection between knowledge and politics. The knowledge sought and collected has been of a varying nature: from rather unsophisticated collections of facts to advanced scientific reports. The close connection between knowledge and politics corresponds to the prevailing attitudes that one should try to plan for the future and try to be anticipatory and innovative. This close connection does not mean, however, that Swedish politics can be said to be a very intellectual and technological process; again and again, it has been emphasised that this very process involves continuous bargaining between a series of well-integrated interests.

The connection between knowledge and politics was especially promoted during the first postwar decades within the framework of the Royal Commissions. The very elaborate system of commissions did not have, and continues not to have, its own research institute, although the idea has been discussed. In contrast, the individual commissions often do have large secretariats with well-qualified personnel. In addition, many commissions go outside their secretariats and initiate commissioned research, generally from the universities. Many commission reports can, in fact, be pure research reports (Foyer, 1969). It is also common to appoint scientists as members of commissions, besides politicians, bureaucrats and representatives of different interests.

Towards the end of the 1960s, and particularly during the 1970s, a conspicuous increase, as well as a change of emphasis, occurred in Sweden's conscious efforts to exploit research and development work (R&D) in the shaping of public policy. Large grants for research and development have been awarded by the ministries in fields such as social welfare, the labour market and communications. These grants have been used by the ministries themselves, by central agencies subordinate to the ministries, or by new bodies set up to initiate research. The expanding resources for R&D were closely tied to the different sectors that the public programmes tended to form. Those in charge of sectors – and not least the bureaucrats working within a sector – should be able to commission research to assist long-term planning, to set goals and methods, as well as to monitor and evaluate what is actually happening within their own sector. Also a large part of this research has been commissioned at the universities. Comparatively little so-called 'in-house research' is carried out in ministries and central agencies; there are also comparatively few research institutes independent of the universities. There is currently much discussion of 'sectorial research' as well as the 'principals of sectorial research' in the country's science policy (Wittrock, 1980). The explosion of this kind of research in the 1970s has, moreover, contributed to a further strengthening of sectorisation.

Increased production of information does not necessarily amount to a complicating factor in policy-making in the same way as bureaucratisation, sectorisation, corporatism and decentralisation. There are, however, two consequences worth mentioning of the increasingly close connection which has arisen between research, concentrated in the universities, and politics and administration. One consequence of this close connection is that few alternative lines of research have been pursued in regard to the solution of social problems. Most research is based on the assumptions of existing administrative agencies and established interests, even though the research is usually independent from those who commission it. This means that official policy proposals, accompanied by extensive research input, are seldom confronted with alternative proposals based perhaps on research from very different perspectives. Another consequence of this close connection is intensified discussion about the difficulties of effectively integrating R&D and the making of policies. The researchers are criticised for not producing research results on time, for being equivocal in their statements about their results, for using a language which makes communication difficult, and so on. The politicians who commission the research are criticised for ignoring the results. In Swedish politics, as in the politics of many other countries, research is utilised for much more than a direct basis for concrete measures: it used as a legitimating device, as a substitute for action, as a basis for discussion or, more generally, to widen the perspective of policy-makers.

The Policy Agenda

There is a final dimension to the increasing complexity in policy-making in the 1970s. This concerns the political agenda itself: the type of issues raised, the speed at which they are raised, and the degree of openness with which they are processed by the policy-makers.

Many issues have been difficult to solve. This has been especially true in the field of nuclear power, a question which has often dominated Swedish politics during the 1970s. It has proved difficult for policy-makers to understand all the technical issues involved, to judge the consequences of the production of this kind of energy in relation to the production of other types of energy, to make sensible projections about future energy production, and so on. The economic crisis, likewise dominating Swedish politics, has also proved very difficult to handle. Even though policy-makers, of course, have been more familiar with economic problems than with all the technical processes which lead to the production of nuclear energy, they have encountered a great many difficulties in trying to solve these problems. Previously applied economic models and recommendations no longer seem to apply.

The 'rhythm' of politics has speeded up. Issues emerge very quickly and are also removed from the agenda quickly. For example, the Swedish economy is very much open to foreign influences, and the problems of the outside world 'spill over' into the country. Domestic mass media, with their great influence, also have a tendency to concentrate attention on a few social problems, stressing their great importance, and then quickly move on to other issues. Yet at the same time, Sweden has its decision-making processes that are slow and thorough in a desire to involve all affected interests. Tensions have always been apparent between this rather sluggish policy process and the rapidly changing political agenda. During the 1970s, however, these tensions increased as external influences on Sweden increased. Nevertheless, the decision-making process has, if anything, become more cumbersome and slow to produce solutions.

This tension is resolved in a number of ways. For example, some decisions have been made outside the framework of the painstaking consultative process regarded as typically Swedish. In order to salvage or to prop up firms which were threatened with liquidation during the economic crises of the 1970s, the government has, for instance, undertaken 'fire brigade' actions, with very limited preparation time. Other decisions have indeed been taken in accordance with the painstaking consultative process, but the tempo of this process has increased considerably. A fully representative Royal Commission investigating the country's energy needs and available energy resources, successfully concluded its work in little over a year. In other cases, commission reports, which have taken a long time to complete, and after all the 'remiss' comments have been sent in, have been shelved because the state of affairs that the commission originally addressed itself to has in the meantime totally changed.

Openness in the making of policy, as well as in its implementation, has also increased. The Swedish policy process has traditionally been one of the most open systems, with public access to virtually all official documents. At the same time, views have existed that negotiations, as part of the ordinary decision-making process, are more effective if they are pursued behind closed doors. Exposure of what happens when decisions are reached, when orders are given and taken, can easily make the actors inflexible and unwilling to compromise. This desire for secrecy has been particularly strong in the Royal Commissions, where a consensus between competing interests had to be reached. Those involved in commission work have, however, also felt a need to constantly inform the interested parties about what is happening; the affected interests have on their part been uneasy about being bound in the future by what was agreed in semi-private. Lately the commissions have increasingly been more open in their investigations and negotiations. In addition, the watchful eye of the press has become keener in relation both to the commissions, and to other stages of the policy process as well. Politicians, as in all democracies, are constantly pressed by the media to discuss current policy problems, in the cause of more open government. This very openness often brings with it, however, greater difficulties in reaching decisions and formulating coherent policy solutions.

Conclusion: The Policy-Makers

Much of our earlier discussion has emphasised the increased difficulty in making and implementing public policies – the deteriorating economic situation and increased social tensions, changing party patterns, weaker government, increased sectorisation and the burgeoning bureaucracy, coordination problems between sectors, increased participation by groups and the speeding up of the policy process. These difficulties affect the capacity of the political system to produce policies which both achieve consensus, and actually solve real problems. Some of the factors discussed in this chapter make it particularly difficult to reach a consensus; others have a particularly adverse effect on the innovative capacity of the policy system. More importantly, the recent developments in the Swedish policy process have made it more difficult to realise at the same time the two types of norms discussed earlier, that is, that policy-makers should seek consensus yet should be anticipatory, innovative and oriented towards solutions which actually work. Ultimately, realisation of these norms is, however, to a large extent dependent upon the desire and the capacity of the central political actors to actually *behave* according to them.

One important characteristic of policy actors in Sweden today is what may be termed a 'loosening' of roles. In traditional textbook descriptions of the political process the main actors in the political system usually have quite distinct roles. Politicians are supposed to take policy decisions; the bureaucrats are supposed to carry out the decisions reached by the politicians; the representatives of different interests are supposed to look after their specific interests; the researchers are supposed to pursue their research in an unbiased manner; the journalists are supposed to record and illuminate events, and so on. In Swedish politics today these distinct roles are no longer maintained. For example, politicians work in central agencies; ex-politicians are appointed to high office within the administration. Civil servants themselves engage in politics and can simultaneously be MPs, as well as playing a key role in advising on the formulation of policy. The representatives of the large interest organisations are active in both politics, and in administration. Interest organisations concern themselves with questions far beyond their original areas of concern; they are represented in Parliament and in a number of central agencies. Researchers take part in politics and administration, as they do to some extent even in the work of the interest organisations; politicians, administrators and representatives of interest organisations influence, for their part, the world of research by virtue of the fact that they are represented on a number of research-initiating bodies. Journalists orchestrate, to a large extent, the political debate and contribute to the determination of the political agenda.

This loosening of functionally determined roles has often been con-sciously pursued and has been justified by reference to the norms relating to policy-making. For example, such justifications have been made when trade unions have been criticised for having opinions and pressing demands in most social areas. They have been said to distance themselves from their real duty, which is to safeguard their members' specific interests, not least in connection with wages. In defence of the trade unions, it has been said that this broad involvement in policy-making is useful in that it encourages the unions to have a sense of responsibility for the whole of society and that this responsibility is desirable just when the unions are trying to press their members' specific interests. A similar justification has also been advanced regarding the representation of different groups in policy-making within different agencies (for example, students in the universities). The critics of this development thought that it was unreasonable for representatives of special groups to take part in all the decisions which could be taken within an administrative agency; their participation should be limited to the business which directly affected them. Again, the wider participation was defended. By participating in a wide area of business and thereby develop-ing a wider societal perspective, purely sectoral and selfish interests might be modified. It is easier, so it has been argued, to reach agreement when everyone is familiar with the broad implications of issues, than when inter-ests are left to take a very narrow sectoral view.

Another characteristic of policy-makers in Sweden today seems to be a greater difference between their language used in private discussion and public debate. A deliberate and calm language tends to persist in non-public discussions. Although the variations are naturally endless, a 'matter of fact' tone continues to be adopted in the commissions and boards where policy decisions are prepared or taken. Participants feel their way carefully; they seldom invoke great principles; they are generally anchored in the present and do not cling to historical traditions or grandiose lines of development; they like to cite surveys and research of different kinds, and so forth. Yet at the same time in public debate, the sweeping, ideologically loaded statements have increased and personal attacks on opponents have intensified. Of course, this new tone to some extent reflects increased tensions in society. It can, however, also be traced back to a climatic change in public debate which affected Sweden, as it did many other countries, in the wake of the events of 1968. A more bombastic and more ideological language became accepted. Finally, the changes in linguistic usage in public debates can also be explained by the intensified competition for political power. The difference in size between the two political 'blocks' has remained very small. A state of political equilibrium easily gives rise to heated public polemics between those of equal strength in the hope of gaining some small advantage over the other. The hard words do not necessarily correspond to equally hard differences.

Other traits of Swedish policy-makers have tended to remain the same and to be conducive to consensus. For example, there exists a reluctance to take up clear positions early in the decision-making process. Naturally, even Swedish political life is full of examples where representatives of parties and interest organisations have felt the need to commit themselves very rapidly, and present very distinct profiles. Still, a tendency prevails to keep options open for as long as possible. There is a desire to avoid the controversial; to seek unity through vague formulations. Even voting, as a way of reaching a decision when there is disagreement, is not particularly usual outside Parliament and local councils, although it naturally occurs from time to time. Great efforts continue to be made to reach decisions through discussion.

The question remains as to whether the attitudes of Swedish policy-makers might have substantially changed during the 1970s, due to the different developments outlined in this chapter. Traditionally policy-makers have been strongly oriented towards reaching agreement and achieving compromise. This was explicitly verified by the previously mentioned survey undertaken in the early 1970s. A number of higher civil servants and MPs were asked: 'In a case of conflict or disagreement in which one side seems to you to be wholly in the right and the other side wholly wrong, do you think that the side which is in the right should stick to its guns or would you personally be motivated to seek a compromise?' Over 60 per cent of both administrators and politicians answered that they were definitely inclined to compromise or at least disposed towards compromise (Anton, 1980). No similar data exist for the early 1980s. It seems, however, very unlikely that any dramatic changes should as yet have occurred in the orientation of Swedish policy-makers toward reaching agreement and achieving consensus. A certain stability persists in what can be called the political culture.

These and other features of stability in the system should, finally, be seen as a reminder of the risks of interpreting events which have not yet run their course. The significance of what has happened can easily be exaggerated. In conclusion, however, it is very clear that different factors, of importance, have contributed to a more complicated policy-making process in Sweden over the last decade and that these factors have also influenced the application of the norms where both consensus and problem-solving are emphasised. Time will tell how deep or long-lasting this influence will prove to be.

References: Chapter 6

Anton, T., 'Policy making and political culture in Sweden', *Scandinavian Political Studies*, vol. 4 (1969), pp. 88–102.

166   POLICY STYLES IN WESTERN EUROPE

Anton, T., *Administered Politics: Elite Political Culture in Sweden* (Boston: Martinus Nijhoff, 1980).
Birgersson, B. O. and Westerståhl, J., *Den Svenska Folkstyrelsen* (Stockholm: Liber Förlag, 1979).
Elvander, N., *Intresseorganisationerna i Dagens Sverige* (Lund: Gleerups, 1969).
Elvander, N., *Svensk Skattepolitik, 1945–70* (Stockholm: Rabén & Sjögren, 1972).
Fleischer, F., *The New Sweden* (New York: McKay, 1967).
Forsebäck, L., *Industrial Relations and Employment in Sweden* (Stockholm: Swedish Institute, 1980).
Foyer, L., 'The social sciences in royal commission studies in Sweden', *Scandinavian Political Studies*, vol. 4 (1969), pp. 183–203.
Gidlund, J., *Aktionsgrupper och Lokala Partier: Tempörara Politiska Organisationer i Sverige 1965–75* (Lund: Liber Läromedel/Gleerups, 1978).
Gustafsson, A. (ed.), *Företagsdemokratin och den Offentliga Sektorn* (Lund: Studentlitteratur, 1979).
Gustafsson, G., *Local Government Reform in Sweden* (Lund: CWK Gleerup, 1980).
Gustafsson, G. and Richardson, J. J., 'Concepts of rationality and the policy process', *European Journal of Political Science*, vol. 7, no. 4 (1979), pp. 415–36.
Hagström, B., *1971 åre Länsförvaltningsreform: En Utvärdering* (Lund: Studentlitteratur, 1978).
Hancock, M. D., *Sweden: The Politics of Postindustrial Change* (Hinsdale, Ill. Dryden Press, 1972).
Lindensjö, B., *Högskolereformen. En studie i offentlig reform-strategi*, Stockholm Studies in Politics 20 (1981).
Lundqvist, L. L., *The Hare and the Tortoise: Clean Air Policies in the United States and Sweden* (Ann Arbor, Mich.: University of Michigan Press, 1980).
Mellbourn, A., *Byråkratins Ansikten: Rolluppfattningar hos Svenska Högre Tjänstemän* (Stockholm: Liber Förlag, 1979).
Petersson, O., *Väljarna och Valet 1976* (Stockholm: Liber Förlag, 1977).
Premfors, R., *The Politics of Higher Education in a Comparative Perspective: France, Sweden, United Kingdom*, Stockholm Studies in Politics 15 (1980).
Premfors, R., 'National policy styles and higher education in France, Sweden and the United Kingdom', *University of Stockholm, Group for the Study of Higher Education and Research Policy*, Report No. 10 (1981).
Richardson, J. J., 'Policy-making and rationality in Sweden: the case of transport', *British Journal of Political Science*, vol. 9 (1979), pp. 341–53.
Ruin, O., *Mellan Samlingsregering och Tvåpartisystem: Den Svenska Regeringsdisk Ussionen 1945–60* (Stockholm: Bonniers, 1968).
Ruin, O., 'Participatory democracy and corporatism: the case of Sweden', *Scandinavian Political Studies*, vol. 9 (1974), pp. 171–84.
Ruin, O., *Studentmakt och Statsmakt: Tre Studier i Svensk Politik* (Stockholm: Liber Förlag, 1979).
Ruin, O., 'External control and internal participation: trends in the politics and policies of Swedish higher education', in H. Daalder and E. Shilds (eds), *Universities, Politicians and Bureaucrats* (Cambridge: Cambridge University Press, 1982).
Rustow, D. A., 'A study of parties and cabinet government in Sweden', in *The Politics of Compromise* (Princeton, NJ: Princeton University Press).
Serner, U., 'Swedish health legislation: milestones in reorganisation since 1945', in A. J. Heidenheimer and N. Elvander (eds), *The Shaping of the Swedish Health System* (London: Croom Helm, 1980).
SOU 1978, 'Lägg besluten närmare människorna', *Statens Offentliga Utredningar*, vol. 52 (1978).
SOU 1980, 'Langtudsutredningen 1980: huvudrapport', *Statens Offentliga Utredningar*, vol. 52 (1980).
Swahn, U., 'Interest representation in Swedish law-making, 1922–78: remiss circulation of Swedish official reports (SOU)', *ECPR Workshop Sessions*, Florence, 25–30 March 1980.

Tarschys, D., *Den Offentliga Revolutionen* (Stockholm: Liber Förlag, 1978).

Tomasson, R. F., *Sweden Prototype of Modern Society* (New York: Random House, 1978).

Tornqvist, K., 'Opinion 80: en opinionsunde sökning hösten 1980', *Psykologiskt Försvar*, vol. 106 (1980).

Wittrock, B., 'Science policy and the challenge to the welfare state', *West European Politics*, vol. 3, no. 3 (1980), pp. 358–72.

Zetterburg, H. L., 'The public's view of social welfare policy in Sweden', *SIFO* (1980).

7

Policy Styles in the Netherlands: Negotiation and Conflict

JAN VAN PUTTEN,
Free University of Amsterdam

Introduction

In Dutch politics a number of competing and conflicting policy styles can be discerned. There are differences not only between the present styles, but also between some present styles and the styles that were practised some twenty years ago. There is also a gap between constitutional norms and actual styles. The differences are due to the rise of new cultural, social and political cleavages in Dutch society, especially in the period since 1960; and to the growth of the size of the government and the administration, accompanied by differentiation and sectorisation.

In this chapter particular attention is paid to: (1) the constitutional norms for policy-making; (2) some recent developments in Dutch political culture, especially their impact on the Dutch party system; (3) sectorisation and the decline of integration and co-ordination.

The Constitutional Norms

The constitution includes important rules for the relations between government, parliament and society. These rules are governed by the idea that government policies should be formulated by deliberation and consultation. In the constitution of 1848, which is still operative, ministerial responsibility to Parliament was introduced. Ministers were no longer held to be responsible to the monarch, but only to both houses of Parliament. Legislation should take place in common deliberation between government and Parliament.

This relation between government and Parliament was defined as dualistic: neither the government, nor the Parliament, can exert power without the other organ. Ministers are appointed by the Head of State, not by Parliament. Unlike the basic law of the German Federal Republic, there is no written rule for the solution of conflicts. There is no provision for motions expressing confidence or lack of confidence. The government may dissolve one or both houses of Parliament (a dissolution has to be followed by general elections); or the members of Cabinet may resign. In the latter case there are no constitutional arrangements for dealing with a Cabinet crisis.

In the first quarter of the twentieth century a growing number of interest groups were formed. They pressed the government to install advisory committees that should be consulted in advance of every government decision. Many politicians questioned this development; they feared a reduction in parliamentary influence. According to the constitution, Parliament is the only form of legitimate representation. In order to control this development, the constitution was amended in 1922, stating that official advisory boards should be instituted only by law, that is, only with parliamentary approval. (As we shall see, only a relatively small number of the official advisory committees are in fact formed in this way.)

The 1922 amendment did not settle the relationship between government and Parliament on the one hand, and organised interests on the other. Especially in Catholic and Protestant circles, there was a strong trend towards a type of corporatist society. In the case of the Catholics (in accordance to the papal encyclicals *Rerum Novarum*, 1891, and *Quadragesimo Anno*, 1931) society was not seen as made up of only two or three conflicting classes, but as an organism, the parts of which were functionally interrelated. The Catholic and Protestant political parties and social organisations stressed the importance of co-operation between the different sections of society. However, they also emphasised the responsibility of the different sectors of society for serving their own sectorial interests (with, of course, due regard to the 'general interest'). They demanded that the government should transfer some of its responsibilities to private organisations of trade and industry in which representatives of employers and employees should 'rule' their own sectors, as organs of public law (Fogarty, 1957).

In 1937 the constitution was amended to allow this. The idea was further developed in an Act of 1950, the 'Wet op de Bedrijfsorganisatie'. This 'publiekrechtelijke bedrijfsorganisatie' however proved to be a failure, especially in the industrial sector where the gap between employers and employees was too wide to be bridged. Nevertheless, the 'Wet op de Bedrijfsorganisatie' is still considered as a milestone along the road to co-operation between the different organised interests in society. It is reasonable to argue that the constitution and the laws based on it reflect the Dutch ideal of decision-making by deliberation, consultation and mutual agreement.

Political Culture

Trends

Although the constitution forms part of the political culture, it is not the only element. There are other elements of political culture that are of great importance in analysing Dutch policy styles. This became particularly clear in the second half of the twentieth century.

In the first half of this century political practice corresponded in many ways with the intentions of the framers of the constitution (and with its amendments). The Dutch reputation for a policy style characterised by appeasement and accommodation (emphasising consultation and negotiation rather than imposition) can, in fact, be attributed to the so-called 'pacification' of 1917. During the forty years that preceded this 'pacification' the political debate was dominated by three themes: state subsidies for religious schools (alongside ordinary state schools); electoral reform; and the improvement of conditions for the working class. There were great differences of opinion on these questions between the governing liberal elite and the recently founded political parties of Protestants, Catholics and Social Democrats. In 1917 agreement was reached on the equality of rights for private and public schools and on the introduction of universal suffrage.

That such a 'pacification' proved possible may be considered as particularly surprising against the background of a social phenomenon that permeated nearly all sectors of Dutch society – namely, the phenomenon of 'pillarisation' (*verzuiling*). By pillarisation we mean the founding of all kinds of organisations on different religious or sociopolitical bases, in such a number and mutually linked with so many ties that the structure of society may be accurately described in terms of clusters of organisations with a common religion or view of life.

Dutch society was split up, in this way, in four 'pillars' (*zuilen*), a Protestant, a Catholic, a socialist and a liberal (or 'general') pillar. There were Protestant, Catholic and socialist trade unions; liberal, Protestant and Catholic organisations of employers, farmers and shopkeepers; Catholic, Protestant and non-religious organisations in the field of education and health care; and, since the 1920s, Protestant, Catholic, socialist and 'general' broadcasting corporations. The party system itself generally reflected this pillarisation. Communication was generally limited to members of one's own 'pillar'. In connection with this organisational and communication structure, a strong feeling of national unity did not (and still does not) exist.

In this pillarised situation pacification and accommodation were possible mainly as a result of the attitudes and the behaviour of the *leaders* of the different 'pillars'. They realised that the country had to be governed, and more or less over the heads of their rank and file, they were willing to negotiate and to compromise. They applied a set of rules that belonged only to the role culture of this elite, not to the 'mass culture'. These rules were not formally or officially decided. They were patterns of behaviour, according to which the political leaders in the era of pacification acted, especially in times of political tension and crisis.

Lijphart (1968), in fact, identifies seven 'rules of the game':

(1)   the business of politics: doctrinal disputes should not stand in the way of getting work done;
(2)   the agreement to disagree; tolerance;
(3)   summit diplomacy;
(4)   the rule of proportionality as a device for problem-solving;
(5)   depoliticisation;
(6)   secrecy;
(7)   the government governs.

The 'politics of accommodation' (Lijphart, 1968) could only succeed because of the relative passivity and docility on the part of the members of the different 'pillars'. Lijphart defined the Dutch political system as 'consociational'. Although his description, and his explanation of some important political phenomena in the Dutch system, was immediately (and still is) subject to sharp criticism (Scholten, 1980), it is the case that political relations in the Netherlands, and indeed policy-making in general, have, for more than fifty years, been characterised by a certain harmony between the largest political parties. In the postwar period this harmony has also characterised relations between the central organisations of employers and labour.

By the mid-1960s this situation had come to an end. This was due to some radical changes in the political culture, corresponding with structural changes in Dutch society. These changes are in many ways similar to those in other West European countries since the Second World War, and were in part the result of developments in the fields of science, technology and industrialisation. The level of education, the standard of living and the social mobility of the population substantially increased. The increasing number of demands from different social and political groups caused an increase in the amount of legislation and an enormous increase in the size of the governmental apparatus itself (Hoogerwerf, 1977). The welfare state was accomplished. Today (1981) some 60 per cent of the national income passes through the public sector, as government and social security expenditures. The government on its different levels (national, provincial and local) is by far the biggest employer: in 1978 3·19 per cent of the population were employed by a government agency (Sociaal en Cultureel Rapport, 1980, p. 273).

In the wake of the structural changes in society, the importance of religion as a factor for organised societal activity declined. This also meant, in many ways, the end of pillarisation. For example, in the late 1960s and the 1970s, the Catholic trade union federation merged with the socialist federation. The Catholic central organisation of employers merged with the Protestant employers organisation. The new organisation co-operates with the much larger liberal organisation of employers. In 1980 after a long period of unification, the largest Protestant political parties, the *Anti-Revolutionaire Party* (ARP) and the *Christelijk-Historische Unie* (CHU), merged with the *Katholieke Volkspartij* (KVP) to form a new Christian Democratic Party, the *Christen-Democratisch Appel* (CDA). In the same period the Christian Democrats have lost much of their support: from seventy-six seats in the Second Chamber (the Dutch House of Commons) in 1963 to only forty-eight in 1981. (The total number of seats in the Second Chamber is 150.)

At the same time new social and political cleavages came into existence, often as a consequence of conflicts, partly along socioeconomic lines, partly around new issues like democratisation, environmental protection, and questions of overseas development aid and foreign and defence policy. Left-wing groups were formed in the established political parties. Two new democratic and radical parties were founded, together with a large number of interest groups and action groups. They mirror the increased structural and cultural differentiation within Dutch society in the post pillarisation era; they forced the introduction of new styles of policy-making. Their existence and their activities have created a new image of Dutch politics.

Writing in 1974 Hans Daalder characterised these developments in relation to Lijphart's earlier work. Thus, he suggested that if Lijphart were writing in 1974 the title of his book would probably have been 'De-pillarization, polarization and revolution in Dutch politics' (Daalder, 1974). In contrast to the seven rules of the game that were identified by Lijphart, Daalder formulated seven new rules which in his view more accurately described the policy styles of the Dutch political parties in the 1970s:

(1)   Instead of avoiding doctrinal disputes, the unmasking of the ideology of the establishment; the necessity of a criticial view of society.
(2)   Instead of the agreement to disagree, contestation and conflict.
(3)   Instead of summit diplomacy, self-management at the grass-roots.
(4)   Instead of the rule of proportionality, polarisation as a means for building an exclusive majority on the basis of a self-determined fixed programme.
(5)   Instead of depoliticisation, politicisation.
(6)   Instead of secrecy, publicity and openness.
(7)   Instead of 'the government governs' the opinion that too much power is concentrated in the government and the civil service, at the expense of the power of parliament.

For many foreign observers, Lijphart's description is still accepted as the way in which divisive issues and conflicts in the Netherlands *are* settled, despite only a minimal consensus. However, even if this description was ever accurate, in the way suggested by Lijphart, it is clear that conditions are very different today. Nevertheless, the situation as described by Daalder, is not entirely accurate for all political parties. The new rules are above all practised by the left-wing parties. But their impact on political decision-making is greater than might be inferred from their numerical strength. Because pluralism is still the main characteristic of the Dutch party system, coalition building and compromise remain necessary conditions for reaching majority decisions. As a result of the adoption of new policy-making styles, coalition-building has become more difficult and it takes longer and longer to reach any decisions.

Changes in Policy Styles of the Political Parties

The recent developments in policy-making are well illustrated by three important policy areas:

(1)   constitutional innovations in the 1970s;
(2)   the formation of the van Agt Cabinet in 1977;
(3)   the legislation on abortion, 1971–81.

Clearly, caution must be exercised in generalising from only three cases. These cases have, however, been selected for two reasons. First, they deal with important political issues on three different levels – the level of the regime itself; the level of the selection of (political) authorities; and the performance of those authorities. Secondly, all three cases illustrate the increased difficulty the Netherlands are experiencing in reaching a majority consensus in Parliament when issues of great political importance are at stake.

Each of the cases illustrate the behaviour of the political parties in Parliament. The Dutch Parliament consists of two chambers, a Second Chamber (directly elected) and a First Chamber (elected by the provincial states). Bills first pass the Second Chamber and then pass to the First Chamber. Although the Second Chamber might be considered as politically the more important (comparable with the House of Commons in the UK), the First Chamber in fact has the final say in legislative questions.

Constitutional Innovations in the 1970s

The first case study deals with attempts, starting in 1966, at constitutional innovation. This case illustrates both the rise of a policy style based on deep-rooted dissatisfaction with the traditional modes of decision-making, and the impossibility of introducing fundamental changes in the constitutional system.

The mid-1960s saw a considerable increase in dissatisfaction, among various categories of citizens, concerning the lack of influence of the ordinary citizen on political decision-making. In 1965 the Cabinet coalition of Christian Democrats and the conservative–liberal *Volksparty voor Vrijheid en Democratie* (VVD) that was formed after the 1963 elections collapsed, and without new elections being held, a new Cabinet was formed. The new Cabinet consisted of ministers of two Christian Democratic parties and the socialist *Partij van de Arbeid* (PvdA). The formation of this coalition, in the absence of a new election, caused an intensification of existing doubts about the efficacy of elections in Holland. The stability of the political system was further put to the test by a series of serious riots in Amsterdam, that reached a climax in 1966.

The political discontent gave rise to a new left wing in the PvdA; radical wings within the Christian Democratic parties; some new parties, among them *Democraten '66* (D'66) and the *Politieke Partij Radikalen* (PPR), and many hundreds of action groups, pursuing a great variety of goals in the political and social sphere. According to the new party, D'66, the Dutch political system was 'ill and tired'. The party demanded the direct election of the Prime Minister and the replacement of the electoral system of proportional representation by a district-based system for the Second Chamber. In the elections of 1967 D'66 obtained seven of the 150 seats. Though the number of seats was rather small, all observers saw this as a great electoral success for the new party. (In the 1981 election D'66 gained seventeen seats.)

The new Cabinet which was formed in 1967 was again drawn from the Christian Democrats and liberals. The new government appointed a Royal Commission to advise the Cabinet on the desirability of amending the constitution and the electoral law. The commission was, in accordance with tradition, politically representative and therefore heterogeneous in its composition. From the beginning it was clear that it would prove impossible to resolve the conflicting views within the commission. With the smallest possible majority, the commission recommended the direct election of the Cabinet 'formateur' (not of the Prime Minister, see below) and the introduction of a new district-based electoral system. The majority report was itself a compromise. The Cabinet, however, ultimately preferred to maintain the existing procedures for the appointment of the members of the Cabinet and for the election of the Second Chamber, and did not adopt the recommendations of the commission.

In the Second Chamber the PvdA, D'66 and the PPR subsequently initiated a Bill based on the majority report. This Bill was defeated by the government parties with support from some small rightist parties. While nearly all politicians strongly supported the need for political innovation, a fundamental reform of the political system proved unattainable.

Only minor changes were carried through. The voting age was lowered to 18 (from 21). A certain amount of democratisation of the universities and the corporations was granted, the former not without severe conflicts within the universities. After ten years of deliberation, a law guaranteeing more openness in government affairs was passed (Brasz, 1977, p. 201), and especially at the local level, procedures for consultation were introduced.

The most lasting legacy from this period seems to be the increased gap between the Christian Democrats and liberals, on the one hand, and the 'progressive parties' (as they call themselves), on the other. Although the progressive parties have as yet not obtained enough seats in Parliament to govern without the support of the centrist Christian Democrats, the most important result of this period seems to be the emergence of what could prove to be a lasting restructuring of the party system into two competing blocks.

The Formation of the Cabinet in 1977

The effects of the new styles of polarisation are particularly striking in the formation of new Cabinets. During the election campaign it is always impossible to predict the coalition that will be built after the elections. This is due to the 'neutral' attitude of the Christian Democratic parties (nowadays the *Christen-Democratisch Appel*, CDA) during the election campaign, in terms of the most 'desired' coalition. In fact, the socialist PvdA and the liberal VVD have, since 1963, refused to co-operate at Cabinet level, and so the Christian Democrats always have to choose between co-operation with either the PvdA, or the VVD. For electoral reasons this choice is only made after the elections have taken place, during the process of Cabinet formation.

No single political party in the Netherlands has ever won an *absolute* majority in Parliament. However, it is generally accepted that a majority Cabinet is by far the best alternative and minority Cabinets are rare in Dutch parliamentary history. In order to secure a majority Cabinet, negotiations and agreements are required, after the elections, between political parties which were often involved in a heated battle during the election campaign. The formation of a new Cabinet is, in consequence, generally a lengthy, complicated process, fraught with problems.

This process is not guided by written rules, but by convention, so-called 'unwritten rules of constitutional law'. The process generally takes the following course. After the elections, the Queen appoints a skilled politician who is given the task either to form a Cabinet, or to inform her about the possibilities of forming a Cabinet, that may count on the support of a majority in Parliament. The 'formateur' or 'informateur' starts negotiations with the qualified political parties about the contents of a government pro-gramme. During these negotiations at least one of the participating parties withdraws or is excluded from further deliberations, because, as indicated, the socialists and liberals have refused to co-operate in a coalition since 1963. Since 1952 Cabinets have consisted of two or three Christian Democratic parties and either the liberal VVD (1959, 1963, 1967, 1971 and 1977), or the socialist PvdA (1952, 1956, 1965, 1973 and 1981), and one or more minor parties (1971, 1973 and 1981).

After agreement on the government programme has been reached, negotiations then follow concerning the number of seats for each of the participating parties in the new Cabinet and the Cabinet-members that are nominated. Over the last fifteen years the PvdA, under the influence of its 'New Left' wing, has opted for a strategy of polarisation and hard negotia-tions. This strategy was fed by distrust of the CDA parties. As a result of this attitude the formation process has become more protracted (Table 7.1).

Table 7.1   *Coalition Formation in the Netherlands*

1959	(after general elections)	68 days
1963	(after general elections)	70 days
1965	(after a Cabinet crisis)	44 days
1966-7	(after a Cabinet crisis)	37 days
1967	(after general elections)	48 days
1971	(after general elections)	63 days
1972-3	(after a Cabinet crisis followed by general elections)	163 days
1977	(after general elections preceded by a Cabinet crisis)	207 days
1981	(after general elections)	108 days*

*Three weeks after the new Cabinet members had been sworn into office they placed their seats at the Queen's disposal as a result of disagreement on economic and financial policies. The solution of the crisis took another three weeks.

The most difficult stage in the process is the first one: the negotiations for the government programme. In 1977 the Queen appointed PvdA leader Joop den Uyl to form a new Cabinet. Den Uyl twice returned his assignment to the Queen, because no agreement could be reached between the PvdA and the CDA on certain parts of the government programme. He gave up a third time because of unsurmountable differences of opinion on the dis-tribution of the seats in the new Cabinet. A later fresh attempt also failed when, at the next stage, no agreement could be reached on the choice of ministers. The CDA then started negotiations with the VVD. Within a month, this resulted in the appointment of a CDA–VVD Cabinet, CDA leader van Agt being appointed Prime Minister.

The PvdA had gained an extra ten seats in the elections of 1977, an unequalled success in Dutch parliamentary history and was, with fifty-three seats, the biggest party in the Second Chamber. Nevertheless, it did not take part in the new Cabinet because of a lack of co-operation between the PvdA and CDA.

Abortion Law Reform

Under the Penal Code abortion until 1981 was considered a crime in Holland. However, an average of 15,000 abortions per year, since 1971, have been performed, two-thirds of them in special clinics. Only rarely was anyone prosecuted. Many efforts have been made, since 1970, to legalise abortion but most of them have failed owing to irreconcilable differences between the parliamentary parties.

In 1970 two representatives of the PvdA (not then represented in Cabinet) proposed a Bill designed to legalise abortion and defining it as a matter concerning only the pregnant woman and her doctor. In 1972 the Cabinet (a coalition of Christian Democrats and liberals) itself proposed that the decision on abortion should be taken not by the woman and her doctor, but by special 'abortion teams' consisting of physicians and social workers. Parliament thus faced two abortion-reform Bills.

After the 1972 elections a new Cabinet was formed, including ministers from the PvdA, D'66 and the PPR, and two of the three major Christian Democratic parties, the ARP and KVP. During the coalition formation process no agreement was reached on a solution to the abortion problem. In such cases the political parties tend to resort to procedural agreements regarding how a decision should be reached. In the abortion case it was decided that the new Cabinet should withdraw the Bill that had been introduced by their predecessors, and leave the initiative entirely to the Second Chamber.

In fact, in the spring of 1975 two Christian Democratic representatives proposed a Bill that in many ways resembled the Bill that had been introduced by the preceding Cabinet. A month later, the *Volkspartij voor Vrijheid en Democratie* also drafted a proposal. Thus, by 1975 *three* different Abortion Bills were being discussed.

Meanwhile, the Christian Democratic Minister of Justice, Dries van Agt (later to become Prime Minister) attempted to close an abortion clinic specialising in late terminations. He failed because women occupied the clinic, and because of objections from a majority of non-confessional ministers in the cabinet; van Agt considered resigning, but (as he admitted two years later) remained in office to prevent more liberal legislation, such as that proposed by the PvdA or the VVD.

In 1976 the PvdA and the VVD opened negotiations and replaced their two separate Bills by one common proposal. The Second Chamber accepted this Bill in September 1976 with a majority of eighty-three to fifty-eight. However, three months later, the Bill was rejected by the First Chamber by a majority of forty-one votes to thirty-four. In contrast to their colleagues in the Second Chamber, most liberals voted against the Bill. As a result the whole procedure had to start again!

After the 1977 election, socialists and Christian Democrats, and in a later stage, Christian Democrats and liberals, again failed to agree on the abortion question during the formation of a coalition. And again they resorted to procedural agreements. The new Cabinet was to introduce a new Bill before 1 January 1979. If the Cabinet failed to do so, the initiative again would be left to the Second Chamber.

The Cabinet succeeded, despite initial disagreement, in presenting a new Bill in February 1979. The Bill proved to be very controversial. Many supporters of legalisation felt that the new Bill made things too difficult for those seeking an abortion. They demanded that the woman herself should have the sole right to decide to terminate her pregnancy. In contrast, many opponents of liberalisation felt that the government proposal went too far. Alternative Bills were introduced, from both sides in the Second Chamber, so that in December 1980 once again three Bills were under consideration. After weeks of tension the Second Chamber accepted, by seventy-six votes to seventy-four, the government proposal. In fact, it was the first time since 1956, the year that the membership of the Second Chamber was extended to 150, that all members were present and took part in the vote! Three months later the First Chamber accepted the Bill with an even narrower margin: thirty-eight votes to thirty-seven.

In the case of the abortion law reform the Dutch political system appeared quite different to the 'accommodational' style suggested by Lijphart. The abortion issue had proved controversial and divisive and extremely difficult to 'process'. Moreover, the final decision had been reached in the parliamentary arena, rather than through any special consociational machinery.

Sectorisation and Integration

Trends

Issues like constitutional reform and abortion law reform are still handled by the political parties in the context of Parliament. Day-to-day politics in the welfare state is, however, handled in another context and the picture of decision-making is quite different: not that of policy-making by both government (as a unity) and Parliament, but policy-making by *sectors*, consisting of individual ministers and their departmental officials, and of corresponding parliamentary committees, advisory boards and interest groups in society. The majority of these sectors display their own policy style.

Thus, party politics is one aspect of the political spectrum, 'sector politics' is another. Cabinet formation and occasionally policy-making in fields where political parties are still virtually the only interest articulators, still belong to the domain of party politics, and are governed by the policy styles as described in the preceding section of this chapter. But wherever interests – in an institutionalised way – are articulated not only by political parties, but also by a wide range of independent interest organisations, the styles of policy-making have become almost independent of the dominant party style. Differences between political parties disappear like snow under a hot sun when, for instance, the interests of the farmers are at stake. The farmers not only possess their own interest groups, but, moreover, each parliamentary party contains one or more 'representatives' of the farmers, that is, members who are farmers themselves or who are recruited from a farmers' organisation. These specialists form the 'green front', defending the farmers' interests against attacks from representatives of other socio-economic groups.

This sectorisation has even influenced the process of Cabinet formation: the Minister of Agriculture is generally drawn from the agricultural sector; his ministerial colleague in social affairs is often a former trade union leader and always a confidant of the trade unions. Similarly, the Minister of Economic Affairs is always a confidant of the employers' organisations.

Sectorisation has given rise to a new dilemma, between unity at the Cabinet level and disagreement within the separate sectors, on the one hand, and peace in each sector but an increasing lack of integration at the Cabinet level, on the other. Increasingly, the dilemma has been resolved in favour of sectorisation by individual ministers and their departmental officials. Thus, the phenomenon of departmentalism, so familiar elsewhere (Richardson and Jordan, 1979, p. 26), has become an important feature of the Dutch policy process. Indeed, the lack of co-ordination became so serious that, in 1979, the government set up a commission to investigate the problem and to formulate recommendations.

In one of its reports, the commission concluded that, starting from the distinction between differentiation and integration, the administration appeared to be made up of two different 'worlds' – the 'world' of the sectors, and the 'world' focused on integration. Every organisational unit performing a specific function was the centre of a clearly defined 'policy community' (Gustafsson and Richardson, 1979, p. 424) of societal organisations and local and provincial authorities. In formal terms parliamentary 'spokesmen' do not belong to these policy communities or 'circuits', but as a result of their specialisation and long service in Parliament they can also be members.

The 'world' focused on integration is quite different. That is the organisational world of the council of ministers, the Cabinet, commissions, the so-called co-ordinating ministers for different government policies and the undersecretaries. In the 'integrative world', relationships are less stable and are subject to tensions. Objectives are often unclear and conflicting, organisational structures are ill-defined and linked by only weak networks. Within the administration differentiation is emphasised at the cost of integration ('Elk kent de laan', pp. 83–4).

Sectorisation has increased in importance during the twentieth century. At the beginning of this century there were only eight ministers, each of them responsible for one department. By 1980 the number of departments had risen to fourteen and the number of ministers to sixteen. Existing departments had been split up to form a number of new departments: Agriculture and Fisheries (1910), Education and Science (1917), Social Affairs (1917), Economic Affairs (1933), Housing and Physical Planning (1945), Social Welfare (1952), Culture, Recreation and Welfare (1965) and Public Health and Environment Protection (1971). One department was abolished, the Department of the Colonies; the War and Navy Departments were merged into a new Department of Defence (1959); and in 1947 a small Department of General Affairs was created to serve the Prime Minister.

Each new department developed its own policy style. It is also possible to detect different policy styles *within* any one department, due to the fact that a new department might have been formed from divisions 'hived off' from different departments. Each division brought with it a characteristic policy style (for example, the Department of Culture, Recreation and Welfare). Further differentiaton, within departments, has been encouraged by the creation of the office of undersecretary in 1948 (in some respects the equivalent of junior ministers in the UK). The undersecretary does not act as a deputy for his minister in the Cabinet Council (only a minister is allowed to deputise for an absent minister), but is responsible for the affairs of a section of the department (under the formal responsibility of his minister). This permits the development of different 'ministerial styles' (Headey, 1974) within the same department.

As suggested earlier, the departmental sectors form the centre of policy-making 'circuits' which include external actors in the policy process, especially the increased number of interest groups and 'action' groups. Moreover, there are the official advisory committees, set up by the government, as intermediaries between society and the administration.

The administration has a large number of such advisory bodies at its disposal. In a study conducted in 1975 some 368 permanent advisory bodies were identified. It is difficult to ascertain the number of ad hoc advisory bodies, but the number is considerable. Of the 368 permanent committees 42 per cent were formed after 1962. Contrary to the constitutional rules, 61 per cent of the advisory committees are not based on a law. Most advisory bodies advise only one minister, itself an indicator of the sectorised nature of many policy-making circuits (WRR, 1977, pp. 43–4).

Sectorisation within Parliament

Parliament has also exhibited a strong tendency to sectorise its activity. Parliament, especially the Second Chamber, is characterised by an ever-increasing number of specialised permanent committees participating in the legislative process and helping to control the government.

In 1948 the Second Chamber had only eight specialised permanent committees. By 1980 the number had increased to twenty-eight. Apart from these permanent committees, the chamber has a large number of ad hoc committees. In 1980 the Second Chamber decided to delegate some authority to the permanent committees. In a number of cases, decision-making on government proposals in a committee does not necessarily have to be approved by Parliament as a whole. This has, of course, intensified sectorisation within Parliament (Table 7.2).

Table 7.2   *Activities of the Second Chamber, 1960–75*

	1960–1	1965–6	1970–1	1975–6
Plenary meetings	85	62	78	108
Number of pages of the Parliamentary Reports	3,200	3,420	3,927	5,616
Commission meetings	342	382	569	685
Number of Bills proposed by the government	174	302	300	285
Number of amendments proposed by MPs	211	203	224	755
Number of motions	25	41	154	387

Sources: van Schendelen (1975), p. 167; van Bussel (1979), pp. 18, 21.

Sectorisation within Parliament has encouraged MPs to be more interested in detailed policy matters. Thus, an MP now feels that he has to justify himself with the interest groups that form part of 'his' circuit. Indeed, the MP–interest-group relationship is of some importance in terms of his chances of re-election. The increased 'parliamentary activism', which is not only the result of sectorisation, but also of other factors (van Schendelen, 1975, pp. 163 ff.), manifests itself in interpellations on all kinds of current issues, followed by the introduction and, subsequently adoption or rejection, of many motions, asking the government to undertake actions or condemning actions that have already been undertaken by governmental agencies. The attention to detail and short-term problems is not balanced by an interest in long-term problems or in government strategy as a whole. Neither is the increased interest in detail associated with increased influence for MPs (van Putten, 1980, pp. 268–70).

The Officials

The increase of the number of policy 'circuits' has important consequences for civil servants. Even if the number of ministers and undersecretaries has increased, they generally cannot take part in the time-consuming negotiations and consultations with all interest groups (and interested individuals) in their sector.

Though Holland subscribes to the same formal system of ministerial responsibility as the UK, it is increasingly a fiction. In many sectors policymaking and policy implementation are in practice the responsibility of the civil servants. There is, in fact, a slight tendency towards greater independence for officials and there are some examples of officials expressing public dissatisfaction with ministerial decisions. There are also a few examples of officials, openly or covertly obstructing their ministers' policies, but generally ministers and undersecretaries praise the loyalty of their officials, even those known to have preferred other policies (Gortzak, 1978).

H. D. Tjeenk Willink has identified four meanings of 'loyalty' – loyalty to the departmental division, loyalty to the department as a whole, loyalty to existing interdepartmental contacts, and loyalty to the minister. In practice, loyalty is often very strongly directed towards the departmental division in which the civil servant is located. This loyalty also includes loyalty to the regular clientele – the interest groups and advisory committees in that particular sector. The primary objective of the civil servant is the preservation and, if possible, expansion of his own division (Tjeenk Willink, 1980, p. 47). Interestingly, Parliament has tried to penetrate these tight circuits or networks and has pressed for the right to examine civil servants in the absence of their ministers. So far, the Cabinet has resisted this proposal.

Different Policy Styles

As we have argued, sectorisation has encouraged a variety of policy styles. In terms of legislation J. M. Polak has argued that each department produces its own 'family of laws', with its own language, formulations and constructions (Polak, 1977). For example, when different departments prepare environmental protection laws, they will display quite different 'family traits'. Differences are particularly marked in terms of procedures and language. Polak goes on to suggest that departments differ in their attitude to regulation by law. In doing so they exhibit quite fundamental differences in their views of society and the role of government within it

(Polak, 1977). Polak's analysis was empirically confirmed in the research project 'Haagse machten' (literally, 'the powers that be in The Hague') conducted during the period 1975–9. In fact, the project was not primarily concerned with the variety of policy styles that might play a role in political decision-making. The central objective was to measure the influence exerted during the adoption of a number of government measures.

Eight government measures were selected from three separate ministries. The measures were of different legal structure in the period 1974–6. The ministries included one of the 'classical' ministries, the Ministry of Justice; one socioeconomic ministry, the Ministry of Economic Affairs; and one ministry in the educational, social services and welfare field, the Ministry of Culture, Recreation and Welfare.

The 'Haagse machten' project dealt with the following eight measures: *Ministry of Justice:* (1) the law on the provisional regulation of a fund for damages due to criminal acts of violence (1974); (2) a general administrative order concerning compulsory breath tests and blood tests for drivers suspected of having drunk too much alcohol (1974); and (3) a resolution regulating the police at Schiphol International Airport (1974). *Ministry of Economic Affairs:* (4) the Selective Investment Law (1974, see below); (5) the Goods and Services Price Regulations 1976 (1975); and (6) the foundation of the LIOF Industrial Bank Ltd, which was mainly set up to facilitate the economic restructuring of the southern part of the province of Limburg (1974). *Ministry of Culture, Recreation and Welfare:* (7) the Press Fund Foundation, set up to advise the minister on the granting of government credit and credit facilities to newspapers (1974); and (8) the regulation of government contributions to local educational and social projects for adults (1976, see below).

The activities of all the participants in the decision-making processes were studied (van Putten, 1980, pp. 9–11). When examining the influence of different categories of actors, the researchers were struck by the *variety* of decision-making processes and by the importance of these differences in terms of possible influence on government decisions. It was also clear that the variety of processes was rarely a matter of conscious choice. In almost every case the very course of the process and its outcome were different from the original intention. During the decision-making processes there were too many rather than too few 'checks and balances', resulting in a large number of concessions being made (Dror, 1968, pp. 81–4).

Due to the differences in the juridical structure of the various measures, as well as in the decision-making processes studies, the circle of participants also exhibited a wide range of differences. This, in turn, affected chances of influencing policy and had implications for policy content. It is, of course, possible to argue that influence can be exerted without direct participation – due to the law of anticipated reactions. However, it seems reasonable to argue that as a rule participation is necessary, if influence over policy is to be achieved. In fact, the results of the 'Haagse machten' study suggest that a large variety of participation opportunities exist. This was true when the legal structure of the measures was held constant and also when the particular ministry was a constant factor. Instead of speaking of 'differences in participation opportunities', it is more accurate to speak of 'inequality of rights': the 'right' to make recommendations or have a say in a matter is acknowledged in one case and not in another. Figure 7.1 illustrates the categories of actors involved in the eight decision-making processes which were studied. In fact, differences in participation rights and levels reflect different policy-making procedures and these, in turn, reflect different policy styles. A comparison of departmental policy styles reveals a number of important differences. For example, the older departments tend to have less developed policy 'circuits' or 'policy communities'.

In the departments that were founded in the nineteenth century Bills and other government proposals are still framed by specialised lawyers working alone and exhibiting strong loyalty to their minister. Much importance is attached to a formal hierarchy and Parliament is still the most important external actor. Gradually, however, even these departments are changing their policy style. The oldest departments are the Ministries of Foreign Affairs, Defence, Domestic Affairs, Finance and Justice. In the past pressure-group activity was concentrated in the fields of economics, social welfare, education, health care and environmental protection. Over the last decade, however, public interest – and consequently the formation of pressure groups – has increased in the fields of foreign policy (NATO, human rights and development aid) and defence (nuclear (dis)armament) and in the domain of the Ministry of Justice (legal aid, privacy and the protection of the rights of aliens). Thus, these older sectors are falling into line in terms of policy style.

A complex structure for consultation and negotiation has been developed by, for example, the Ministry of Culture, Recreation and Welfare for the development of welfare policies. Three distinct official channels of communication have been devised:

(1)   between the department, the Union of Dutch Municipalities and the co-ordinating body for the eleven provinces; decentralisation policies are negotiated through this channel;

(2)   between the department and the organisations of employers and employees in the field of social and cultural welfare; conditions of work are negotiated through this channel;

(3)   between the department and the private peak organisations in the field of social and cultural welfare.

Important policy proposals are discussed in each of these three circuits. The communication patterns between the Ministry of Education and Science

Figure 7.1 *Involvement of various categories of actors in eight policy-making processes (van Putten, 1980)*

	1	2	3	4	5	6	7	8
organisations and/or persons concerned informed before official promulgation of the government measure in question	×	×			×	×		×
involvement of the First Chamber	×	×		×	×			
involvement of the Second Chamber (xx) or members of the Second Chamber (x)	×	×	×	xx	xx		xx	
submitted to the Council of State (for advice)	×	×		×	×			
discussed in the Council of Ministers	×	×		×	×			×
public hearings								
interested persons privately consulted	×	×		×	×	×		
consultation of advisory committees	×	×		×			×	
tentative draft published				×				×
interdepartmental co-operation at the end of the policy-making process	×	×		×	×		×	×
interdepartmental co-operation at the start of the policy-making process	×	×	×	×	×		×	×
drawn up by individual officials		(x)	×	×			×	(x)
drawn up by commission predominantly consisting of government officials	×		×			×	×	×
drawn up by commission outside the administration					×	×	×	×

| | 1 | 2 | 3 | 4 | 5 | 6 | 7 | 8 |

Key: (1) Law on fund for damages   (5) Goods and services price regulations
(2) Compulsory blood test for drivers   (6) Founding of LIOF Industrial Bank Ltd
(3) Role of police at Schiphol Airport   (7) Press Fund Foundation
(4) Selective Investment Law   (8) Educational projects for adults

and its environment are even more impressive. In the field of education many hundreds of pressure groups of very different backgrounds and composition are active. J. M. G. Leune distinguishes three kinds of contacts between the representatives of these organisations and the official decision-makers:

(1) Formal contacts through the advisory committees. In 1976 there were sixty advisory committees in education and science. Some 108 organisations were represented in these committees.
(2) Informal contacts with the minister, the undersecretaries and the top officials. In fact, these 'functionaries' are themselves often former leaders of pressure groups in the field of education.
(3) Relations between pressure group leaders and Members of Parliament.

Education appears to exhibit the phenomenon of rather wide consultation alongside a form of 'inner-circle negotiation' (see Chapter 4). Thus, the former Minister of Education, J. A. van Kemenade, has argued that policy-making in the field of education bears the characteristics of a 'closed circuit' (J. M. G. Leune, in: J. A. van Kemenade, 1981, pp. 400–78).

In order to appreciate the complexity of the Dutch policy styles, it is, however, important to study examples in some detail. Space does not permit a full analysis of the 'Haagse machten' project. However, the processes involved in the Selective Investment Law and legislation concerning education for adults, have been selected because they exhibit many of the similarities between sectors as well as exhibiting sectoral differences.

The Selective Investment Law

The Selective Investment Law (1974) imposes a system of licensing and levies on investments in commercial buildings and installations in the west of the Netherlands. The Ministries of Economic Affairs and Housing and Physical Development are responsible for the scheme. A preliminary draft of the Selective Investment Law was framed in the Ministry of Economic Affairs and then submitted to the Social and Economic Council for advice. (The government is obliged to submit all its important social and economic policies to the council for consideration. The Council consists of forty-five members; fifteen are appointed by the unions, fifteen by the employers' organisations, and another fifteen, as 'independent' members, by the Crown.)

The Social and Economic Council drew up two reports on the draft Selective Investment Bill. In the first report a number of specific recommendations were made, but 'on due consideration' government officials and ministers concluded that they could not accept the council's advice. The second report was more general and civil servants thought it too vague. However, the vagueness did have certain advantages in that it did not restrict the responsible ministers in their Cabinet deliberations.

Another advisory body which was consulted was the Advisory Council on Physical Planning, which includes experts in the field of urban and regional planning. This Council wrote an extremely sceptical report, in which a great deal of doubt was expressed as to whether the selected means would bring about the desired results. In fact, shortly afterwards, the draft Bill was considerably altered. The changes were, however, not the result of the report written by the Advisory Council on Physical Planning. A new Cabinet had been formed with a different political composition and with a different Minister of Economic Affairs. It appears, therefore, that in this case the *formal* advisory bodies had little influence.

In contrast, individuals and organisations *outside* the formal machinery may be directly involved in the policy deliberations. For example, during the negotiations to form a Cabinet in 1971, the President of the Netherlands Bank and the chairmen of the three main trade unions made it very clear to the individual in charge of selecting the Cabinet candidates just exactly what their standpoints were on curbing investment activities in the western part of the Netherlands. During the drafting of the Bill at the Ministry of Economic Affairs, representatives of (mainly large) firms and of employers' organisations were also involved in discussions. As soon as the draft Bill was published, it provoked numerous reactions on the part of private interest groups and from the provinces and municipalities. Later, during the parliamentary discussion of the final Bill, many of them were to express their opinion again. Similarly, the president of the Netherlands Bank and the director of the Central Planning Agency were also active (either by the request of the department, or on their own initiative) in trying to influence the policy process. Moreover, if the interests do not get their way at the ministry, they can always try again as members of the Social and Economic Council.

The civil servants also consulted certain 'experts' from the world of trade and industry, to check that all the important points were covered in the preparatory stage of policy-making. These individual experts were, in fact, not particularly 'neutral'. One of them threatened to transfer the investments of his firm abroad! The senior official dealing with the particular problem – the levies to be paid on capital investments – took the criticism very seriously and responded by suggesting possible alternatives. The ease of access to civil servants in the ministry was particularly striking as was the flexible response of the officials. For example, the various representations do seem to have affected the scale of levies on investments.

External attempts to exert influence were of course not solely directed at the ministry, but at Parliament as well, particularly the Second Chamber. More or less 'stripped', the Bill was then published in the government gazette (*Staatsblad*). Careful scrutiny suggests that less notice had been taken of the objections by economic and administrative opponents than they themselves would have liked. Nevertheless, the history of the drawing up of the Selective Investment Law indicates the difficulties of introducing regulatory legislation in the face of pressure from economic interest groups.

The study of the drawing up of another measure by the Ministry of Economic Affairs, the goods and services price regulations (1976), also revealed something of a consultation model between the Ministry of Economic Affairs and the industrial organisations. In particular, the talks with the various employers' organisations were of a 'negotiation' nature whereby, within narrow margins, a *do-ut-des* principle was applied. The greatest degree of 'negotiation' was to be found in the relations between the ministry and the organisations of industrial employers. In contrast, there was far less 'negotiation' between the ministry and the traders' associations. This is not to suggest that the ministry gave way to the industrial employers on most points. In practice, fewer of their requests were rejected than was the case with the organisations of independent tradesmen. This is probably related to differences in negotiation tactics. The organisations of tradesmen largely formulate their demands in view of what is desirable, whereas the organisations of the leading employers mainly formulate their demands in view of what is feasible.

Indirectly, the trade unions exerted more influence on the price policy than all the employers' organisations together. In exchange for co-operation with the goverment's restrictive wages policy, they successfully demanded a very rigorous price policy. Negotiations with the employers were, therefore, conducted against this rather constraining background.

Regulation of Government Contributions to Local Educational Projects for Adults

The regulation of government contributions to local educational projects for adults (1976) provides for payments by the national government to municipal authorities in order to finance municipal educational projects, and to subsidise privately run educational projects for adults. This measure also contains rules for decision-making, which municipal authorities have to follow when drawing up their policies regarding subsidies. The responsible minister was the Undersecretary of Culture, Recreation and Welfare.

In 1970 the Minister of Culture, Recreation and Welfare asked a non-official commission to draft a regulation for subsidising local educational projects for adults. The Ministry of Culture usually chooses non-official commissions (that is, commissions existing entirely of representatives of private organisations and of external experts) for this kind of work. After two years the departmental officials discovered that the commission intended to recommend measures quite different from the policies preferred by the civil servants. The civil servants, therefore, decided to bypass the commission and a departmental working group was set up in 1974 in order to formulate the department's own recommendations.

The departmental working group prepared several drafts. The ninth draft was submitted to the responsible undersecretary, and then to other divisions within the department as well as to other relevant departments. A new draft was drawn up after the departmental units and the other departments had reacted and this became the 'first final draft'. The first final draft was made public and sent to a large number of private and administrative organisations in the field of education and welfare. Some fifty responses were received as a result of this consultation.

Meanwhile, developments extraneous to the policy sector had occurred. In 1973 a new Cabinet had been appointed. The new minister had appointed a committee to consider the organisation and co-ordination of welfare policies in general. (The committee was composed of three civil servants, two university professors and four representatives of organisations in the field of social and cultural welfare.) One of the most serious problems was the lack of co-ordination in the welfare field. The committee recommended that responsibility for the co-ordination and financing of welfare work should be transferred from central to local authorities. Local authorities should receive guidelines from the Ministry of Culture, Recreation and Welfare and financing from the Ministry of Finance. The committee considered that such a decentralisation would contribute to a better co-ordination of welfare activities. They also felt that it would make these activities more accessible to the population. The Cabinet and the Second Chamber shared this view. As a result the 'first final draft', providing for direct subsidies from the department to the private organisations, had to be thoroughly remodelled. Financial contributions would now be given to the municipal authorities and they, in turn, would subsidise welfare activities, according to guidelines formulated by the department. The comments from private organisations were also taken account of in this redrafting process. The initial non-official commission was also reactivated. The 'second final draft' resulting from all these activities was sent to and discussed with some other departments, the Union of Dutch Municipalities (the pressure group for the municipal authorities in the Netherlands) and to the co-ordinating body for the provinces. After these discussions, a 'third final draft' was drawn up. This draft was, as with the 'first final draft', made public and widely distributed. At the same time the organisations in the field of welfare were invited to a meeting at the ministry to discuss the draft.

Soon after the completion of this further stage in the consultation procedure, the Department of Culture, Recreation and Welfare was surprised by a somewhat malevolent letter from the Minister of Education. A territorial dispute had arisen as the Ministry of Education objected to the activities of the Ministry of Culture in the field of adult education. Was not education the responsibility of the Minister of Education? Clearly, the Education Ministry had paid insufficient attention to the first and second 'final' drafts and had not recognised this 'invasion' of its sector. The letter from the Minister of Education (who, in fact, was of the same party as the Undersecretary for Welfare!) proposed some modifications. In fact, the undersecretary was threatened with putting the issue on the Cabinet agenda if the modifications were not accepted.

The undersecretary tried to make the best of it, discussed the matter with the Minister of Education, and promised to remove the impression that his department was intruding the Ministry of Education's sector. At the beginning of 1976 the regulation was at last published in the government gazette. However, one element in the package remained to be settled – the salaries of the personnel employed by the welfare organisations. The department had failed to reach agreement on this with the unions because of excessive wage demands.

The Second Chamber had not taken an active part in the decision-making process. The chairman of the Welfare Committee had made an arrangement with the undersecretary that the committee would be informed of all important drafts and comments. Only if irreconcilable differences of opinion emerged between the department and the private organisations, would the committee interfere. In that case the committee intended to hear the organisations first, and then to discuss the problem with the under-secretary. This reactive attitude of the parliamentary committee is typical of the policy style in the sector. In other sectors, for example, foreign affairs and defence, Parliament generally has a quite different attitude and often tries to take an initiative.

Central Co-Ordination

Sectorisation and differentiation within the administration, reflecting differentiation within society, conflicts with the need for integration and unity of government policies as a whole. The Cabinet is, of course, supposed to promote integration and unity.

In fact, the position of the cabinet has always been rather weak. The constitution mentions only individual ministers, to be appointed or dismissed by the head of state. It does not specify the function of Prime Minister and now does not even mention the Council of Ministers as a permanent body.

Until 1947 the chairman of the Council of Ministers was also responsible for one of the departments, usually domestic affairs or finance. Since then he has no specific departmental responsibility and is charged only with chairing meetings of the cabinet and its commissions, and with the promotion of integration. This does not imply that he has more formal power than his Cabinet colleagues. He is still *primus inter pares*. In this respect his position fundamentally differs from that of the British Prime Minister or from that of the Bundeskanzler in the German Federal Republic. Unlike the British Prime Minister, he is not allowed to replace members of the Cabinet, and unlike the Bundeskanzler, he does not decide upon the main lines of government policies. These are matters of common collegial decision-making.

Some writers, especially jurists, argue that collegial decision-making in the Council of Ministers might be seen as a counterbalance to the promotion of specialised interests in political and social life (van Maarseveen, 1969, pp. 32, 33). In reality, this seems to be a dubious claim. It is increasingly clear that the Cabinet performs its integrating functions ineffectively. Much of the discussion in the Cabinet is concerned with the details of proposed measures. The Cabinet is essentially a body where disputes between various ministers are settled, and is only to a very limited degree a body where colleagues join in a true decision-making process (van Putten, 1980, p. 258). The same is true of the budgetary process (Koopmans, 1968, pp. 130–44).

The contrast between the 'normative style' of Cabinet policy-making and reality was very evident in the Third Report of the Commission on the Organisation of the Administration. On the basis of interviews with a great number of ministers and former ministers, the commission reached the following conclusion: 'In the council of ministers much time is devoted to the settling of conflicts between two or more ministers. Moreover, the flooding of the agenda with matters of lesser importance may serve as a legitimation for keeping really important problems with a broader and farther reaching character from the agenda.' The commission blamed time constraints and the political ambition of the individual ministers for the way the Cabinet conducted its business.

The commission saw the lack of integration-oriented activities as due to such factors as constitutional and administrative law, political opportunism and organisational difficulties. In terms of constitutional law, the principle that all ministers are equal implies that they have equal rights in deciding the agenda of the Cabinet Council. In terms of administrative law, each minister has his own legal 'competence' which has to be respected by the Cabinet. Thus, laws and other regulations keep them captive in the departmental and sectoral net. From a political viewpoint, ministers, knowing that their period of office is likely to be short, are scarcely motivated to give priority to issues that are complex or politically risky (*Elk kent de laan*, 1980, p. 94). The disintegrating influence of sectorisation is reinforced by coalition politics. Where Cabinets are composed of competing partners, the political profit to an individual minister's own party often outweighs the common responsibility for the unity of the government.

The problems of differentiation and integration are, of course, not new and over the years some mechanisms have been devised for the promotion of co-ordination between individual ministers and their departments. In spite of these attempts, the lack of co-ordination remains a serious problem. Thus, the Commission on the Organisation of the Administration concluded, 'generalising, the interdepartmental relations might be characterised as a jungle' (*Elk kent de laan*, p. 147).

Conclusion

When describing and explaining the major policy styles in a political system, it is useful to consider them in the context of major contemporary sociopolitical processes. Dahl and Lindblom distinguish between four central sociopolitical processes: the price system, hierarchy, polyarchy and bargaining. Hierarchy is a process in which leaders control non-leaders. In a polyarchy leaders are controlled by non-leaders. Bargaining is a process in which leaders control each other (Dahl and Lindblom, 1953, pp. 22, 23).

It appears that policy-making in the Netherlands contains elements of all these processes, especially of polyarchy, hierarchy and bargaining, and that differences in policy styles might be explained in terms of these central sociopolitical processes. Polyarchy (in terms of relations between voters and Parliament and between Parliament and the Cabinet) and hierarchy (within the administration) were, over time, partly pushed aside by sectoral bargaining, the policy style corresponding with sectorisation.

That administration gave way to bargaining can in part be explained by changes which took place within the administration itself. Traditionally the administration was the preserve of lawyers. The growth of the welfare state, accompanied by the creation of a number of new departments, involved the recruitment of relatively new disciplines into the government bureaucracy: economists, sociologists and political scientists.

The older ministries tend to follow the tradition of the liberal constitution state, preferring government policies to be passed by formal law, in co-operation between government and Parliament. For many of the officials of these departments, democracy is so strongly associated with law-making by government and Parliament together that they sometimes totally neglect the fact that representation is not the direct, but only an indirect, expression of the principle of popular sovereignty.

The newer departments have a much higher proportion of economists, sociologists and political scientists. They are not so influenced by the principles of classical representative democracy and are more inclined towards effective and efficient problem-solving. They recognise social differentiation and pluralism and stress the importance, in the policy-making process, of hearing interested individuals and groups. They sometimes readily ignore the constitutional norm that the only 'legitimate' form of representation is through Parliament.

The 'Haagse machten' project confirmed these differences. Policies from the Ministries of Economic Affairs and Culture, Recreation and Welfare were formed in a closer co-operation with interest groups in the sectors under consideration than policies from the Ministry of Justice. On the other hand, there was a greater degree of involvement by Members of Parliament in these policies (see Figure 7.1).

In terms of the distinction between negotiation and imposition, policies in the Netherlands are generally negotiated. The original negotiation was between government and Parliament. Now the negotiations are increasingly between (parts of) the administration and advisory bodies and interest groups in the different sectors of society, with the Cabinet and Parliament losing much of their preponderance.

Expressed in terms as active or reactive, the policy styles of the leftist political parties, especially the PvdA, might be labelled as active, and those of the more conservative parties (CDA and VVD) tending to be reactive. In the PvdA activity stems from discontent with society, distrust of non-left political parties and impatience. An impatient individual or group is obviously more inclined to imposition than to negotiation. But reality is much tougher: the voters support a plural party system, and within that system socialists have never gained a majority in Parliament. Despite themselves, they too are doomed to negotiate.

In this chapter attention has been paid to three different 'worlds' with different policy styles: the conflict-ridden world of party politics; the strong and differentiated world of the sectors; and the weak world of the Cabinet. In the period of economic growth (until approximately 1974) the existence of these different worlds in one political system did not cause much damage to the rather smooth functioning of the system. Maximising of benefits took place in the context of affluence, of a steady increase of public resources to be distributed among many competing actors.

But since 1975 the growth of available resources has slowed down rapidly. Many interest groups initially maintained their high levels of expectations and refused to make sacrifices, because they were not convinced that the sacrifices they were asked for by the government were matched by the sacrifices that were being asked from others. Annual efforts, undertaken by the government to conclude a 'social contract' with the trade unions and employers, broke down (Ramondt, 1980). In some cases the intransigence of the interest groups was supported by one or more political parties (especially by the Opposition) and also made its influence felt in the Cabinet meetings, where the different ministers strongly defended the interests of their own sector.

Compromise in the Cabinet was difficult enough to reach. These difficulties were multiplied when Cabinet compromises were presented to

Parliament. This was the case, for example, with a series of expenditure cuts in 1978–80. In many cases the Cabinet yielded to parliamentary pressure, but in 1979 ministers did decide to make a stand. Government proposals were pushed through under the threat of a Cabinet crisis. Faced with a choice between loyalty to their 'circuits' and loyalty to the Cabinet, the governmental parties agreed to support the Cabinet. In this case imposition replaced policies aiming at consensus.

The Cabinet's victory was, however, only a temporary triumph as public expenditure continued to grow. The problem of financing this expenditure, in a period of diminishing economic growth, became so acute that in 1980 the Minister of Finance refused to accept further compromises and resigned. (The other ministers stayed in office, and the Minister of Agriculture was appointed Minister of Finance.) At the end of the 1970s the three worlds seemed to merge in a *bellum omnium contra omens*, a battle of all against all: between competing interest groups; between interest groups and their sectoral department; between interest groups and political parties; between competing political parties; between political parties (not only those belonging to the Opposition) and Cabinet-members; between Cabinet-members; and, finally, between the Cabinet and the governor of the Bank of the Netherlands, the last bulwark of financial propriety.

The Dutch political system has, therefore, entered an extremely difficult and stressful period, in which policy-making and implementing has become much more 'difficult'. In particular, it is very difficult to reach consensus in the policy field. Only when the level of expectation falls in such a way as to nearly match financial resources, will the conflict subside.

In fact, there is an awareness of the need to increase the rationality of policy-making. However, the problems which need to be tackled are very serious. There have been many efforts to increase *sector* rationality (Gustaffson and Richardson, 1979). The structures developed by the Ministry of Culture, Recreation and Welfare (see p. 184) point in that direction. There is also recognition that sector rationality can in the end prove to be quite irrational because of the lack of co-ordination and attempts are being made to integrate the objectives of different sectors. The recommendations of the Commission on the Organisation of the Administration aim at strengthening co-ordinated rationality. This requires, as Gustafsson and Richardson emphasise, that the Cabinet itself clearly defines its overall objectives. The commission stresses the need of an 'action programme', to be drafted by the Cabinet immediately after its appointment, and to be adapted yearly to changed circumstances. The commission also recommends functional and territorial decentralisation in order to prevent an overcrowding of the Cabinet agenda. In terms of functional decentralisation, the commission advocated the creation of independent agencies, not to be covered by ministerial responsibility, as is the case with many agencies in Sweden and, to a lesser extent, the USA.

Many models, however, aiming at increasing rationality in policy-making and starting from the formulation of *objectives*, tend to overlook the fact that power is needed to implement desired policies, included any policy to increase rationality in policy-making (Kuypers, 1980). 'Irrationality' is often the result of a relatively unco-ordinated flow of external power and influence on the decision-making system. Once external influence has been allowed – albeit only once – a vested interest has been created which can prove difficult to remove. Once gained, power is not easily surrendered. Co-ordinated rationality, especially, requires an ultimate centre of legitimate decision-making, invested with a large degree of power. The Netherlands, like many Western European countries, at present lacks such a centre.

The problem becomes even more complicated when considered in relation to democracy, or democratic decision-making. Co-ordination on the base of negotiation and consensus seems possible only when the basic objectives of the different actors do not show a great divergence and when time is irrelevant as a factor in the decision-making process. At present, these two conditions are seldom met. Most Western societies show a high degree of differentiation and rapid change. In such circumstances lessons of rationality might not be easily applied, especially when democracy, as it should be, is cherished as a value of great human importance.

References: Chapter 7

Brasz, H. A., 'The Netherlands', in I. Galnoor (ed.), *Government Secrecy in Democracies* (New York: Harper & Row, 1977).

van Bussel, G., *De overbelasting van de Tweede Kamer en haar werkwijze* (Amsterdam: Vrije Universiteit, 1979).

Daalder, H., *Politisering en lijdelijkheid in de Nederlandse politiek* (Assen: Van Coreum, 1974).

Daalder, H., 'The Nethlerlands', in S. Honig (ed.), *Political Parties in the European Community* (London: Allen & Unwin, 1979).

Dahl, R. A. and Lindblom, C. E., *Politics, Economics and Welfare: Planning and Politico-Economic Systems Resolved into Basic Social Processes* (Chicago: University of Chicago Press, 1953, 1976).

Dror, Y., *Public Policy-Making Re-Examined* (New York: Chandler, 1968).

Elk kent de laan die derwaart gaat, Derde Rapport van de Commissie Hoofdstructuur Rijksdienst ('s-Gravenhage: Staatsuitgeverij, 1980).

Fogarty, M. P., *Christian Democracy in Western Europe* (London: Routledge & Kegan Paul, 1957).

Gortzak, W., *De kleine stappen van het kabinet-Den Uyl* (Deventer: Kluwer, 1978).

Gustaffson, G. and Richardson, J. J., 'Concepts of rationality and the policy process', *European Journal of Political Research*, vol. 7, no. 4 (1979), pp. 415–36.

Headey, B., *British Cabinet Ministers* (London: Allen & Unwin, 1974).

Hoogerwerf, A., 'Government growth in the Netherlands since 1900: size, development, imbalance and overload', paper presented for the ECPR Workshop on Overload, Berlin, 1977.

van Kemenade, J. A. (ed.), *Onderwijs: bestel en beleid* (Groningen: Wolters-Noordhoff, 1981).

Koopmans, L., *De beslissingen over de rijksbegroting* (Deventer: Kluwer, 1968).

Kuypers, G., *Beginsel en van beleidsontwikkeling*, 2 vols (Muiderberg: Coutinho, 1980).

Lijphart, A., *The Politics of Accommodation, Pluralism and Democracy in the Netherlands* (Berkeley, Calif./Los Angeles: University of California Press, 1968).

van Maarseveen, H., *De heerschappij van de Ministerraad* ('s-Gravenhage: Staatsuitgeverij, 1969).

Polak, J. M., 'Stellingen met toelichting over de 14 wetsfamilies', *De 14 wetsfamilies* ('s-Gravenhage: VNG, 1977).

van Putten, J. (ed.), *Haagse machten, Verslag van een politicologisch onderzoek naar de totstandkoming var acht regeringsmaatregelen* ('s-Gravenhage: Staatsuitgeverij, 1980).

Ramondt, J., *Spelende elites, een essay over continuïteit en verandering in de Nederlandse arbeidsverhoudingen* (Alphen aan den Rijn: Samson, 1980).

Richardson, J. J. and Jordan, A. G., *Governing Under Pressure: The Policy Process in a Post-Parliamentary Democracy* (Oxford: Robertson, 1979).

van Schendelen, M. P. C. M., 'Groei en achtergronden van parlementair activisme', in U. Rosenthal, M. van Schendelen and G. H. Scholten (eds), *Ministers, ambtenaren en parlementariërs in Nederland*, (Grongingen: Tjeenk Willink, 1975).

Scholten, I., 'Does consociationalism exist? a critique of the Dutch experience', in R. Rose (ed.), *Electoral Participation: A Comparative Analysis* (London: Sage, 1980).

Sociaal en Cultureel Planbureau, *Sociaal en Cultureel Rapport* ('s-Gravenhage: Staatsuitgeverij, 1980).

Tjeenk Willink, H. D., *Regeren in een dubbelrol*, Achtergrondstudie nr. 1, uitgebracht aan de Commissie Hoofdstructuur Rijksdienst ('s-Gravenhage: Staatsuitgeverij, 1980).

WRR, 1977: Wetenschappelijke Raad voor het Regeringsbeleid, *Externe adviesorganen van de centrale overheid*, Rapporten aan de Regering, Nr. 12 ('s-Gravenhage: Staatsuitgeverij, 1977).

8 Convergent Policy Styles in Europe?

JEREMY RICHARDSON, University of Strathclyde

The Value of Policy Style as a Concept

The reader alone must judge the efficacy of the concept of policy style. This book is intended as an *exploration* – an attempt to discover if sufficiently clear patterns can be discovered for us to be able to identify the main characteristics of the policy process in the six countries studied. Have individual countries developed standard operating procedures which are *usually* used to formulate and implement public policies? In particular, do they adopt a *characteristic approach to problem-solving*, and do they have a *characteristic relationship between government and other actors in the policy process*? Are particular policy-making 'arenas' more likely to be used than others? (For example, are policy problems normally processed in the parliamentary arena, or in a rather closed world of bureaucratic/interest-group consultations and negotiations, or in a broader electoral arena?) Are there any trends, within the policy process, which can be discerned for particular countries and are these trends common throughout Western Europe?

It is hoped that some of these questions have at least been partly answered in this volume. Thus, it appears that most European countries find it increasingly difficult to adopt an anticipatory approach to problem-solving. For example, even Sweden, with its long-established reputation for radical and innovative policy change directed at creating a particular kind of society, now finds it much more difficult for government to play such an active role. Nearly all societies appear to be subject to a high degree of sectorisation of policy-making. And nearly all societies are finding that policy-making and implementing processes have to accommodate increased numbers of increasingly active interest groups. It, therefore, appears that there is indeed a drift towards the top right-hand segment of the simple typology described in Chapter 1, that is, societies seem to be emphasising a consensus relationship between government and other actors combined with a reactive, rather than an anticipatory, approach to problem-solving.

It must, however, be recognised that we still lack really systematic detailed data for a wide range of Western European states. The Norwegian case is almost certainly the best documented, thanks to the so-called 'power project', conducted at the University of Bergen over several years. In the other cases presented in this book (with the possible exception of the 'Haagse machten' project in Holland) there are no comprehensive data on the policy process across a wide range of different policy sectors and over a long period of time. At the outset we recognised that each author would be, to a considerable degree, trying to make sense out of an incomplete and sometimes confusing picture. The reality of policy-making and implementing is often too 'messy' for it to exactly fit our simple typology as formulated in Chapter 1. For example, in the French case it appears that the policy process has a multitude of 'faces', seemingly in conflict with one another. Thus, Hayward (Chapter 5) discusses the 'immobilisme' in the case of the Rhine–Rhône canal yet reminds us that a study of French nuclear energy policy would present a radically different (indeed heroic) policy style. Similarly, in the Norwegian case Olsen *et al* (Chapter 3) points out that although policies are often settled in the bureaucratic-corporative machinery (we might perhaps see the bureaucratic-corporative system as the characteristic Norwegian policy style), other policy-making arenas are important too. Though bureaucratic negotiation with the affected interests may be the commonest way to reach policy decisions, many decisions are reached outside the bureaucratic-corporative arena either because the Norwegian Parliament has managed to increase its power somewhat, or because there has been a significant degree of political mobilisation around an issue. This type of qualification would also be true of the UK. The tendency to 'privatise' policy-making and to negotiate and bargain with interests does not always hold true. Some policies can be seen as non-negotiable, or largely so, and on other occasions issues manage to escape the closed world of policy communities based on Whitehall and are decided in the parliamentary arena or are subject to much wider public debates. In Sweden, too, the normally well-ordered and peaceful policy process can seemingly blow a fuse and considerable conflict can result (say) over nuclear energy or in the normally well-ordered world of labour relations.

A particular difficulty in trying to identify a predominant policy style over time is that the power of the legislature may vary, depending on the party balance at any one time. In the UK, for example, electoral de-alignment (Crewe *et al.*, 1977) has sometimes produced 'untidy' election results, with governments having either a very slim majority in the House of Commons, or no majority at all. This has allowed the House of Commons to achieve some increase in its influence on the policy process and has shifted some issues back into the parliamentary arena of decision-making. Both the

Swedish and Norwegian cases may also be examples of an increased incidence of issues being processed in the parliamentary arena because governments lacked clear parliamentary majorities for their programmes. In the Dutch case the complex party bargaining, described by van Putten, can also play a central role in the policy process particularly by influencing the composition of Cabinets. We have yet to see the impact of the socialist presidential and assembly victories in France, but there is at least a possibility that France will show its radical heroic policy style more often. The increased volatility of electorates has also increased the importance of policy *issues* during election campaigns, and elections may therefore have greater relevance to the policy process than in the past. It also appears that all Western European states are witnessing greater political mobilisation around certain issues (abortion and nuclear energy being two spectacular examples), and this, too, can prise issues out of the closed predictable world of policy communities into the more uncertain public arena.

If the policy process is now more unpredictable, where does this leave the concept of a characteristic policy style? In fact, the picture which has emerged for each country in this volume is not entirely unpatterned. Though it appears that there is more than one policy style in any one country, certain styles are relatively common. Moreover, it is important to note the sheer *volume* of policy-making and policy-implementing activity in the modern state and that available case studies will probably concentrate on the most spectacular (controversial and contested) examples of policy activity. Thus, it may well be that for every case of a decision being taken in the parliamentary or electoral arena, or in the context of high political mobilisation, there are several hundred taken in the less visible world of government–interest-group negotiations. The concept of policy style may also help us to identify the *preferred* policy processes for each country – what might be termed a *procedural ambition* on the part of policy-makers. The British and Swedish cases may be particularly illuminating in this respect. In both cases there appears to be a natural inclination for policy-makers (be they politicians, civil servants, or interest-group leaders) to 'process' problems by incorporating interest groups into the policy process. Thus Olof Ruin, writing before the current intense concern with corporatist trends, saw Sweden as responding to criticisms of corporatism by introducing yet more corporatism (Ruin, 1974). In concluding his discussion of participatory democracy and corporatism in Sweden he observed that the demands for more individual-oriented participation could be seen as a reaction against a too successful integration of interest-group elites in the governmental process. He noted that

now, however, the responses to these demands imply again the creation of an integrated elite, although on a lower level in the process. A reaction might again occur. We seem to some extent to be involved in a vicious (or

virtually self-flagellating?) circle. Traits of corporativism evoke dissatisfaction that evokes more corporativism, and so forth. (Ruin, 1974, p. 163)

In Britain, too, there seems to be a very strong tendency to attempt to
process even the most difficult issues through corporatist type (often
simply tripartite, government–Confederation of British Industry–Trades
Union Congress) machinery. The perceived need to consult, to negotiate
and to reach agreement severely limits the policy options open to government, as the former Head of the Home Civil Service in the UK has
observed. Similarly, Ashford has noted that 'the policy-making constraints
of British politics are derived from the requirements of consensual politics
as enshrined in the British constitution, institutions and parties' (Ashford,
1981, p. 263). In the Norwegian case, too, Olsen *et al.* suggest that, notwithstanding increased mobilisation and confrontation, the styles of problem-
solving, bargaining and self-governance will dominate. The implication
of Chapter 3 seems to be that the Norwegian policy style has a gyroscopic
effect which as yet has managed to withstand countervailing forces. Yet
policy styles may under certain circumstances have to change as a result of
new factors (such as increased mobilisation, more unconventional participation), both internal and external to the political system. Thus, in the
West German case Dyson suggests that is possible to identify a shift of
dominant policy style in the 1960s from regulation and status preservation
to concertation and status preservation. He sees this gradual change as a
growing recognition of the disruptive power of both well-organised groups,
and ad hoc citizen action groups (Chapter 2). In the Dutch case, too, van
Putten suggested that there is now more emphasis on bargaining, even in
those more traditional policy areas which in the past have tended to exhibit
a more formal, constitutional policy style (Chapter 7).

One of the main difficulties in the concept of policy style is that it can, of
course, mean all things to all men and can be used in such a flexible way as
to lose all heuristic value. We have tried to strike a balance in this volume
between forcing each author to fit the analyses of his country into the very
simple typology of Chapter 1 and allowing each author to develop his own
unique typology. Like all such compromises the results can be disconcert-
ing, although in this case the act of asking the question: '*is there a common
policy style, in terms of the simple typology?*' has, we believe, increased our
understanding of the policy processes in Western Europe. It has also
pointed to some common trends all of which appear to make the business of
government at all levels more difficult.

Some Common Trends in the Policy Process

An important trend to emerge from our study is the strengthening of the
forces noted in Chapter 1 – namely, the sectorisation and segmentation of

the policy process. The segmented state has seemingly become a primary feature of the political landscape. Policies often emerge from specialised 'policy communities' in which there is a very high degree of group incorporation. These policy communities can be rather closed secretive informal structures. The great mass of the citizenry are generally excluded from most stages of the policy process, which has become professionalised. Yet in another sense the policy community system can be seen as rather open. Entry to the policy communities in any given policy sector is, contrary to popular belief, not always difficult, provided that groups and individuals are prepared to accept certain community rules and constraints on their behaviour. These rules impose costs as well as benefits (see Olsen, 1981), but the advantages of 'insider' status (Grant, 1978) usually outweigh these costs. Europe has seen a strong 'participation movement' (particularly in Scandinavia), with participation and greater access being emphasised as important political objectives in themselves. Writing in 1958 Finer criticised the term *pressure* group on the ground that it implied that groups had to *force* their way into the policy process, whereas they are usually pressing against an open door. Some twenty-three years later, participation rights have been extended to a much wider range of governmental and non-governmental policy processes as a result of the participation movement. However, even quite disruptive and disapproved of behaviour, when it does occur, can be an effective means of gaining access and insider status (Grant, 1978). Western democracies are at times capable of amoeboid-like behaviour in their capacity to 'injest' all sorts of apparently hostile groups. Sweden may be one of the more extreme examples of this capacity to absorb and accommodate almost any interest. As one writer on a so-called underground newspaper in Stockholm remarked, it is difficult to be 'underground' in Sweden – as soon as the government finds out they step in and give you a subsidy! Even extremely hostile groups, professing total alienation from the system (for example, some black groups in the UK) can find themselves being drawn into the 'establishment' machinery (Jacobs, 1978). Rioting, too, as the people of Toxteth, Liverpool, discovered in 1981, can be quite effective in bringing concessions from government. The relative openness of policy communities to groups (if not to individual citizens) is, in fact, suggested by the phenomenon of overcrowding of policy sectors. Thus, a marked feature of the European democracies has been their willingness to accommodate new interests in each policy sector. For example, Heisler and Kvavik (in formulating a more systematic characterisation of what they term the 'European polity') see 'a decision-making structure characterized by continuous, regularized access for economically, politically, ethnically, and/or subculturally based groups to the highest levels of the political system – i.e. the decision-making subsystem', as one of the central features of their 'European polity' model. They see the pattern of group access as regularised, taking a structural form and as essentially a system of co-optation (Heisler and Kvavik, 1974, p. 48). Furthermore, the act of co-optation binds the participants to the system by giving them a vested interest in the continued operation of the structure. Structured co-optation becomes even more important as the numbers of participating groups expands, *an expansion which has gone so far that 'most groups have already been coopted – virtually without regard to their supportive or opposing orientations to the regime or its norms'* (Heisler and Kvavik, 1974, p. 57; emphasis added). Peters (in an interesting attempt to classify the modes of interaction between pressure groups and bureaucracies) has also emphasised the role of groups in the policy process. He argues that 'one of the dominant features of the post industrial society is the return to pressure groups as a dominant input mechanism. Another is the growing influence of bureaucracy over policy. Thus, the correlation between these two institutionalised actors becomes crucial for understanding the nature of government in advanced societies' (Peters, 1977, p. 45). The Western European policy style thus has as one of its key features the desire to accommodate all 'relevant' interests, with a widening definition of 'relevant'. Thus, Lijphart's term 'the politics of accommodation' seems a good description of the Western European policy style, even if we do not accept the concept of pillarisation which is normally associated with that term (Lijphart, 1968). France, of course, remains difficult to fit into this broad generalisation, particularly if as Hayward reminds us, one notes the divergence between the normative policy style and the diversity of actual behaviour of participants in the policy process.

The willingness to accommodate and absorb new interests, in an amoeboid fashion, does, as indicated in Chapter 1, present problems. Thus, in the West German case Dyson demonstrates that the health policy community was much more complex by the end of the 1970s than it was in the 1950s and was rent by more divisions. In the USA, too, Fritschler has shown that the policy community relating to the tobacco industry changed as a result of wider participation in the policy area. In effect 'the small group of people in Congress, in the agencies, and in the tobacco groups lost control of the policymaking processes ... the new tobacco subsystem is likely to be a much different one from that which preceded it and was powerful until the early 1960s' (Fritschler, 1975, p. 152).

As policy communities expand they can, of course, lose the sense of *community* which can exist when small numbers of participants are involved. Policy-making in (say) the 1950s may have been best characterised as akin to life in a small village with relatively small numbers of participants, with much personal contact and a strong sense of belonging. Increasingly the 'policy villages' have expanded into small 'policy towns' and even 'policy cities' with a much-reduced sense of cohesion and loyalty, and with greatly increased problems of control. Achieving order and stability in the much-enlarged policy communities which have developed in at least some sectors is proving to be a much more difficult task than 'policing' the small villages of the 1950s. Having been relatively willing to admit newcomers to the village, policy-makers have the task of themselves adjusting to a new form of urban life. The *structured* nature of the communities, suggested by Heisler and Kvavik, can be so eroded that a rather loose and expanding 'issue network' is created. Jordan sees issue networks as fragmented, open and extraordinarily complex and ill-structured for resolving conflicts and reaching authoritative decisions (Jordan, 1981, p. 114). Heclo has also suggested that 'looking for the closed triangles of control we tend to miss the fairly open networks of people that increasingly impinge upon government' (Heclo, 1978, p. 88). Even in France, as Hayward suggests, there is increased pressure to accommodate new interests. Thus, 'the leaders of the proliferating protest or outsider movements cannot successfully be ignored as irresponsible activists ... some have the power to disrupt society and so must either be repressed or accommodated' (Hayward, this volume, p. 119). France, of course, also provides a warning that broad generalisations will not always fit, as at least one 'model' of the French policy process sees pressure groups as pressured and as playing a much diminished role compared with groups in (say) Sweden (see Chapter 5; Wright, 1979, pp. 173–85; Cerny and Schain, 1980).

The intensification of sectorisation, together with the need to accommodate more groups into the many stages of the policy process (not least of which is the implementation stage – it is perhaps at this stage that the groups are at their most powerful), has at least two important consequences for the policy process – both of which make policy-making and implementing more difficult. First, sectorisation commonly causes a disintegration of the centre. The Dutch case appears to be an extreme example of this disintegration – so much so in fact that sectorisation was openly recognised as a serious problem warranting the setting up of a special investigatory commission. Too often we speak of *the* government as though it was a monolithic institution with one will. In reality, like all large organisations it is several organisations, each with its own will (Pressman and Wildavsky, 1973, p. 92). The more clients a ministry has to represent within the central machine, the more it is under pressure to fight its corner against all other sectoral interests. Ministers become, typically, absorbed with and bound by their own policy sectors (both in terms of avoiding conflict within their sector and in terms of winning resources for their sector), rather than by their contribution to collective decision-making within the government. The system of 'departmental pluralism' *within* government brings with it serious problems of co-ordination. Secondly, the increased participation by groups, which has been identified in all six countries under examination, can cause a degree of 'immobilisme'. The greater the number of participants involved in any one policy decision, the less likely it is that agreement will be achieved. This is all the more so if the groups resort to 'unconventional' participation. As Dyson's discussion of West German nuclear-energy policy illustrates, unconventional participation (such as in Brokdorf in 1976) can totally disrupt the working of well-defined policy communities. In their study of attitudes to political action Barnes and Kaase suggest that the increase in the potential for protest is a lasting characteristic of mass publics (Barnes and Kaase, 1979, p. 524). And as Muller suggests, 'the resort to unconventional action signifies that, to some extent, institutional channels of representation and conflict resolution may be inadequate or defective' (Muller, 1979, p. 5). Yet the growth and impact of unconventional participation is, in fact, an area demanding much greater research effort. As Budge notes in reviewing the Barnes *et al.* study, even that work tells us more about *attitudes* to action than about protest behaviour itself (Budge, 1981). Whatever the actual incidence of unconventional participation the pressure to accommodate more and more groups into policy-making and implementing processes has, as we have seen in the six country studies, intensified. Herein possibly lies the key to the stability of West European political systems. Do the advantages of increased incorporation and accommodation of groups (in terms of reducing disruptive opposition to government and in terms of producing policies which more accurately meet the needs of citizens) outweigh the disadvantages of somewhat overcrowded policy communities? Can the new groups be socialised, through participation in the policy communities, into the norms which facilitate compromise, consensus and problem-solving? These difficult questions have to be resolved in the context of a reduction in the power of the centre (either of Cabinets or Parliaments and they, too, are sectorised) to impose solutions on the separate sectors and in the context of a resource squeeze which itself limits the capacity to 'buy off' discontent. In a period of resource expansion it was relatively easy to adopt solutions in which everyone who mattered gained. Thus, the policy process in the period of steady expansion in public expenditure was not unlike the Dodo's caucus race in *Alice in Wonderland* in which everyone won and everyone got prizes. Not surprisingly a race in which there are winners and losers is more difficult to manage.

Overloaded and Bankrupt Government or a Period of Adjustment to a New Game?

We have seen, then, a picture of societies under increasing stress – aptly summarised by Olof Ruin's title for his chapter on Sweden, 'Sweden in the 1970s: policy-making becomes more difficult'. Many authors over the last decade have also noted the increased difficulty of governing and the notion of overloaded government has emerged as one of the central concerns of political science. For example, in 1975 King demonstrated that Britain had become harder to govern in the 1970s, because

> at one and the same time, the range of problems that government is expected to deal with has vastly increased, and its capacity to deal with problems, even many of the ones it had before, has decreased. It is not the increase in the number of problems alone that matters, or the reduction in capacity. It is the two coming together. (King, 1975, p. 294).

Rose, too, has placed very great emphasis on the degree to which modern governments are overloaded and on the seriousness of the threat which this presents to contemporary government (Rose and Peters, 1978; Rose, 1979; 1980; 1981; see also La Porte, 1975; Ionescu, 1975; Douglas, 1977).

Our own studies have highlighted such problems as lack of central co-ordination, increased numbers of groups having to be accommodated in the policy process, acts of unconventional participation and the development of obvious immobilist tendencies in many policy sectors. Particular attention has been paid by some authors and, indeed, policy-makers themselves, to the possibility that the *funding* of public policies presents itself as a central problem to Western governments in the 1980s. For example, Rose and Peters, in asking the question 'Can governments go bankrupt?' have emphasised the limits of the capacity of governments to keep raising revenue through taxation. They argue that at a certain point, if government spending continues to grow, the taxation required to support it will cause a real decline in take-home pay (Rose and Peters, 1978, p. 63). This, in turn, threatens political bankruptcy for a government. In practice, the 1980s, so far, look like confirming fears that governments simply cannot cope with the conflicting demands for an expansion of government activity (for example, in reducing unemployment) while restricting or reducing the tax burden on individuals. Virtually all of the Western economies have seen high inflation, high unemployment and the creation of a huge 'debt-mountain' as a result of deficit financing by governments.

Yet as Rose himself recognises, caution is needed in predicting doom. Thus, he notes that Clark's (1945) warning about the dire consequences of government spending going beyond 25 per cent of GNP has proved to be ill-founded, and that Milton Friedman's warnings about the consequences of public expenditure exceeding 60 per cent of GNP are not supported by any social science evidence (Rose, 1981, p. 11). In fact, the evidence about the effects of government expenditure and of increased taxation is at best contradictory. One simple, though important, qualification is that the percentage of GNP absorbed by public expenditure and the levels of taxation do vary widely in the Western democracies and that the degree of 'difficulty in governing' (if, indeed, that could be measured) may not correlate with high levels of public expenditure and high taxation. The specific issue of the impact of levels of taxation on the level of support for governments seems fraught with difficulties. As Hibbs and Madsen note there is little doubt that public resistance to the growth of taxation and tax expenditure has increased in many Western industrial societies in the last decade, yet Denmark is the only country in which a sizeable backlash movement has significantly disrupted the traditional electoral order (Hibbs and Madsen, 1981, pp. 413, 417). They suggest that the composition of the tax burden is of central importance and 'that the long-run cause of welfare state backlash is the expansion of the system based on rapidly rising, highly visible general revenue taxes ... from a political point of view, the optimal tax system thus relies heavily on indirect and programmatic (earmarked) taxes' (p. 434). Other writers have argued that swopping between direct and indirect taxation is more or less cosmetic (Beenstock, 1979, p. 15). The more technical question of whether tax rates are already at such a high level that the maximum tax revenue is close to being obtained may be of central importance to Western governments – for if resources for public policies *can* indeed be expanded, through increasing tax revenue, then many of the problems of overload can be ameliorated. Rose suggests that 'as big government grows bigger still, it can put at risk the marginal effectiveness of its fund-raising policies. The reason is simple – the more money that government seeks in taxes, the greater the marginal incentive to citizens to avoid or evade taxes' (Rose, 1981, p. 16). Yet some economists have seriously questioned this view. Thus, Hemming and Kay conclude

> that the evidence runs strongly against the argument that tax rates in Britain, or any other country, are at levels such that the maximum available tax revenue is close to being obtained ... if we ask the question 'would it be possible, if it were thought desirable, to raise substantially more tax revenue than is at present derived in the UK?' then we believe that the answer is yes. (Hemming and Kay, 1980, pp. 86–7)

Moreover, it is possible to argue that ultimately citizens will come to realise the benefits of taxation, as well as the costs (Tufte, 1980, p. 568). It is perhaps prudent while noting that the resource squeeze has certainly made the job of governing much more difficult, as we suggested earlier, it may be wrong to assume that public resources might not expand again once citizens have had direct experience of the effects of reduced public expenditure, alongside tax reductions.

In fact, this suggests a more general reason for being extremely cautious in predicting the possible demise of the existing forms of government in Western democracies. We must not underestimate the capacity of governments and societies to adjust and respond to new situations. For example, one common response to 'overload' is to hive off functions from central government either to semi-autonomous public agencies (Hood, 1978), or to decentralise them to regional and local government (Sharpe, 1979). The 'exporting' of difficult problems from the centre may mean that some problems are more effectively dealt with. At a minimum, as Dyson notes in the case of health care and also currency management in West Germany, there are *political* benefits in exporting difficult problems to decentralised institutions. The West German example also suggests that it may be more possible to solve the problems of co-ordination in a decentralised context. Thus, Dyson suggests that comprehensive planning was able to establish a firmer grip at the state (*Land*) level than in the federal government. (See also Gustafsson and Richardson, 1979, pp. 429–30, for a discussion of decentralisation as a possible response to overload; and Olsen *et al.*, this volume.) Another possible response is for governments to manipulate expectations in an attempt to manage the policy process more effectively. For example, Edelman has emphasised the power of governments to affect the behaviour of citizens. Thus, 'government affects behaviour chiefly by shaping the cognitions of large numbers of people in ambiguous situations. It helps create their beliefs about what is proper; their perceptions of what is fact; and their expectation of what is to come' (Edelman, 1971). Much of politics, he argues, can therefore be seen as 'symbolic action'. More specifically governments can and do increasingly resort to 'placebo' policies in an attempt to manage the political agenda (Gustaffson and Richardson, 1979, p. 417). The UK, for example, in the early 1980s appears to lend some support to the view that expectations may change, particularly in response to a crisis. In the heady atmosphere of crisis, as the Thatcher government was attempting to implement a tight monetary policy, structural change, which had earlier proved quite impossible, was achieved. Thus, in the industrial field massive restructuring took place in the British Steel Corporation and in British Leyland Vehicles – both state-owned. The arrival of a crisis can itself be the necessary spark for radical change to take place, without a significant threat to the political system. Chapter 3, by Olsen *et al.*, suggests other responses that may mitigate problems of overload – namely, the co-optation of groups and causes. Though recognising that there may be limits to what can be achieved through organisational means, they suggest that those limits are not given and, indeed, that the limits may be stretched through more knowledge of the actual effects of various organisational forms in public policy-making.

We might, therefore, conclude on a reasonably optimistic note. Our studies have indeed emphasised the increased difficulty in governing in Western Europe. But as Samuel Beer has recently pointed out in the context of the USA, we should not exaggerate. Having concluded that the USA had failed to develop a new public philosophy, he nevertheless concluded that

> there is such a thing as equilibrium without purpose. The balance of
> social forces today tends towards a kind of peace. Moroever, a great

hinterland of common belief, the American political tradition, helps to hold conflicts within manageable limits and to enable exchange, economic and political, to flourish. (Beer, 1978, p. 44)

Another skilled American observer, Aaron Wildavsky, has also reminded us, that despite the gloom, we should not ignore the achievements of the modern state. When we point to the many policy failures of modern governments, we should, he suggests, ask ourselves whether we would trade these problems for those we used to have. Policies do have unpleasant side-effects, but we would not wish to go back to an age when race, poverty, environment and a host of other problems were ignored (Wildavsky, 1979, p. 5). In the European context we might also conclude that much has been, and still is being, achieved and that we too have strong traditions on which to draw. We might also reasonably expect that policy-makers will gradually learn to manage more complex policy-making and implementing processes. New political skills will need to be developed and it is to be expected that the learning process will not be easy. It may prove impossible to consciously *choose* a particular policy style in the face of increased complexity – but the likelihood is that none the less we will muddle through. We may conclude by drawing upon W. J. M. Mackenzie's *Power, Violence, Decision*. In noting that the institutions of adaptivity are continually threatened by the institutions of violence he quotes from Sophocles' *Antigone*: 'And he [man] has taught himself speech and wind-swift thought and the temperament of a city-dweller . . . he contrives for everything, and he is not without resources for whatever the future may bring. From death only will he find no escape' (Mackenzie, 1975, p. 238).

References: Chapter 8

Ashford, D. E., *Policy and Politics in Britain* (Philadelphia, Pa: Temple University Press, 1981).

Barnes, S. H., and Kaase, M., *Political Action: Mass Participation in Five Western Democracies* (Beverley Hills, Calif.: Sage, 1979).

Beenstock, M., 'Taxation and incentives in the UK', *Lloyds Bank Review*, no. 134 (October 1979), pp. 1–15.

Beer, S. H., 'In search of a new public philosophy', in A. King (ed.), *The New American Political System* (Washington, DC: American Enterprise Institute, 1978).

Budge, I., review of Barnes and Kaase (1979), *American Political Science Review*, vol. 75, no. 1 (1981), pp. 221–2.

Cerny, P. G. and Schain, M. A. (eds), *French Politics and Public Policy* (London: Methuen, 1980).

Clark, C., 'Public finance and changes in the value of money', *Economic Journal*, no. 55 (December 1945), pp. 371–89.

Crewe, I., Särlvik, B. and Alt, J., 'Partisan dealignment in Britain, 1964–74', *British Journal of Political Science*, vol. 7, no. 2 (1977), pp. 129–90.

Douglas, J., 'The overloaded crown', *British Journal of Political Science*, vol. 6, no. 3 (1976), pp. 483–505.

Edelman, M., *Politics as Symbolic Action: Mass Arousal and Quiescence* (New York: Academic Press, 1971).

Fritschler, A. L., *Smoking and Politics: Policymaking and the Federal Bureaucracy*, 2nd edn (Englewood Cliffs, NJ: Prentice-Hall, 1975).

Grant, W., 'Insider groups, outsider groups and interest group strategies in Britain', University of Warwick, Department of Politics, Working Paper No. 19 (May 1978).

Gustafsson, G. and Richardson, J. J., 'Concepts of rationality and the policy process', *European Journal of Political Research*, vol. 7, no. 4 (1979), pp. 415-36.

Heclo, H., 'Issue networks and the executive establishment', in A. King (ed.), *The New American Political System* (Washington, DC: American Enterprise Institute, 1978).

Heisler, M. O. and Kvavik, R. B., 'Patterns of European politics: the "European polity" model', in M. O. Heisler (ed.), *Politics in Europe* (New York: McKay, 1974).

Hemming, R. and Kay, J. A., 'The Laffer curve', *Fiscal Studies*, vol. 1, no. 2 (1980), pp. 83–90.

Hibbs, D. A., Jr, and Madsen, H. J., 'Public reactions to the growth of taxation and government expenditure', *World Politics*, vol. XXXIII, no. 3 (1981), pp. 413–35.

Hood, C., 'Keeping the centre small: explanations of agency type', *Political Studies*, vol. XXVI, no. 1 (1978), pp. 30–40.

Ionescu, G., *Centrepetal Politics: Government and the New Centres of Power* (London: Hart-Davis, MacGibbon, 1975).

Jacobs, B., 'Public policy and local interest groups in Britain', Ph.D. thesis, University of Keele, 1978.

Jordan, A. G., 'Iron triangles, woolly corporatism, or elastic nets: images of the policy process', *Journal of Public Policy*, vol. 1, pt 1 (February 1981).

King, A., 'Overload: problems of governing in the 1970s', *Political Studies*, vol. XXIII, nos 2–3 (1975), pp. 162–296.

La Porte, T. R. (ed.), *Organized Social Complexity: Challenge to Politics and Policy* (Princeton, NJ: Princeton University Press, 1975).

Lijphart, A., *The Politics of Accommodation: Pluralism and Democracy in the Netherlands* (Berkeley, Calif./Los Angeles: University of California Press, 1968).

Mackenzie, W. J. M., *Power, Violence, Decision* (Harmondsworth: Penguin, 1975).

Muller, E. N., *Aggressive Political Participation* (Princeton, NJ: Princeton University Press, 1979).

Olsen, J. P., 'Integrated organizational participation in government', in P. Nystrom and W. Starbuck (eds), *Handbook of Organizational Design*, Vol. 2 (Oxford: Oxford University Press, 1981).

Peters, B. G., 'Insiders and outsiders: the politics of pressure groups influence on bureaucracy', *Administration and Society*, vol. 9, no. 2 (August 1977), pp. 191–218.

Pressman, G. L. and Wildavsky, A., *Implementation* (Berkeley, Calif.: University of California Press, 1973).

Rose, R., 'Ungovernability: is there smoke behind the fire?', *Political Studies*, vol. XXVIII, no. 3 (1979), pp. 351–70.

Rose, R. (ed.), *Challenge to Governance* (Beverley Hills, Calif.: Sage, 1980).

Rose, R., 'What, if anything, is wrong with big government?', *Journal of Public Policy*, vol. 1, no. 1 (1981), pp. 5–36.

Rose, R. and Peters, G., *Can Government Go Bankrupt?* (New York: Basic Books, 1978).

Ruin, O., 'Participatory democracy and corporativism: the case of Sweden', *Scandinavian Political Studies*, vol. 9 (1974), pp. 171–84.

Sharpe, L. J. (ed.), *Decentralist Trends in Western Democracies* (Beverley Hills, Calif.: Sage, 1979).

Tufte, E. R., review of Rose and Peters (1978), *American Political Science Review*, vol. 74, no. 2 (1980), pp. 567–68.

Wildavsky, A., *Speaking Truth to Power: The Art and Craft of Policy Analysis* (Boston, Mass.: Little, Brown, 1979).

Wright, V., *The Government and Politics of France* (London: Hutchinson, 1978).

Index